Collin College Library
SPRING CREEK CAMPUS
Plano, Texas 75

D0254676

SCC
22.95

Affirmative Reaction

NEW AMERICANISTS
A Series Edited by Donald E. Pease

Collin College Library
SPRING CREEK CAMPUS
Plano, Texas 75074

AFFIRMATIVE REACTION

New Formations of White Masculinity

HAMILTON CARROLL

DUKE UNIVERSITY PRESS
Durham & London 2011

© 2011 Duke University Press
All rights reserved
Printed in the United States of America on
acid-free paper ∞

Designed by Jennifer Hill
Typeset in Garamond Premier Pro
by Achorn International

Library of Congress Cataloging-in-Publication Data
appear on the last printed page of this book.

CONTENTS ☙

ACKNOWLEDGMENTS ∽

THE WRITING OF THIS BOOK has taken place across two continents, three countries, four cities, and four educational institutions. It began in the final weeks of my time as a graduate student at Indiana University and was completed during my first period of study leave from the School of English at the University of Leeds. Postdoctoral positions at the Georgia Institute of Technology and at the Clinton Institute for American Studies at University College Dublin served as the transition points between student and teacher. I am grateful to the many people— friends, teachers, and colleagues—who have offered support, encouragement, enthusiasm, instruction, criticism, goading, humor, and respite as needed along the way.

While this book is not a revision of my doctoral thesis (that book is yet to come) and contains only ten heavily revised pages from it, it would not look as it does without the advice and encouragement I received during work on that project. As such, my first thanks belong to the members of my dissertation committee, Jonathan Elmer, Tom Foster, and Joan Hawkins. Most especially I am grateful to my director, Eva Cherniavsky, without whom this book would not exist in this, and possibly any, form. Thanks to Robyn Wiegman for asking the question and suggesting the text from which this project first grew.

Many of these chapters were given their first public airings during the Futures of American Studies Institute (my home away from home) over the past ten years. Many thanks to my wonderful friends Don Pease, Colleen Boggs, Lara Cohen, Elizabeth Dillon, Marty Favor, Donatella Izzo, Cindi Katz, Eric Lott, and Jolie Sheffer who made those airings so rewarding and refreshing. Thanks also to the many plenary speakers, participants, and guests who have engaged with my work at the Institute. To Catherine Carey and Liam Kennedy, thank you both for your help and support during what turned out to be a significant transition year.

Thanks to Matt Bowen, James Murphy, Doreen Piano, Tyrone Simpson, and Robert Stalker for lively conversations about individual portions of this book and for their friendship more generally. To my fellow Americanists at Leeds, Bridget Bennett, Denis Flannery, Jay Prosser, and Andrew Warnes, I extend my deepest thanks for your generosity.

To my brother, Jerome, and to Miranda, Ellie, and James, many thanks and all my love. To my sister, Rowan, my love and gratitude always. For her support during an earlier stage on this journey, many thanks and much love to Abby Nardo. My heartfelt thanks also to Mickey and Sharon Nardo. To my mother, Lynn, and my stepfather, Simon, thank you (from Mif and Jef, as well!). Thanks also to my father, Julian. For his support, encouragement, and stellar example when I took my first tentative steps toward an intellectual life, I owe more than I can say to Steve Brown, and it is to him that I dedicate this book.

At Duke University Press, Reynolds Smith (who greeted the project with encouraging enthusiasm), Courtney Berger (who inherited it from him), Sharon Torian, Jade Brooks, and Mark Mastromarino combined to make the publication process as smooth as possible, for which they all have my thanks. Thank you to the anonymous readers for the press whose care and attention have made this a better book.

My deepest and final thanks are due to Lourdes Orozco, who—with wit, patience, love, and enthusiasm—carried me through to the end.

Audiences at the Futures of American Studies Institute, Dartmouth College; Indiana University; University of Leeds; Clinton Institute for American Studies (University College Dublin); University of Swansea; School of English, University College Dublin; MLA Annual Conference; American Studies Association Annual Conference; and British Association for American Studies Annual Conference have listened as I presented portions of this work in progress and have helped me refine my ideas and develop my thinking. Portions of this work were written while I was a research fellow at the Clinton Institute for American Studies, University College Dublin.

An earlier version of chapter 1 was published as "Jack Bauer e la Sua 'Extraordinary Rendition': L'Etica della Tortura e il Melodrama del Neoliberalism" in *Acoma: Revista Internazionale di Studi Nordamericani*, no. 36 (2008). A version of chapter 3 was published as "Men's Soaps: Automotive Television Programming and Contemporary Working-Class Masculinities" in *Television and New Media* 9.4 (2008). An earlier version of chapter 6 was published as "Romancing the Nation: Family Melodrama and the Sentimental Logics of Bourgeois Nationalism" in *Comparative American Studies* 5.1 (2007).

White Masculinities and
the Politics of Representation

What then is the American, this new man?
J. HECTOR ST. JOHN DE CRÈVECOEUR, *Letters from an American Farmer*

American Manhood was under siege. . . . The men I got to know . . .
had without exception lost their compass in the world.
SUSAN FALUDI, *Stiffed*

IN HIS AFTERWORD to the 2005 reprint of his
best-selling novel, *Fight Club*, Chuck Palahniuk explains why he wrote the original short story: "The
bookstores were full of books like *The Joy Luck Club*
and *The Divine Secrets of the Ya-Ya Sisterhood* and
How to Make an American Quilt. These were all novels that presented a social model for women to be together. To sit together and tell their stories. To share
their lives. But there was no novel that presented
a new social model for men to share their lives."[1]
Palahniuk's complaint, and the sentiment behind it,
is exemplary of the appeals to injury or claims of disproportionate representation that figure prominently
in late twentieth-century discourses about the plight
of white manhood in American culture. Such claims
are, on the one hand, laughable. Surely culture is *full*
of social models for men? Surely white men are more
often the instigators than the victims of discrimination? On the other hand, Palahniuk is far from
alone in his assessment of the paucity of emotionally

fulfilling outlets for male self-expression. In Hollywood feature films, prime-time television shows, self-help books, newspaper columns, conservative talk radio, news magazine cover articles, and presidential speeches the discourse of masculinity in crisis is clearly evident.

Embedded in this so-called crisis of masculinity is the claim that white men, whose franchise on opportunity in the United States has putatively been revoked, are those most adversely affected by the social transformations of the post–civil rights era. The discourse of masculine crisis attempts to account for and to reorient these transformations; white male injury, phantasmagoric though it may be, is a phenomenon that attempts to recoup political, economic, and cultural authority in the face of a destabilized national consensus. As the labor and sociocultural landscapes of the contemporary United States have shifted, white masculinity has reacted defensively.[2] David Savran argues, for example, that the new interest in, or visibility of, white masculinity should be seen as "an attempt by white men to respond to and regroup in the face of particular social and economic challenges," the most significant of which is "the end of the post–World War II economic boom and the resultant and steady decline in the income of white working- and lower-middle-class men."[3] But Palahniuk's claim is not about labor, but about social interaction: transformations in labor opportunity are being *felt* as transformations in social opportunity. What does it mean, then, for Palahniuk to bemoan the failure of contemporary culture to equip men with the necessary tools for social interaction?[4] And given the success of cultural objects such as Palahniuk's novel and David Fincher's film adaptation of it, why do these claims seem to resonate so strongly with audiences in the contemporary United States? What *work*—cultural, social, and political—does this discourse of crisis do? What are the reactive strategies that maintain white masculine privilege in the face of the broader transformations of labor and social life? Why does white masculinity need to defend itself in such ways? *Affirmative Reaction* investigates how such appeals to injury and claims of disproportionate representation incorporate and mobilize failure as a constitutive force for the reorientation of posthegemonic forms of white masculinist privilege; I chart the devices and strategies that maintain heteronormative white patriarchal privilege in contemporary American culture.

White F(l)ight: The Discourse of Crisis and Disavowal

Affirmative Reaction proceeds from the belief that the new forms of white masculine identity constituted through claims such as Palahniuk's are symptomatic and opportunistic responses to the twin pressures of domestic multiculturalism and identity politics, on the one hand, and the globalization of labor and economics, on the other. The crisis of masculinity is a local (i.e., nationally specific) response to a global phenomenon, for while globalization accounts for some of the most profound transformations of modern American society, the national is still the level on which such transformations are most commonly felt, negotiated, and understood. The erosions of masculinist privilege at both the global and the national levels produce a dialectics of crisis in which the politics of identity serve as a lure for the problems of labor—which affect all people, not just white men. Thus the macrological transformations of labor produced under the shift to a global service economy are often interpreted and understood at the micrological levels of home, family, and male psychology. As such, white men place responsibility for a broad series of shifts in labor opportunity at the feet of the women and people of color who have displaced them. As David Wellman points out, "Political-economic troubles are experienced as racial and gendered, rather than class, grievances."[5] Such erosions of patriarchal enfranchisement produce marked effects across the spheres of work and family that are clearly visible in contemporary American cultural representations of masculinity as shifts in gender expectations, representational status, employment prospects, and political power all work to transform the status of white masculinity.

In concert with the broader transformations of labor under global neoliberalism, postwar transformations in the labor economy of the United States have, as George Lipsitz has pointed out, "worked to detach individuals from the traditional authority of work, community, and family."[6] In the United States this detachment from "traditional authority" has produced an understanding of worker disenfranchisement that manifests itself along predictably gendered lines as transformations in labor roles require the reconstitution of domestic labor in the private sphere of home and family. Mike Hill suggests that "the conditions of labor now impinge on the traditional domestic arrangements that it once required, with the consequence of diminishing the real numbers of traditional male-headed heterosexual families."[7] The domestic, therefore, becomes a location, both real and symbolic, where sociocultural change is not only felt but also negotiated and managed.

Thus in *Stiffed*, her study of the "betrayal of the American man," Susan Faludi claims that the decline in traditional "masculine" jobs has led to a rise in insecurity in the American male psyche. Increasingly marginalized in the postindustrial service economy of contemporary capitalism, American men are caught between America's "industrial past" and its "corporate future."[8] Hobbled by a lack of education and a cultural climate that views the majority of available service and knowledge work as feminized (and feminizing), the working-class male in the contemporary United States has become the foremost victim of the postindustrial service economy.[9] In a now familiar way Faludi cites the transition from manual to mental labor as deleterious for men: "[An] important aspect of [traditional] masculinity was the importance of commanding the inner skills to work with materials. Workmanship generated a pride founded in the certainty that what you did bespoke a know-how not acquired overnight.... Out of that security grew authority—an authority based, as in the root meaning of the word, on having *authored* something productive." The "middle managers" of the new corporate ethos, in contrast, "had no such connections, no such abilities, and were imbued with no such confidence."[10]

While there can be no doubt that broad transformations have radically altered the landscape of labor and opportunity in the United States and elsewhere, arguments such as Faludi's participate in the broader and more pernicious culture of white male injury or victimhood that cites women and people of color as the beneficiaries of those transformations at the expense of white male enfranchisement. This belief persists despite much evidence to the contrary. While more and more people live in poverty in the United States and working-class and middle-class opportunities decline as the rich continue to get richer, these class-based facts do not follow racial lines. According to the U.S. Department of Labor, whites—and white men in particular—continue to earn considerably more than their black and brown counterparts. In 2006, for example, the median weekly earnings for white men were $761, while median earnings for black men were only $591, and Hispanic or Latino men earned even less, $505. White women earned $609; black women, $519; Hispanic or Latino women,

$440. Correspondingly, in 2006 71 percent of eligible white men sixteen and older were employed, compared to only 60 percent of black men.[11] At the same time wages have fallen considerably. As Wellman points out, median income for white men dropped from $34,231 to $31,012 between 1973 and 1992. This drop, however, was equaled by a corresponding drop in wages for black and Latino men. Over the same period the earnings of corporate bosses rose considerably.[12] As Wellman suggests, "Lost ground does not mean lost advantage."[13] But white men persist in seeing it that way.

White injury is clearly more perception than reality, but it is a perception that has extraordinary sociocultural heft. One of the interesting facts about the perception behind these statistics is the refusal to see disadvantage as a class rather than a racial or gender issue. We might ask not only why the disparities between white and minority earnings are invisible to white men, but also why the gulf between the low- and high-wage earners among white men is equally invisible. The most obvious answer to these questions is many Americans' persistent belief in the American Dream. Claiming white injury is a way of protesting the erosions of white men's historical advantage while denying that advantage ever existed. Richard Dyer, speaking of whiteness more broadly, points out that whites are unable to see their privilege because the assets that accrue to it are "part and parcel of the sense that whiteness is nothing in particular, that white culture and identity have, as it were, no content." More than lack of content, however, whites' inability to see privilege while it is so clear to others is a result of their belief in the status of the individual. "It is intolerable to realize," Dyer writes, "that we [whites] may get a job or a nice house, or a helpful response at school or in hospitals, because of our skin colour, not because of the unique, achieving individual we must believe ourselves to be."[14] In the American context the currency of this belief is tied to the ideologies of possessive individualism that anchor the American Dream. For white men to see themselves as disadvantaged by the successes of other white men would place them in an untenable position in relation to their beliefs in the economic and social mobility guaranteed as the inalienable rights of U.S. citizenship.

As a libidinal fantasy, white injury is at once a response to very real erosions of opportunity and a response to what Thomas DiPiero has described as a "contemporary push toward opening up new raced, gendered, and sexual identities that do not take the white male as their normative ground."[15] In a process of willed misrecognition or scapegoating, this culture more often than not locates the source of white male disenfranchisement at the feet of women and ethnic minorities. This is, in part, what Palahniuk is doing when he compares *Fight Club* to novels such as *The Joy Luck Club* and *How to Make an American Quilt*. This comparison is a reactive strategy in which white masculinity makes its own appeal to injury. Savran argues that the phenomena of white male injury "represent[s] an attempt on the part of white men to recoup the losses they have allegedly suffered at the hands of those women and persons of color who, in fact, have had to pay for the economic and social prosperity that white men have historically enjoyed."[16] If there is one aspect that separates the current crisis of masculinity from those that have come before, it is white masculinity's turn to the representational politics of identity. One of the most fascinating aspects of this contemporary discourse of crisis is the way it mobilizes the very politics of identity that it believes are responsible for the disarticulation of privilege from white male bodies in the first place.

White/Male: The Dialectics of Identity

Critical conversations about race, gender, and sexuality in the United States after the civil rights era have tended to focus on the concepts of difference and representation, specifically on issues of particularity. These concepts are of prime importance in understanding how privilege functions to exclude and deny power to marginalized others, yet this focus not only obfuscates other mechanisms that secure white masculinist privilege, but also, and perhaps more significantly, ignores how difference itself has become a key strategy for maintaining and recuperating that privilege.[17]

One of the principal tools of that recuperation, I would argue, is the transformation of white masculinity from the universal into the particular, whereby the particular becomes a location from which privilege can be recouped. As the normative ground of white masculinity erodes, patriarchal privilege seeks new locations to stake its claims; as the politics of representation transform the grounds of identity, white masculinity turns to a reactive strategy under which it redefines the normative by citing itself as a marginal identity. It is this strategy that I uncover as I analyze the varied locations that currently secure white masculinist privilege. As such, this book departs from and develops arguments such as those made by Sally Robinson about "white masculinity in crisis." Robinson primarily considers how white men were visible in American culture between the late 1960s and the late 1980s. She examines how white men managed their newfound visibility and how they sometimes used the strategies of identity politics to do so. She believes middlebrow culture positions an injured white masculinity as a visible identity.[18] The figure of the white male as injured subject that is central to Robinson's study (and to Fred Pfeil's) is more peripheral to my own. I examine how white masculinity places itself in other identity locations (white trash, queer, blue-collar, Irish) in order to disavow that it is normative. This, I believe, is one of the book's unique contributions: it maps the multiple locations where a single identity formation maintains privilege through a process of disavowal and transformation. I argue that once it has become visible (in the ways Robinson examines) white masculinity reworks the meaning of that visibility by locating itself elsewhere. No longer able—if in fact it ever was— to rely on its status as unremarkable or normative, white masculinity attempts to manage the stakes of its own fragmentation by co-opting the forms of representational meaning secured by women, gays, and people of color over the preceding decades. How, then, can we think through the relationship between white supremacy and the representational politics of particularity? If identity is defined most clearly by being contrasted to its putative opposites, then white masculinity is defined through a process of negation that functions, most clearly, at the levels of race and gender.

White masculinity holds for itself the privilege of definition: to be white is to be *not* black; to be male is to be *not* female. Added to this is the privilege of invisibility. Lipsitz argues that "as the unmarked category against which difference is constructed, whiteness never has to speak its name, never has to acknowledge its role as an organizing principle in social and cultural relations."[19] Ruth Frankenberg likewise claims that "whiteness makes itself invisible precisely by asserting its normalcy, its transparency, in contrast with the marking of others on which its transparency depends."[20] To be white, these authors assert, is to be nothing—and to be nothing can be a very good thing. Increasingly, however, and in response to the erosions of privilege produced by identity politics after the women's rights, gay rights, and civil rights eras, white masculinity has undergone its own process of particularization; it has found a need to "speak its name" and most regularly does so in the very discourses of difference and representation that have previously unsettled its claims on the universal. The processes through which white masculinity recodes difference require critical attention and new ways of thinking about the relationships between skin color, gender, and privilege. We need ways to think both beyond identity and through its multivalent uses in order to fully understand how difference functions in contemporary American culture and society. As Robyn Wiegman claims, "To the extent that critical race theorists have assumed that the power of whiteness arises from its appropriation of the universal and that the universal is opposed to and hence devoid of the particular, we have failed to interpret the tension between particularity and universality that characterizes not simply the legal discourse of race . . . but also the changing contours of white power and privilege in the last three centuries."[21] White masculinity's turn to the differential structures of identity politics suggests that to think of whiteness and masculinity as merely unmarked, invisible, or normative categories that define, describe, and fix bodies and subjects is deleterious to a full understanding of the mechanisms by which privilege is accrued and maintained.[22] Without a full sense of the interplay between whiteness and masculinity in contemporary culture, it is too easy to lose sight of the symbiotic imbrications of these two identitarian terms; it becomes possible to think of them separately only after they have been properly understood together.

By mapping out the contingent nature of white masculinity we can reconceptualize the terms that explain its sociopolitical effects. White masculinity functions dialectically in relation to specific productions of classed, raced, gendered, and sexualized identities. It does not stand in a fixed relation either to its own other constituent parts (race, class, gender, sexuality) or to those others against which it defines itself, but inhabits a contingent space in which it is altered, both structurally and symbolically, in relation to them. As *Affirmative Reaction* shows, the appropriation of the identitarian discourses of mid- and late twentieth-century U.S. political discourse by white masculinity recuperates hegemony by articulating it to difference. Only by placing pressure on the point of this dialectical articulation can we examine just how incoherent, reactive, and contingent whiteness and masculinity really are. But how can we discuss one of these formations without losing sight of the other?

Hegemonic whiteness requires a complex process of maintenance as the pressures against which privilege is constructed alter over time. Frankenberg writes, "In times and places when whiteness and white dominance are being built or reconfigured, they are highly visible, named, and asserted, rather than invisible or simply 'normative.'"[23] In this account the project of white dominance is to achieve stability, to attain (or regain) the position of invisible or unmarked subject putatively inherent in whiteness. Arguably, however, white privilege is *always* being built or reconfigured; whiteness is (as Frankenberg herself acknowledges) a process. The reasons for this are twofold. On the one hand, white privilege is always under assault; on the other, whiteness is a very slippery, illusory base on which to build any notion of identitarian privilege. When relying on the logics of identity, whiteness is engaged in a constant process of boundary maintenance and reconstitution. This is a problem inherent both in white masculinity as an identitarian category and in those categories that function in opposition to it. As Hill suggests, "When identities are sealed, valued, or derided absolutely, change lapses into becoming a game of ontological leapfrog, in which 'I' want what my oppressor has and, in so wanting, reproduce him as myself."[24] Hill is describing the fact that difference structures meaning both relationally and absolutely. Representation therefore runs the risk of merely reproducing discrimination in an ongoing process whereby one group gains at the expense of another. The other face of Hill's observation, of course, is that such ontological structures are open to manipulation. This, I suggest, is how white masculinity currently contests its dismantling: as it is made visible, marked, or particular, white masculinity recalibrates the orientation of those transformations from its position of dominance. White masculinity has, in short, learned how to manage the stakes of its own failure, thereby turning that failure into a profoundly powerful form of success. Whiteness, says Hill, is "the struggle to be ordinary."[25] It is that struggle that I place at center stage here. As white masculinity becomes visible, it makes that visibility mean what it wants, which, of course, is hardly to be visible at all; as white masculinity can no longer rely on the normative status of either term, it transforms the meanings of both into something else.

My central theoretical claim in *Affirmative Reaction* is that the true privilege of white masculinity—and its defining strategy—is not to be unmarked, universal, or invisible (although it is sometimes one or all of these), but to be mobile and mutable; it is not so much the *unmarked* status of white masculinity that ensures privilege, but its *lability*. *Labile* as a scientific term used in chemistry and physics offers a useful series of descriptive categories for an understanding of the mechanisms of heteronormative white masculinity. To be labile, the *Oxford English Dictionary* tells us, is to be "prone to undergo displacement in position or change in nature, form, chemical composition, etc." Lability includes both mobility and mutability. Understanding white masculinity in relationship to lability allows us to keep in mind both its ability to shift locations and its ability to change its nature. The interconnectedness of these two processes requires us to think beyond universalism on the one hand, and alterity on the other.

Labile, however, also means to be "liable or prone to lapse," to be "unstable," to be "prone to fall into error or sin," and, in financial terms, to be "lapsable." Thinking about white masculinity in this sense allows us to recognize its *reactive* nature, to see how it *responds* to sociopolitical transformations. This is the true power of white masculinity. As Eva Cherniavsky has pointed out, it may very well be the "capacity to incorporate (appropriate) difference that consolidates rather than prostrates white personhood."[26] White masculinity has responded to calls for both redistribution and recognition by citing itself as the most needy and the most worthy recipient of what it denies it already has. It is this sleight of hand that I examine as I consider the various strategies by which white masculinity has transformed the universal into the particular as a means of restaging universality.

"Their Tragedy Is Universal": *Brokeback Mountain* and the Gendering of Queers

In his gushing review of Ang Lee's film the critic Roger Ebert makes much of its purported universality: "*Brokeback Mountain* could be about two women, or lovers from different religious or ethnic groups—any forbidden love." He takes this line of argument one stage further, saying, "I can imagine someone weeping at this film, identifying with it, because he always wanted to stay in the Marines, or be an artist or a cabinetmaker."

"Their tragedy is universal," he says of the film's central characters.[27] What Ebert is identifying as the film's positive attribute—its universality—is precisely what I wish to examine as I show how the film's central love story is subordinated to a latent story of white male disenfranchisement which is routed through the affective structures of melodrama. *Brokeback Mountain* takes the particular story of same-sex desire in the face of an oppressive social regime and abstracts it to a universal story of love and loss. This transformation ultimately focuses on the very erosions of white masculine privilege in which the film might otherwise seem to be participating; the film, in other words, uses its story of repressed gay men to erase the very contexts in which such subjects might be seen to matter. Homosexuality provides a form of particularization that allows the film to address its central concern—white male opportunity—in the intimate private sphere of male relationships. *Brokeback Mountain* uses its pseudo-queer melodrama to chart the transformations of patriarchal enfranchisement in the postwar United States. As such, the film should be understood in relation to the history of labor that serves as its historical backdrop. Despite its ostensible focus on male same-sex desire, the film is less an example of the minority politics of recognition than it is a reorientation of the imperative for minority representation.

Adapted from a short story by Annie Proulx first published in *The New Yorker* in 1997, *Brokeback Mountain* tells the story of two cowboys, Ennis Del Mar (Heath Ledger) and Jack Twist (Jake Gyllenhaal), who meet in the summer of 1963 while herding sheep for a Wyoming rancher. The two young men begin an affair that lasts, on and off, until Jack's death in 1982. The film garnered both critical and commercial success, and its status as a serious prestige picture of outstanding quality was reflected in overwhelmingly positive reviews from critics in the mainstream press.[28] Like Ebert, many reviewers took the film's representation of same-sex desire to be secondary to the broader, and less threatening, concept of forbidden love conceived more generally, and much was made of the film's melodramatic sentimentality. Writing for the *New York Times*, Stephen Holden remarked on the "lonesome chill [that is] as bone deep as the movie's heartbreaking story of two cowboys who fall in love almost by accident." Owen Gleiberman of *Entertainment Weekly* called the film a "big Hollywood weeper with a beautiful ache at its center" and a "wistful epic of longing and loss."[29] In their descriptions of the film as a universal story of love and loss these reviewers highlighted the degree to which *Brokeback Mountain* is possibly the least queer film about same-sex desire imaginable. This is not a problem of tone—the film makes no claims for its own status as a queer text—but is a reflection of the fact that the film is less concerned with homosexuality or queerness than with the socioeconomic erosions confronting men in the United States of the 1960s, 1970s, and 1980s. What interests me about the film is less what it has to say about homosexuality—ultimately not very much—or love, but what it has to say about white masculinity in the contemporary United States. *Brokeback Mountain* is more about labor than love. The film turns to the structures of identity and uses the plight of its repressed male subjects as a means to represent a more hegemonic form of white masculinist disenfranchisement; it produces a space within which white men can regain center stage by calling them something else: gay men.

The way the film subordinates Jack's and Ennis's forbidden love to its reclamation of center stage for white masculinity is perfectly illustrated in two consecutive scenes that bear close attention for what they tell us about the film's take on the transformations of masculinist privilege in the postwar United States. Both scenes take place during Thanksgiving in 1977. In one Jack and his wife, Lureen (Anne Hathaway), host a Thanksgiving dinner for Lureen's parents; in the other Ennis visits his ex-wife, Alma (Michelle Williams), and his daughters in the house they now share with Monroe (Scott Michael Campbell), Alma's second husband. The first of these scenes does not appear in Proulx's original short story, but a version of the second does. In the first Jack's failings as a role model for his son are highlighted as he engages in a series of skirmishes with his father-in-law at the dinner table: "Whoa, now, Rodeo. . . . The stud duck does the carving around here"; "You want your boy to grow up to be a man, don't you, daughter?"; "A boy should watch football." Jack actually stands up to his father-in-law in this scene (a fact that induces a small moment of pride in Lureen, which contrasts with the dismay she shows when she overhears a group of farmers dismiss his rodeo career in an earlier scene). That Jack regains a measure of authority in his own house—"This is my house, this is my child, and you are my guest," he tells his father-in-law—is unusual because the film has done so much to highlight Jack's irrelevance. This momentary display of authority suggests the film's ambivalence about the status of the protagonists in relation to the traditional values they have failed to meet or transcend.

In contrast to the masculine conflicts over carving and football that structure the Twists' Thanksgiving dinner, Ennis is confronted with an electric carving knife and figure skating on television. He can do nothing about either. As Monroe carves the turkey with his electric knife, Ennis responds to his daughter's request for stories about his brief rodeo career with the admission that it lasted "only 'bout three seconds."[30] Whereas Jack seems to regain a measure of control in the first scene, the masculinity Ennis embodies is shown to be thoroughly outmoded in the second: this isn't his house, these are no longer his children, and he is the guest. Symbolically trapped between the overbearing patriarchal ideals of Jack's father-in-law and the new masculinity of Alma's feminized second husband, a grocery store manager, Jack and Ennis inhabit a no-man's-land of unmet expectations and personal failure that the film could not produce without the lure of its universalizing love story.

Brokeback Mountain is as much a film about fathers and sons as it is about same-sex desire. Both Jack and Ennis have or had problematic relationships with their own fathers, and Jack is caught in a running conflict with a father-in-law who detests him. These conflicts illustrate the film's use of the intimate sphere of home and family as it charts the declensions of patriarchal authority in contemporary American culture. For Ennis the figure of the father looms large as a symbol of patriarchal authority. Early on we learn that Ennis's parents were killed in a car crash and that he was raised by his older brother and sister. Before his father died, however, he precipitated a foundational event in the young boy's life that Ennis relays to Jack. Shortly after they have been reunited after a long separation, Jack suggests that the two men could buy a small ranch together. Ennis explains to him why that can't happen by relating a story about his father that illustrates the gulf between his father's world and his own. When he was a young boy, Ennis tells Jack, his father took him and his brother to see the mutilated corpse of a local gay man, Earl, who had been lynched by some of the townspeople and then dragged behind a pickup truck by his genitals. Ennis admits to Jack that he believes his father might have been one of the perpetrators. In his retelling of this story Ennis reflects the degree to which he has internalized the boundary-policing logic of vigilante violence, and it is Earl's fate that he imagines for his friend when Jack's

wife describes his death to him at the end of the film. This form of patriarchal supremacy acts *on* Ennis and not, as it does for his father, *through*
him; he is the victim and not the perpetrator of such violence.

Taken directly from Proulx's short story, published in 1997, this scene
foreshadows the lynching of Matthew Shepard in Wyoming in 1998 and
of James Byrd Jr. in Texas in the same year and the less well-known murder
of Billy Jack Gaither in rural Alabama in 1999. Unlike the short story, the
film was made with full knowledge of these horrific murders and the ensu-
ing debates about hate crime laws in the United States. As the film evokes
the memories of Shepard, Byrd, and Gaither, it also yokes these men's stories to the longer history of lynching and racial terrorism in the United
States. Therefore the homophobic violence of this lynching situates Ennis's
memories of his father within a structural form of white supremacy that,
as Wiegman notes, "produc[es] the threat of [white masculinity's] own
extinction as the justification and motivation for violent retaliations."[31]
Brokeback Mountain, however, renders this history of white supremacy
ahistorical. By making this a story about Ennis's relationship with his father, the film displaces the very real histories of lynching and vigilante
violence in the United States and relocates its conflict at the level of the
domestic. The film obfuscates the institutional structures of homophobia
by routing them through the patriarchal space of family and generational
inadequacy and anxiety. That the bourgeois family has traditionally been
the primary location where homophobia is reproduced goes unaddressed.
The structural and systemic homophobia that this story should bring to
the fore is obfuscated by the film's sentimentalized discourse of familial
melodrama. As it elides the homophobia in American society the film is
able to maintain its focus on Jack and Ennis as particular individuals and
to avoid mapping their experiences onto these broader societal structures.
There is, in short, no real critique being produced in these scenes. The
story tells the audience how hard it is to be Ennis's father's son, not how
hard it was to be a gay man in the rural United States during the 1970s.
Melodrama substitutes for politics.

Jack's patriarchal tribulations are of a more mundane but equally telling nature. His career as a rodeo cowboy is largely a story of personal failure and cultural transition, but it is also a source of generational conflict.
In an early conversation Jack tells Ennis that his father was a successful

rodeo cowboy at a time when that "meant something." Despite following in his footsteps, however, Jack is equally failed by his father: "My ol' man was a bullrider," he tells Ennis, "pretty well knowed in his day, though he kept his secrets to himself. Never taught me a thing. Never once come to see me ride" (14). Jack's failure as a bull rider is conflated with his father's paternal failings, which the film later links to Jack's own fatherhood, and provides another example of the film's sense of the narrowing opportunities for men in the contemporary United States.

When his rodeo career dries up, Jack becomes a salesman at the farm machinery company owned by his father-in-law, L. D. Newsome (Graham Beckel). This job is evidence of the transition from a laboring to a service economy in which men like Jack and Ennis cannot survive. Unable to measure up in the masculine world of the rodeo, Jack has moved into the emasculating world of the service industries: he is selling farm machinery, not using or repairing it. Jack is first seen in his new job showing a tractor to some farmers. As he drives the tractor around the forecourt one farmer turns to the other and asks, "Didn't that piss-ant used to ride the bulls?" "He used to *try*," the other responds (55). This lack of respect, of what Faludi calls "authority," is linked slightly later to Jack's own parental authority in a brief scene in which he is seen driving another piece of heavy farm equipment with his son, Bobby, on his lap. Letting his son take the wheel, Jack exclaims, "It's all yours, Bobby. It's all yours" (59). As the film makes clear, though, what is being symbolically passed from father to son here comes through L. D., who is both father-in-law and boss to Jack, who has been removed from the patrilineal structure of inheritance, a point brought home by the fact that the scene takes place on the Newsome Ranch. Bobby's status as more L. D.'s grandson than Jack's son is also highlighted in an earlier scene, set in the hospital after Lureen has given birth. Lureen's mother, who is holding the baby, turns to her husband, holds the baby up to him, and exclaims, "Oh, L. D.! I can already see who he looks like." "He's the spittin' image of his grandpa," L. D. replies (43). In this scene as in the others, Jack's status as biological father to Bobby is rendered entirely irrelevant. Lureen moreover is a more successful businessperson than Jack is and holds a managerial position of authority over him in her father's company. Unable to support his family without the assistance of his father-in-law, Jack, like Faludi's middle managers, has fallen

Ennis is framed by fireworks on the Fourth of July. From *Brokeback Mountain* (2005).

outside the realm of masculine authority to become less than a man. As such, the film situates Jack, as much as if not more than Ennis, as a primary victim of the socioeconomic transformations it charts.

Although traditional models of masculine behavior are no longer adequate, the film is ambivalent about discarding them altogether, and it evinces a curious habit of citing both Jack and Ennis as "real men" and patriotic Americans. In one particularly telling scene Ennis confronts a pair of drunken bikers who are making lewd comments about the women in the crowd at a Fourth of July fireworks display he attends with his family before his divorce. On the one hand, this scene is one of many that highlight the violence in Ennis's character, a violence that the film repeatedly and insistently relates to his homosexuality: he's violent because he's repressed. On the other hand, though, it represents Ennis as a patriotic and family-oriented American. After the bikers move away, Ennis is shown framed against the red, white, and blue of the fireworks display. This framing and the scene as a whole cite him as an upholder of the very family values of conservative America he might otherwise be seen to fail and that, more important, might be seen to fail him.

Brokeback Mountain unyokes white masculinity from its usual structures of power and enfranchisement, thereby allowing white masculinity to return to center stage. In its presentation of two gay men trapped in a social regime in which they cannot speak the name of their love, *Brokeback*

Mountain transforms the universal into the particular and cites particularity as universality's defining characteristic. The story of a repressive social regime in which same-sex desire is forbidden is routed through domestic melodrama and subordinated to the film's representation of the erosions of white masculinist privilege; thus *Brokeback Mountain* turns its queer subjects into disenfranchised white men. This turn to universality and intimacy produces an erasure of history in which the structural inequalities of American society are rendered moot. The film is able to produce the universalism that Roger Ebert so loudly applauds only by separating the history of oppression from structures of power and domination.

Same-sex desire in *Brokeback Mountain* produces a homosocial space of intimacy that is located outside the traditional realms of family and domesticity, in which the film's protagonists find themselves lacking. In the process, though, that desire itself is transformed into something altogether less interesting.[32] The film's reconstruction of the universal obfuscates too much of the history of the mechanisms that maintain patriarchal privilege in the United States as it displaces the actual histories of repression and of the struggles for equal rights that have consumed women, people of color, and gays for much of the twentieth century (and before). Jack and Ennis are saved from the putative irrelevancy of white men in contemporary American culture by being remade as gay men. As such, white masculinist privilege is reauthorized in the very locations where its authority has been disrupted. Authority is regained in the turn to minority representation.[33] Reading beyond the film's manifest content of same-sex desire and universal love uncovers the conservative resolutions and mores that subtend that primary melodrama. As the universal transits through the particular only to become universal again, we are offered the story of Jack and Ennis as our own—whoever we are and whatever our own stories might be. The particular is abstracted into a universality that claims, once again, the responsibility and the prerogative to speak to, and for, us all.[34]

Archive and Structure

Affirmative Reaction is not a book about the facts of white masculinity (whatever they might be), but a book about the representational strategies by which white masculinity attempts to hold on to privilege; it is a book about representation as both politics and culture. I analyze the

WITHDRAWN

SPRING CREEK CAMPUS

contemporary structures of white masculinist privilege in a broad range of contemporary popular culture texts: Hollywood feature films, premium cable television reality shows, rap music, broadcast television dramas, comic books, celebrity figures, CD liner notes, and September 11 commemorative news magazine issues. While some, perhaps all, of these textual artifacts might seem ephemeral, each provides rich evidence of the sociocultural conditions I seek to chart. Popular cultural artifacts are often consumed or dismissed without a full understanding of precisely what they are portraying and how. It is not enough to dismiss popular culture as lowbrow, irrelevant, or unworthy of consideration. Popular culture is a complex and variegated terrain on which the concerns of society at large can often be mapped. Through a series of close textual readings of popular culture artifacts, each of which condenses the broader mechanisms of white masculinist privilege, I reflect on cultural practice as cultural politics.

Affirmative Reaction is divided into three sections, each of which pairs two texts. The second text in each section also produces a pair with the first text from the next section; thus chapter 2 could also be paired with chapter 3, chapter 4 with chapter 5, and chapter 6 with chapter 1. This structure and its attendant foci highlight the disparate array of mechanisms through which white masculinity carries out its maintenance project while also suggesting the connections between seemingly disparate, even oppositional locations of identity.

Part I, "9–11/24–7: Affective Time and the War on Terror," situates the book's broader concerns with whiteness and masculinity within the specific sociocultural contours of the United States after September 11, 2001.[35] In this section I argue that the events of September 11 produced an acceleration or amplification of preexisting American cultural formations and thus limn the broader historical processes of masculinist recuperation that are the book's central concern. In the responses to and aftermath of the events of September 11 white masculinity found its most expressive modality. In chapter 1, "Jack Bauer's Extraordinary Rendition: Neoliberal Melodrama and the Ethics of Torture," I analyze the ways Fox TV's highly successful drama *24* conjoins the privatization of citizen responsibility produced under neoliberalism to the state of exception invoked by the Bush administration in its response to the threat of global terrorism. Conceived and piloted before September 11, the show suggests a clear link between the retrograde masculinities required by the War on Terror and the postconsensus masculinities that are the focus of this book. The show 24 provides an example of a form of masculinity, common since September 11, which reworks traditional paradigms of heroism. I use this reading of 24 to consider the relationship of what Foucault terms governmentality to contemporary neoliberalism. The ethical imperative that endows the show's hero, Jack Bauer, with the capacity to act as an autonomous subject unconstrained by normal rules situates him as a sovereign subject. These issues are manifest in the relationship between Bauer's function as a public servant and his responsibilities as a private citizen. In the space between citizenship and patriarchy Bauer is able to deem who constitutes a legal subject with rights to the processes of the justice system. Linking public responsibility to private desire, 24 transforms contemporary geopolitics into domestic melodrama. The show's formal concatenation of time and space produces an affective logic for the ticking-time-bomb scenario in which those actions are the only response to extraordinary circumstances. As both father and counterterrorist operative, Bauer is a model of exemplary citizenship. By conjoining the relativist imperatives of the War on Terror and traditional models of patriarchal authority, 24 finds a new home for an old hero.

Chapter 2, "Future Perfect: 'Everyday Heroes' and the New Exceptionalism," examinines the figure of the everyday hero that emerged immediately after September 11 in relation to contemporary models of U.S. exceptionalism. I link the recuperative models of masculinist action encoded in the figure of the firefighter to the concomitant belief in the exceptional nature of September 11. Firemen in particular came to stand as exemplars of a way of life that was encoded as particularly and typically American: selfless, heroic, individually brave citizens rising in a moment of need to serve the common good. I argue that the fireman as everyday hero produced a white ethnic masculinity that recodes multiculturalism as whiteness and heroism as the domain of masculinity; the New York City fireman became an exemplary white ethnic, working-class hero. At the same time, a time immemorial was produced in which the events of September 11 signified both an end and a new beginning for America. Often portrayed as a fantasy terrorist attack on the Statue of Liberty, this temporal ellipsis provided a stage on which the newly minted everyday hero could rehearse for the public a version of September 11 with a different ending. In the nationalist fantasy of revenge and reclamation the Statue of Liberty often stood for both the future and the heroic past of the nation. This fantasy reoriented and forestalled the deconstitution or interruption of American master narratives by transforming the inassimilable into the exceptional. I chart the construction of this recuperative figure through readings of a variety of cultural texts: Marvel Comics' miniseries *The Call of Duty*, various comic book publishers' commemorative collections, and mainstream news magazines' issues commemorating September 11. As the events of September 11 ruptured the fabric of the nation, the concatenation of the New York City fireman as everyday hero and the Statue of Liberty as exemplary victim inaugurated a recuperative fantasy future perfect in which the United States would not fail to act. This fantasy reinstalled traditional models of gendered behavior while also transforming white working-class men into ethnic subjects.

The second section of the book, "Embodying Difference: Whiteness, Class, and the Postindustrial Subject," examines the celebratory attention given to blue-collar, working-class, and white trash masculinities in postindustrial America. In these chapters I explore the ways white masculinity uses class as a recuperative identity. This analysis focuses on representations of the white trash and laboring body. Chapter 3, "Men's Soaps: Automotive Television Programming and Contemporary Working-Class Masculinities," uses the Discovery Channel's highly successful reality-based television show *American Chopper* to examine contemporary discourses about the relationship between gender, class, and work. *American Chopper* presents an idealized realm of masculine interaction that reproduces traditional divisions of public and private, masculine and feminine, labor and leisure, while updating those divisions in the face of the corrosive pressures of the postindustrial service economy. As it collapses the separate spheres of public and private, work and home into the pseudo-domestic world of fraternity and labor that is the mechanics' workshop, *American Chopper* valorizes a form of working-class manual labor at precisely the moment when such labor has all but disappeared in the United States. In its discourse of commensurate affect the show produces a form of blue-collar patriotism that situates the American worker as a nostalgic figure. By producing the laboring subject as a consuming subject—and the "proper" recipient of the promise of the American Dream—the show incorporates the very losses it elides into the structures of possibility it celebrates.

Chapter 4, "'My Skin Is It Startin' to Work to My Benefit Now?': Eminem's White Trash Aesthetic," charts the interconnections of embodiment, race, and gender in the figure of the white rapper Eminem and his self-representation as white trash through an analysis of the pseudo-biographical film *8 Mile* and Eminem's self-presentation as a marginalized white trash subject. In the case of *8 Mile* this reorientation of white male privilege becomes most apparent as one reads the film's narrative teleology against the grain of its conflated politics of white agency and disavowal. I argue that Bunny Rabbit, the film's fictional protagonist, mobilizes a cross-racial identitarian politics of class affiliation to overcome forms of social disenfranchisement. For all the film's seeming progressivism its coalitional politics of difference, in which class trumps race, actually enables a traditional tale of white male enfranchisement by yoking identity politics to the traditions of American individualism. This racial shell game is evidenced most clearly in the relationship between Rabbit's self-identification as white trash and the film's capitulation to a traditional American narrative of individual responsibility. The mobilization of white trash allows whiteness to be recast as a minoritized identity such that class becomes a means of performing whiteness while simultaneously claiming that race no longer matters. White trash becomes a celebratory form of minority affiliation by transforming the embodiment of race into the embodiment of class. As white becomes white trash it loses the stigma of privilege it previously held. It is the very differentiation of whiteness through class that recuperates privilege. White trash is then related to forms of celebrity as, like his fictional counterpart, Eminem is able to celebrate and overcome his own racial identity by transforming the affective meanings of his own body. White trash provides a marginalized identity position by which white masculinity can regain a celebratory status.

In the third and final part of the book, "Daddy's Home: Family Melodrama and the Fictions of State," I argue that the family melodrama has become, perhaps again, a paradigmatic site for the recuperation of white patriarchy. I explore the ways the domestic has become a contested site of masculinist recuperation, a location to which patriarchal figures can retreat only after they have reoriented their relationship to it. In chapter 5,

"The Fighting Irish: Ethnic Whiteness and *Million Dollar Baby*," I show how Irishness enables a sentimentalized form of white paternal identification by recasting whiteness as an ethnic identity. This transformation is also a recuperation of masculinist privilege. I read beyond the film's plot of female empowerment and argue that *Million Dollar Baby* (directed by Clint Eastwood) is primarily concerned with the recuperation of white patriarchy. I situate this analysis in a reading of the relationships between Frankie Dunn and the film's two other principals, Maggie Fitzgerald and Eddie "Scrap-Iron" Dupris. By adopting Maggie as a pupil, Frankie redeems his past failures as a father and a friend. This redemption is encoded in his ability to transform Maggie from waitress to boxer and from white trash to Irish. Like *8 Mile*, *Million Dollar Baby* makes explicit links between ethnicity and class; unlike the former, however, in *Million Dollar Baby* white trash is debased and Irishness is a transcendent form of whiteness. While *8 Mile* celebrates the white trash body, *Million Dollar Baby* rejects it. Maggie's transformation from trash to Irish requires her to harness the body's impulses, to control its urges, to become a properly consuming citizen. As Maggie becomes Irish she becomes a recuperated and recuperating subject. Newly minted as Irish, Maggie becomes both a surrogate daughter and a platonic lover for Frankie, freeing him from the prison of his earlier failures: her recuperation is ultimately his. I go on to situate this reading of patriarchal redemption in relation to Clint Eastwood's career as an actor and a director, arguing that the transformation from Dirty Harry to Frankie Dunn evidences a similar tale of agency and disavowal.

Chapter 6, "Romancing the Nation: Family Melodrama and the Sentimental Logics of Neoliberalism," uses Steven Soderbergh's film *Traffic* to examine how the structures of sentiment help shore up the putatively waning authority of white masculinity by yoking patriarchal authority to a nationalist discourse of individual responsibility most prominently displayed in the private domains of family and home. Soderbergh's film finds conservative resolutions within its liberal politics as it mobilizes a fantasy of paternal triumph that coalesces around the domestic space of the paradigmatic bourgeois family. The preservation of the patriarch-centered family is concomitant with the preservation of national patriarchy, and one is seen as a model for the other. The pragmatic force of neoliberalism is oriented toward the transnational, but it still finds its most generative affective force at the heart of bourgeois nationalism and its keenest protector in the figure of the white father. The chapter concludes by situating *Traffic* within a contemporaneous cycle of left-leaning liberal critiques produced in Hollywood (*Syriana, Good Night, and Good Luck, Crash*) in order to highlight the reactionary nature of the resolutions offered by a supposedly progressive liberalism and to suggest the profound degree to which the agendas of neoliberalism organize the contemporary political horizons of both the right and the left. Tracing the structures of feeling the family melodrama produces, the conclusions of this chapter return us to the beginning of the book and the issues raised by *24* as, again, white patriarchy finds old solutions for new problems.

Throughout *Affirmative Reaction* I chart the various locations of identitarian difference to which white masculinity turns as it attempts to hold onto majority privilege. Whether these locations are traditional sites of minority difference (Irishness, white trash, domestic melodrama) or reworked traditional sites of masculinist investment (laboring bodies, public sphere politics, vigilantism) the outcome is the same: the foregrounding of white masculinity in relation to women, people of color, and the non-heteronormative. As Coco Fusco has famously suggested, to ignore white ethnicity is to redouble its hegemony by naturalizing it. Without specifically addressing white ethnicity there can be no critical evaluation of the construction of the other.[36] By foregrounding the strategies white masculinity currently uses to produce itself as difference we can more easily see how privilege is accrued and maintained. Collating a range of seemingly disparate cultural artifacts and showing the strange connections between them, I offer evidence for the extraordinary labor involved in the maintenance project of white masculinist enfranchisement. If, as I argue, white masculinity is neither unmarked nor invisible, but labile—constantly in motion, constantly in flux, constantly at work on (and for) itself—what does it look like when we make it sweat?

Affective Time
and the War on Terror

1

JACK BAUER'S EXTRAORDINARY RENDITION ᴄᴈ◟

Neoliberal Melodrama and the Ethics of Torture

The important thing here to understand is that the people that are at Guantánamo are bad people. I mean, these are terrorists for the most part.
VICE PRESIDENT RICHARD CHENEY

At the very moment when it would like to give lessons in democracy to different traditions and cultures, the political culture of the West does not realize that it has entirely lost its canon.
GEORGIO AGAMBEN, *State of Exception*

THE FOX TV DRAMA *24* conjoins the privatization of citizen responsibility produced under neoliberalism to the state of exception invoked by the Bush administration in its response to the putative threat of global terrorism: the War on Terrorism after the attacks on September 11, 2001. The show's hero, Jack Bauer (Kiefer Sutherland), is a sovereign figure and its plots are melodramas of state and family. The show's focus on individual responsibility and domestic melodrama effects a regulatory state fiction that negotiates the transformations of citizenship under neoliberalism and the sovereign paradigms of the War on Terror. It reproduces traditional forms of American heroism that are then transformed in relation to the dictates of neoliberal forms of capitalist accumulation. In its frequent evocation of extralegal processes of abduction, rendition, execution, and torture, *24* instantiates a cultural representation of the suspension of law through which the Bush administration fomented a state of exception that has held both U.S. citizens and the world hostage since September 11.

In its updating of masculine identity, which it routes through exceptionalist forms of patriotism and heroic masculinity, *24* provides a cultural instantiation of the exemplary neoliberal citizen. The events of September 11 and their aftermath have produced a set of conditions for the transformations of the relationship between the subject and the state under which the forms of self-regulation and governance required by neoliberal capital are cited as the proper response to global terrorism. While it is important therefore to understand how the Bush administration's responses to the events of September 11 altered the geopolitical landscape, it is equally important to understand how those responses fit into a longer history of the transformations of politics and capital in contemporary society. The War on Terror provided the Bush administration with the rationale for a series of domestic and global projects that predate the events from which they ostensibly stem. With a production history that likewise predates the events of September 11, *24* serves as a generative site for the working-through of these interconnections and differences.[1] Examining the relationship between neoliberal subjectivity, sovereignty, and masculinity allows the irruptions and continuities to become visible and allows for a more nuanced interpretation of not only the links between the nationalist project of the War on Terror and the market imperatives of neoliberalism, but also of the links between cultural production and what Georgio Agamben calls the "political culture of the West."[2]

The show is set in the Los Angeles branch of a fictional Counter Terrorism Unit (CTU). In each season Jack Bauer and the other CTU operatives attempt to thwart an increasingly complicated series of terrorist plots against the United States. The plot of the first season revolves around the attempted assassination of presidential candidate David Palmer (Dennis Haysbert) on the day of the California Democratic presidential primary.[3] This assassination attempt is part of a larger plot to exact revenge for a covert U.S. military operation carried out in the Balkans some years before, in which Palmer and Bauer were key actors. As part of their convoluted plan to assassinate Palmer and ruin Bauer, the terrorists kidnap Bauer's daughter, Kimberly (Elisha Cuthbert), and threaten to kill her if Bauer does not assist them. In the season finale Nina Myers (Sarah Clarke), a coworker with whom Bauer had an affair, is revealed to be a terrorist and kills Bauer's wife, Teri (Lisa Hope). The primary plotline of the show's second season—written and produced after September 11—revolves around the attempt of a group of terrorists led by Syed Ali (Francesco Quinn) to detonate a nuclear bomb (over) Los Angeles.[4] The season also includes an attempt by the vice president, Jim Prescott (Alan Dale), who is in collusion with a group of powerful business leaders, to seize the presidency by way of the 25th Amendment.

In addition to its elaborate plotlines *24* is notable for its form. As the show's name suggests, each season consists of twenty-four hour-long episodes taking place over a single day. The action unfolds in real time, even taking into account the elapsed time of commercial breaks. The producers of the show utilize a variety of structural devices to keep the viewer constantly aware of its real-time nature. Commercial breaks are bookended by an onscreen digital clock that counts down the number of seconds before and after each break, supplemented by the sound effect of an analog clock ticking off seconds. All the telephones at CTU Headquarters have the same ringtone, and the sound of ringing phones is foregrounded in the audio mix. Action taking place in different locations is often shown in split screen, with as many as six events displayed simultaneously. These formal and structural manipulations contribute significantly not only to the show's appeal for viewers—and to their sense of its originality—but also to the affective responses *24* evokes.

"Sure, If You Have a Warrant": *24*'s Sovereign Paradigms

> I got into acting to avoid politics and so I can remain in a fantasy world, and you guys are kind of bringing me out of it.
> MARY LYNN RAJSKUB, who plays CTU Technician Chloe O'Brien on the show *24*

> We also have to work, though, sort of the dark side, if you will. We've got to spend time in the shadows.
> VICE PRESIDENT RICHARD CHENEY

The show *24* situates the actions of its protagonist and hero in relation to the complex transformations of sovereignty and citizenship under neoliberalism and the War on Terror.[5] In each season Bauer's relationship with

CTU is fraught with complications. He has been suspended, under investigation, incarcerated, unemployed, in hiding, undercover, or, at the beginning of season 6, imprisoned in a Chinese torture camp. As a figure who is frequently both a state functionary—an employee of CTU—and a rogue agent, Bauer inhabits a liminal position in relationship to the legal system. It is his status as at once both inside and outside the law that enables him to be an effective agent. Arguably, then, Bauer is merely an example of the traditional models of masculinist heroic action that are so pervasive in American culture. Even as 24 updates them for the neoliberal state, the narratives of American heroic invincibility that it presents rely on common tropes of heroism and valor. As such, Bauer is an example of the outlaw and official hero that Robert B. Ray describes as one of the organizing myths of American culture.[6] While traditional American mythologies offer myriad examples of these competing figures of heroism, they are often joined by a third, composite type that Ray calls the "reluctant hero," who is drawn to action by outside forces. The reluctant hero is often a family man who must weigh the consequences of public action on private life. Jack Bauer is just such a man, drawn against his will into a conflict not of his own choosing. By mobilizing traditional tropes of masculinist heroism 24 produces the self-regulating neoliberal subject as hero.

In the figure of Jack Bauer 24 illustrates the transformations of U.S. citizenship after September 11 and yokes those transformations to traditional models of American exceptionalism and heroic action. In so doing the show makes legible and, more importantly, palatable the changes it charts. The actions of the Bush administration are made normal by situating them in relation to traditional forms of U.S. belonging. In "The Global Homeland State: Bush's Biopolitical Settlement," Donald E. Pease suggests that, through legislation such as the Homeland Security Act, in the aftermath of September 11 the Bush administration effected a "mass denationalization" under which the citizenry has been "dislocate[ed] from the national imaginary through which their everyday life practices become recognizably 'American.'" In this transformation the population has become an "unprotected biological formation whose collective vitality must be administered and safeguarded against weapons of biological terrorism."[7] As the example of 24 suggests, this "mass denationalization" takes place, almost paradoxically, through the manipulation of the very national narratives it disrupts. The exemplary forms of citizenship 24 evinces rely on a spectacle of hyperpatriotism through which the citizenry willingly abdicates its civil liberties in the name of national security, thereby negating the very values of liberty and possessive individualism the nation putatively embodies.

In its capitulation to this climate of fear *24* suggests at once the post–September 11 transformations in the United States from democracy to continuous state of exception, the forms of self-governance and self-regulation required of the citizenry under neoliberalism, and the profound connections between the two. Arguing that it usually takes six weeks to establish effective undercover status, Bauer has the lead witness in a federal case brought to CTU (illegally) and then shoots and beheads him in order to present his head as a trophy to the leader of a criminal organization he must infiltrate. "You want to find the bomb?" he asks his superior, who expresses concern at his methods. "This is what it's gonna take. That's the problem with people like you, George, you want results but you're not willing to roll up your sleeves and get your hands dirty. . . . I'm going to need a hacksaw." The Bush administration's post–September 11 actions, Judith Butler suggests, have produced "a new exercise of state sovereignty" that requires both a suspension of the law and "an elaboration of administrative bureaucracies in which officials now not only decide who will be tried, and who will be detained, but also have ultimate say over whether someone may be detained indefinitely or not."[8] The show brings together the "new exercise of state sovereignty" Butler describes with a traditional representation of American heroism that renders the state of exception legible by situating the exception within traditional ideologies of heroism and masculine action. The state sovereignty Bauer manifests is masked by the normalizing logics of heroic action. It is in the subtle reiterations of sovereignty that the power of the state of exception lies. The suspension of law that Bauer's actions exemplify is easily recoded within the paradigm of heroic action in which the heroic figure stands outside the law in order to ensure that justice is carried out. That contemporary forms of extralegal action produce sovereignty rather than justice is a phenomenon that is easily missed.

For the Bush administration law became what Michel Foucault calls a tactic: "With government, it is a question not of imposing law on men but of disposing things: that is, of employing tactics rather than laws, *and even of using laws themselves as tactics*—to arrange things in such a way that, through a certain number of means, such-and-such ends may be achieved."[9] The Bush administration's adherence to the law functions in just such a way, and it is not hard, as Butler suggests, to see the "instrumental uses to which the law is put in the present situation." The administration has produced a spectacle of the law. Claiming a strict adherence to the letter of the law while flagrantly breaking or ignoring numerous actual laws, the administration uses the law as a tactic in its ongoing pursuit of executive power, and the spectacle of sovereignty inaugurates the state of exception that suspends the law behind which it inaugurates itself. As such, sovereignty is exercised in what Butler calls the "self-allocation of legal prerogative." It is therefore in the very relationship between the administration's adherence to some laws and its suspension of others that the sovereign and the state of exception lie. The suspension of law, Butler writes, "produces sovereignty in its action and as its effect."[10] The precise relationship between the law and the state of exception under the Bush administration is complex and often contradictory, however.

While the Bush administration flaunted its contempt for international law and the United Nations, it also went to great lengths to prove the legality of certain positions.[11] Attorney General Alberto R. Gonzales, for example, first rose to prominence when his "Torture Memo" to President Bush of 25 January 2001 became public.[12] Timothy Brennan and Keya Ganguly argue that the administration's continuous attempts to provide legal precedent for its unlawful acts belie the claim of a renewed state of exception and sovereign power: "[President Bush] has sought not to suspend the law but vigorously to observe its letter, enlisting allies within the judicial system to deploy legal briefs on behalf of his favored interpretations. At the same time, he has been in open violation of the law, including the constitution. He is not therefore sovereign and above the law but, in practical terms, a criminal; and these are not versions of the same thing.... Naked power and the law have worked together in complementary rather than contradictory fashion." The authors dismiss the concept of sovereignty because Bush has attempted to prove the legality of his every move, but this underplays the intricate nature of the relationship between sovereignty and governmentality, or what the authors themselves call "naked power and the law."[13] If, as Foucault suggests, law has become a tactic of government, then the administration's adherence to some laws, and the extent to which it has gone to show that adherence, offers further evidence that the law has come to serve as a means rather than an end. The Bush administration is less interested in upholding the law than in maintaining power. That power is manifest most clearly in the very spaces in which the law is suspended. "Sovereignty," Butler argues, "is reintroduced in the very acts by which [the] state suspends law, or contorts law to its own uses."[14] Using the events of September 11 as a rationale, the Bush administration produced the affective conditions for a totalizing state of exception.

It is of course in the state of exception that functionaries, what Butler calls the "newly invigorated subjects of managerial power," become sovereign.[15] In the figure of Jack Bauer the state functionary becomes sovereign hero.[16] Frequently acting outside the law, Bauer embodies the sovereign subject produced under the state of exception. Pease claims that "in order to protect the rule of law . . . the state declared itself the occupant of a position that was not subject to the rules it must protect."[17] Bauer is a sovereign subject who stands outside the law in order to ensure that it is upheld. Acting from necessity and in times of great duress, he presents an image of sovereignty that belies the subordination of ethical concerns and human rights at the heart of the War on Terror.[18]

The ethical imperative that endows Bauer with the autonomy to act within the state of exception as an autonomous subject unconstrained by normal rules situates him as a sovereign subject with the right to decide what constitutes a legal subject. For Agamben, the state of exception is "that temporary suspension of the rule of law that is revealed instead to constitute the fundamental structure of the legal system itself."[19] In an episode from the first season Bauer complains to a policewoman whom he has recruited to help him apprehend a suspect, "I wish you hadn't called for backup." "Why?" she asks. "Because cops have to play by the rules and I may have to break a few with this guy." Minutes later, immediately after the policewoman has been shot and killed, Bauer tells a police chief, "Please forget about the damn chain of command. I need to see this man now. Just for a few minutes." Slavoj Žižek suggests of *24* that, "while [the CTU agents] continue to act on behalf of the legal power, their acts are no longer constrained by the law."[20] In the figure of Jack Bauer *24* provides a model of heroic behavior that belies the erosions of civil society it claims to protect.

Butler argues that contemporary sovereignty is "animated by an aggressive nostalgia [that] reanimates a spectral sovereignty within the field of governmentality."[21] Since September 11, however, Bush has arrogated to himself an increasingly shadowy and complicated series of sovereign powers. This authority is yoked to the construction of a reinvigorated masculinist prerogative in which the War on Terror provides the raison d'être for the recuperated forms of nostalgic masculine authority. If, as Wendy Brown writes, governmentality names the moment in which the "homology between family and polity dissolved," the War on Terror resolves that homology and situates heroic action as the patriotic defense of both the home and the homeland.[22]

"You're Going to Have to Trust Me": Melodramas of Homeland Security

> 24 is hardly a documentary. We'll use specific devices to create drama, and for that to be confused with what is happening in the real world is silly.
>
> KIEFER SUTHERLAND, who plays Jack Bauer on 24

> We have spoken to soldiers with experience in Iraq who say, for young soldiers, there is a direct relationship between what they are doing in their jobs and what they see on tv.
>
> BRIGADIER GENERAL PATRICK FINNEGAN

Jack Bauer is both a public servant and a family man, and especially in its early seasons 24 is as much a family melodrama as it is a political thriller. In the first season Bauer's daughter, Kim, is kidnapped after she has snuck out late at night to hang out with a friend (who is later killed) and to meet two young men who subsequently turn out to be working for the Drazens, the criminal family who are plotting the assassination attempt around which the season's plot centers. At first Bauer and his wife believe Kim's disappearance is a domestic parenting issue. Bauer has only recently moved back in with his wife and daughter after a period of separation in which he had an affair with a CTU coworker, Nina Myers, and unresolved family tensions are highlighted early on. When the audience first sees Bauer he is playing chess with Kim late at night. During their conversation Kim's dedication to her father—she calls him "Daddy"—is established in opposition to her distrust of her mother, whom she blames for the Bauers' marital problems. "So, is she still giving you the cold shoulder?" Kim asks him. Moments later the viewer sees a photograph on Kim's bedside table of her with her father. In this first episode Bauer is established as a caring and concerned parent; if he is not a loyal husband, then certainly he is a dedicated father—and it is fatherhood that the show ultimately finds to be more important.

Bauer's status as a caring father is a central aspect of his identity, and the show's focus on fatherhood is one way it attempts to inaugurate a recuperative state of masculinist action. Stella Bruzzi equates modern masculinity with "fragility" and the "notion that men's greatest battles [are] now the internal rather than the external ones"; in contrast, *24* reweaves the competing imperatives of home and nation and regenerates a prior mode of masculine action.[23] In this way the show is in keeping with the generally reactionary and revisionist nature of post–September 11 constructions of masculine identity during which, Elaine Tyler May writes, media portrayals of heroism "reinforced gender constructions that date back half a century."[24] The fact that the show's first season, which does so much to establish the narrative patterns that follow, was conceived and plotted prior to the events of September 11 only serves to highlight the discursive continuities of pre– and post–September 11 renegotiations of masculinity that are often facilitated by the reclaiming of domestic space as a site of masculinist action and recuperation.

Scaled down to the level of domestic melodrama, the imperatives of the state are flattened into the emotional requirements of paternal responsibility. The relationship between Bauer's desire to save his family and his obligation to his country is complex, and these two imperatives, unsurprisingly, are often at odds with one another. At the beginning of each episode the tension between family and nation is highlighted for the audience as a voice-over from Bauer states, "Right now terrorists are planning to assassinate a presidential candidate. My wife and daughter have been kidnapped. And the people I work with may be involved in both. I'm Federal Agent Jack Bauer. And this is the longest day of my life." It is often difficult to establish whether Bauer's actions are related to the threat against Palmer or the kidnapping of his wife and daughter; many of his extralegal activities are attempts to save his wife and daughter and not part of his duties as a CTU officer. Viewers are often kept in a state of confusion about Bauer's motives and are frequently required to suspend their own moral faculties and to rely on Bauer's.

In episode 1 a CTU coworker (who later turns out to be an enemy mole) tells Bauer that she will hack into a computer system and access private Internet passwords only if he has a warrant. "And if I didn't have a warrant?" he asks her. She asks in turn whether the information he's looking for is important. "It's pretty important," he concedes. "Go," she acquiesces. The email password he wants turns out to belong to his own daughter, and he is trying to work out who she might have snuck out to meet. This episode highlights the breakdown between public and private that animates so much of the show's narrative drive. The scene takes place at CTU headquarters after Bauer has been called in to attend to the national crisis while he is in the midst of his family crisis. At this point neither Bauer nor the audience knows that the two events are related. Because Bauer's actions are motivated by his desire to find his daughter (and later his wife), his transgressions of civil liberties and the right to privacy are excused; as the public and the private are conflated, the illegal actions of a federal agent are forgiven when they turn out to be the actions of a concerned father. Transforming the actions of the state into the actions of a father, 24 obfuscates the ethical debates that might otherwise cloud its clear vision of right and wrong. Bauer has a clear moral vision and an unwavering sense of justice.[25] As a father he is a public servant the citizenry can trust.

Even when Bauer shows a blatant disregard for the law or the "damn chain of command," his actions are clearly motivated by his concern for the good of both nation and family, although his responsibilities toward his family are not always coterminous with those public imperatives. Unlike traditional models of heroic endeavor in which the public good might intrude on family life but ultimately ends up being reconciled with it, 24 sees the two to be in a state of constant, if often productive tension. The elevation of family over state reaches its apotheosis in the final episodes of season 1, when Bauer persuades Palmer to pretend that an assassination attempt on his life has been successful so that the assassins will release Kim. Palmer agrees to the request because, as he tells his wife, "Jack Bauer saved my life not once, but twice." Personal honor is at once both more important than public responsibility and a requirement for it. Moreover it is in this moment that Palmer becomes a presidential candidate. He is in fact so disgusted with his wife after she leaks the fact of his survival to the press that he leaves her, claiming, "I just don't think you're fit to be the first lady." Like Palmer, who lies to the nation to help save Kim's life,

Bauer evinces the correct response to the terrorists' manipulations. In a final moment of vigilante justice, after being told that Kim has been killed, Bauer singlehandedly storms the dockside hideaway of the Drazens and kills all the henchmen. Private justice overcomes public responsibility at the close of this scene, when Bauer kills Viktor Drazen rather than taking him into custody.

If *24* takes the home and the nuclear family to be the proper locations within which patriarchal or paternal authority is effected, it also suggests the sacrifices required in the name of that authority. At the end of the final episode of season 1 Teri Bauer is murdered, apparently unnecessarily, when the mole attempts to escape from CTU. While Teri's death could be read as a punishment for Bauer's imperious and impulsive actions, it is more accurate to say that her death frees him from the problematic responsibilities of family. Bauer has shown that he is more than equal to those responsibilities and therefore can now be freed of them. In the final scene of the season finale he is shown holding Teri's corpse, crying, "I'm so sorry, I'm so sorry." This scene runs concurrently in split screen with a sepia-tone flashback to early moments of family reconciliation from the first episode. Returned to a moment from the beginning of the season— yet less than twenty-four hours earlier, in the show's narrative time—the viewer is reminded that the story began with the Bauers' attempted reconciliation, which was interrupted by the requirements and responsibilities of public action. The viewer is brought full circle and reminded of Bauer's personal commitment to the family values his public actions have sought to uphold. Bauer sacrifices his own family so that the nation can remain intact. As CTU Director Richard Walsh (Michael O'Neill) exclaims in the opening episode, "If Palmer gets hit—the first African American with a real shot at the White House—it'll tear this country apart."

Through his public actions and private sacrifices Bauer prevents this shearing of the fragile fabric of the nation. Ray suggests that the reluctant hero composite yokes together such contradictory traditions—individualism and community—and thus foregrounds what he calls "the general pattern of American mythology: the denial of the necessity for choice."[26] This denial inaugurates the sense of innocence that allows the citizenry to believe that its own behavior is exemplary; through the figure of the reluctant hero Americans are able to imagine themselves as actors *because* they have been acted upon. This belief was evoked by President Bush in relation to the events of September 11 and reiterated by his White House press secretary, Scott McClellan. "The terrorists started this war," McClellan said, "and the President made it clear that we will end it at a time and place of our choosing."[27] We have been subject to irrational and unprovoked attack, this logic suggests, but we shall respond in ways appropriate to our national character and strengths.

The similarities between the traditional models of heroism Ray delineates and the new heroic figures produced after September 11 suggest the profound ways in which standard U.S. national narratives have been translated in the current moment. Jack Bauer is a new kind of hero for a new kind of war only inasmuch as he updates the paradigmatic features of Americans' belief in masculinist heroic action. One of the defining features of the concatenated outlaw and official hero is his liminality; while the official hero, often a schoolteacher, a lawyer, a mayor, is a figure of order and stability, the outlaw hero inhabits the limits of society and thereby defines its center. "By discouraging commitment to any single set of values," Ray explains, "[the outlaw and official hero] mythology fostered an ideology of improvisation, individualism, and ad hoc solutions for problems depicted as crises."[28] The typical heroic figure of the cowboy, for example, stands removed from the civilizing social order. The cowboy manifests the violent or regressive characteristics the social order denies in itself; unconstrained by the rules of law, the outlaw hero is able to protect society from external threats because he is willing to behave in ways the social order annexes. In these ways, Ray suggests, the outlaw hero produces justice outside the law (and when the law has failed). The outlaw hero is a liminal figure outside the law and the social order who, paradoxically, ensures their survival. Jack Bauer functions in precisely this way as he oscillates between state functionary and rogue agent. In the space between the failure of the law and the state of exception, Bauer becomes sovereign.

In the immediate aftermath of September 11 Bush evoked just such a figure of vigilante justice when, during an appearance at the Pentagon, he responded to the question "Do you want Bin Laden dead?" by claiming, "I want justice. There's an old poster out west, as I recall, that said, 'Wanted: Dead or Alive.'" When asked for further clarification, Bush responded, "I just remember, all I'm doing is remembering when I was a kid I remember that they used to put out there in the old west, a wanted poster. It said: 'Wanted, Dead or Alive.' All I want and America wants him brought to justice. That's what we want."[29] By describing the invasion of Afghanistan and the attempt to capture Osama bin Laden in these terms, Bush was linking the response to September 11 to the long-standing tradition of American heroism Ray describes. By situating the hunt for bin Laden in the "old west" Bush was able to produce a narrative of recuperative justice in which the United States would not fail to act and within which the citizenry could produce the correct affective responses to the coming war(s).[30] Most fascinating, though, is Bush's claim that "all [he's] doing is remembering." Regardless of whether Bush grew up in Texas or Connecticut, in this memory he conflates the history of the nation with its mythic archetypes. What Bush remembers is a fiction. Conflating history with popular culture, he situates the War on Terror within a commonly held set of beliefs about American masculinity. At the same time that he linked contemporary events to the nation's mythic past, he produced an affective relationship between vigilante justice and the citizenry when he claimed, in the same speech, "The world will see that the strength of this nation is found in the character and dedication and courage of everyday citizens."[31] Such tests of character have become a core component of the Bush administration's rhetoric of masculinity and further suggest the links between traditional and neoliberal forms of masculinist action. September 11 allowed for a return to prior forms of masculinity that had been called into question by the sociocultural transformations of the past half century. In *24* Bauer not only stands as an exemplar of traditional American values of community and individuality, but also reflects the exemplary masculinity repeatedly evoked by Bush in his presentation of the War on Terror: "Bring it on," "Mission accomplished," "Wanted: Dead or Alive." The administration used the mythic values of American popular culture to create a powerful narrative backdrop against which the War on Terror could be played out.

At the center of that backdrop was the figure of the president himself. The "character" and "courage" of the everyday U.S. citizen Bush evoked is embodied most typically in figures of patriarchal authority, and the president is citing himself, as president and as a Texan and a Washington outsider, as the proper heir to the morally certain mythic heroes of the Old West. If the War on Terror requires proper enemies—the Taliban, Saddam Hussein—it also requires proper heroes. In her discussion of Bush's infamous "Mission accomplished" stage show aboard the aircraft carrier USS

Abraham Lincoln in May 2003, Dana D. Nelson writes, "The Bush team has made presidential manliness central to its mission and image."[32] The goal of this presidential machismo, however, was not to provide stability or security to the nation, but exactly the opposite. The masculine hyper-militarism of the domestic and foreign policies of the Bush administration were specifically designed to maintain—not allay—the sense of fear that gripped the nation after September 11. The show *24* produces a version of that fear in both its plotlines and its formal narrative structure.

"Events Occur in Real Time":
The State of Exception's Anxious State

> America wants the War on Terror fought by Jack Bauer. He's a patriot.
> JOEL SURNOW, cocreator and executive producer of *24*

> My impression is that what has been charged thus far is abuse, which I believe technically is different from torture. I don't know if it is correct to say what you just said, that torture has taken place, or that there's been a conviction for torture. And therefore I'm not going to address the "torture" word.
> SECRETARY OF DEFENSE DONALD RUMSFELD

The sense of anxiety that the Bush administration manufactured by barraging the public with incessant terror threats and security alerts required Americans to internalize the administration's policies at the level of affect rather than rationality; U.S. citizens were, as a rule, required to *feel* scared. The show *24* instantiated this feeling in its own formal devices. As Bauer's actions—as both father and counterterrorist operative—provide a model of exemplary neoliberal citizenship, *24*'s syntactical concatenation of time and space manifests an immediacy in which those actions were the only response to exceptional circumstances. The split screens, ticking clock, and onscreen clock that have become the show's signatures produce a sense of anxiety that functions as spectacle and affect. The sense of real-time immediacy compels the forward momentum of the plot and manipulates the viewer into a state of constant nervous tension. The viewer becomes a spectator of a television event that is seemingly more real and has more immediacy than the carefully orchestrated sound bites of the evening news. The show's formal manipulations provide the affective rationale for the more macabre elements of its plotting. Always tied to temporal necessity, Bauer's actions gain a moral imperative that transcends the normal ethical parameters of responsibility. The torture of suspects, detainees, coworkers, and even family members is a regular event on *24*, and the show frequently replicates the smoking gun as mushroom cloud logic behind the ticking-time-bomb argument. There is never time for reflection in *24*, and decisions must be made in relation to a future perfect in which potential acts of terror have *not* taken place because of Bauer's and others' ability to decide on and pursue a course of action unconstrained by the rules of law.

In its formal manipulations of time *24* produces a state in which the moral relativism that lies behind the Bush administration's argument makes sense: the threat of global terrorism requires that the state's actions must be considered in relation to its overall goals and to particular threats rather than to international standards of human rights or responsibilities. "The Bush administration's military policies in coordination with its new Department of Homeland Security," Nelson observes, "have excelled at extending the time of fear and its masculinist compensations."[33] In its formal manipulations of narrative time and space *24* perfectly reflects this "time of fear" and provides us with a heroic figure who can navigate the postethical terrain of torture and rendition. Bauer's actions are always tied to an ethical imperative toward forward movement in which every second counts.

In its production of a state of nervous anxiety in which immediate results are required and must be achieved by whatever means, *24* replicates the ticking-time-bomb scenario mounted most famously in recent years by Alan Dershowitz in his defense of the use of torture by the United States in its pursuit of suspected terrorists. The first episode of season 2, for example, opens with a scene in which a group of South Korean military personnel torture a man while U.S. military officers wait in an adjoining room. "When?" one of them asks when the head torturer enters the room. "Today," the torturer responds. "Somewhere in the city of Los Angeles," the president declaims after he is told of the imminent threat, "there's a terrorist with his finger on the trigger, and we've got to get him." This imminent threat—"What I'm about to tell you, Mr. President, is triple sourced"—serves as reason enough for any course of action. Therefore it is deemed acceptable that, for example, Bauer shoot his supervisor

The pressures of family and work collide for Jack Bauer. From 24, season 1, episode 24 (originally broadcast 21 May 2002)

in the leg with a tranquilizer gun because he suspects—incorrectly—that he is a mole (season 1); carjack and kidnap a waitress while he is a fugitive (season 1); shoot and behead the key witness in a federal narcotics trial in order to establish cover (season 2); force a suspect he is interrogating to watch the staged assassination of his son on a live video feed (season 2); become addicted to heroin to infiltrate a Mexican drug cartel (season 3); shoot a detainee in the leg during an interrogation session to expedite the extraction of information (season 4); and torture both the brother and the estranged husband of his girlfriend because he suspects them—again, incorrectly—of being terrorists (season 4).

The ticking-time-bomb scenario attempts to account for situations in which it would be acceptable to torture detainees. Is it acceptable, the scenario asks, to resort to torture in the face on an imminent threat such as a nuclear bomb or other large-scale attack? In his essay "The Rules of War Enable Terror" Dershowitz argues that torture is an acceptable method of extracting information from detainees and that international torture treaties must be modified to allow for such eventualities: "The treaties against all forms of torture must begin to recognize differences in degree among varying forms of rough interrogation, ranging from trickery and humiliation, on the one hand, to lethal torture on the other. They must also recognize that any country faced with a ticking-time-bomb terrorist would resort to some forms of interrogation that are today prohibited by the treaty." Leaving aside the issues of credibility surrounding information obtained under torture, such a perspective produces a sliding scale of the value of human life and a relative and relational construction of responsibility and agency. Condoning the murder of civilians in the pursuit of terrorists, Dershowitz claims, "Civilians who are killed while being used as human shields by terrorists must be deemed the victims of the terrorists who have chosen to hide among them, rather than those of the democracies who may have fired the fatal shot."[34] Secretary of State Condoleezza Rice famously used a version of this argument to justify the U.S. invasion of Iraq when, in an interview with CNN's Wolf Blitzer in September 2002, she claimed, "The problem here is that there will always be some uncertainty about how quickly [Saddam Hussein] can acquire nuclear weapons. But we don't want the smoking gun to be a mushroom cloud."[35] It is this neo-con relativism that *24*'s ticking clocks and real-time hysteria mirror as they rationalize Bauer's vigilante sovereignty at the level of affect. The temporal imperatives of the War on Terror, in which threats are both constant and imminent, require a return to decisive masculinist action and a retreat from liberal relativism and the constrictions of international law.

Time in *24* is both slowed down and sped up, often at the same time and through the same devices; temporality is simultaneously expanded and compressed in a way that unmoors the audience from the standard conventions of forward narrative momentum. At the same time, the show's use of split screens shatters the representational space within which the narrative action takes place. Presented with simultaneous screens displaying multiple characters, locations, and time frames, the audience is overloaded with information. There is often too much going on for the viewer to take it all in. In and of itself this produces a sense of anxiety as viewers attempt to account for what they might have missed at any given moment. As the visual field splits into multiple screens and the digital clock appears accompanied by the ticking sound effect viewers are made to feel that they cannot absorb, let alone make sense of, the masses of data with which they are confronted. This sense replicates the information overload under which U.S. citizens are required to be hypervigilant and to trust the government to parse information for them.

The rapid acceleration of time is accompanied by an equally radical and disorienting slowing down of time. Because the narrative never jumps to later points of action, every event unfolds in excruciating slow motion. In the first season, for example, Kim Bauer's friend Janet (Jacqui Maxwell) is killed by their kidnappers. The events that precipitate Janet's death unfold over three or four episodes and Janet dies over the course of three or four real-time hours. For the audience, however, her death takes a month, the length of time required in the broadcast schedule to air three or four episodes. This manipulation of time alters the audience's perception of the events and produces a contradictory sense of what their outcome will be. Because she is constantly about to die, there is always the possibility that Janet will be rescued; because she never is, her death seems inevitable. She dies both too slowly and too quickly. In this way time is both expanded and compressed: events are always taking place interminably, but they are also always taking place too quickly. This simultaneous sense of haste and the lack of forward momentum produce an affective reaction in which events are at once inevitable and always precipitant. This feeling of narrative inevitability is an affective version of the state of perpetual war justified by the Bush administration. Even if torture is the last resort, the last resort is where *24* always seems to be. The "too soon" nature of the show's narrative momentum is always linked to the "just in time" nature of action and resolution that Bauer exemplifies.[36]

The show *24* does not participate in the conversation about the ethics of torture, but produces a torturer, Jack Bauer, in whom we are encouraged to place our faith. The audience is to trust not only that Bauer acts outside the law only at moments of extreme necessity and when no other recourse is left to him, but also that he is capable of deciding for himself when those moments arise. The necessity for immediate action in the face of unknown, indefinite, and constant danger requires that his coworkers trust him without requiring any explanation of his actions or of the deeds—usually illegal—he asks them to perform. The sovereign authority that resides in Bauer, that which allows him to decide who is guilty and innocent and who should be considered expendable, is vested not in any specific authority (for this is something he often exceeds), but in his person and, more significantly, in his character. This location of sovereign authority in the subject of the state functionary leads, as Susan Sontag has suggested of the Bush administration's production of an endless war, "to the demonizing and dehumanizing of anyone declared . . . to be a possible terrorist: a definition that is not up for debate and is, in fact, usually made in secret."[37] Bauer becomes the location in which justice resides—he is judge, jury, and executioner—and (as the viewer frequently hears) the nation is lucky to have such an exemplary citizen watching over it in such harrowing times. "You saved my life," President Palmer tells Bauer when he tries to persuade him to return to CTU in the first episode of season 2. "I trust you as much as I trust anyone."

The show foregrounds character and trust in place of laws and facts, and Bauer's tautological mode of empathetic argumentation—"It's pretty important"—is not dissimilar to the methods of persuasion used by Bush in his appeals for support during the War on Terror. Bush, for example, evoked the question of character during a surprise visit to Iraq on 13 June 2006, when he told U.S. troops, "[I came] to look Prime Minister Maliki in the eyes and determine whether or not he is as dedicated to a free Iraq as you are. And I believe he is."[38] Statements such as this—and there were many of them—illustrate the renewed focus on tests of character and faith that seemingly motivated the Bush administration's foreign policy: the United States has the right to act however it sees fit just as long as it *believes* that it is acting in a just way. For the conservative theorist Robert D. Kaplan the twenty-first century will be one in which the United States will "initiate hostilities" and will "justify it morally after the fact." "The moral basis of our foreign policy," Kaplan continues, "will depend upon the character of our nation and its leaders, not upon the absolutes of international law."[39] That character, not international law, will dictate U.S. foreign policy became a truism of the Bush administration. In a time of such uncertainty, as Kaplan implicitly argues, we must trust in character and moral vision. The show *24* presents a world in which character is enough, and Jack Bauer's character is exemplary.

In an article on *24* published on *Salon.com* in 2003 the television critic Charles Taylor wrote, "At times the deepest horror of the show has been that of watching good men choose to act in ways they never dreamed of acting." After describing a number of torture scenes from the show, Taylor says, "If this sounds like pulp overkill, it didn't play that way. These scenes were appropriate to a time when America is having a previously unimaginable conversation about the ethics of torture. It's hardly cold realpolitik to believe that torturing an informant would be worth preventing a nuclear explosion. But at the same time, '24' didn't pretend that those methods would not diminish us somehow as a nation."[40] Unfortunately *24 does* pretend that such methods won't diminish us as a nation.[41] The "unimaginable conversation[s] about the ethics of torture" that Taylor describes are rationalized and normalized in *24*—even dismissed as irrelevant—as it presents a world in which the alternative to torture is equally unimaginable; what is required by the show's real-time immediacy is decisive action. Like Kaplan, the show suggests that the character of its central protagonist is capable of withstanding the burden of this responsibility. There is never a time when Bauer is called on to consider other options, nor to reflect on why the tactics he does employ are so often ineffective or that his victims are so frequently innocent. Žižek suggests that the lie of *24* resides not only in its presentation of a world in which it is "possible to retain human dignity in performing acts of terror," but also in its insistence "that if an honest person performs such an act as a grave duty, it confers on him a tragic-ethical grandeur."[42] Because he is a figure of trust, Bauer's actions are sacrosanct; even when he engages in illegal activity he is doing so for the right reasons. Moreover even the U.S. citizens Bauer tortures—friends, family, coworkers—are quick to forgive and even quicker to return to action as their country needs them.[43]

The show *24* did not create the policies of preemptive strike, the neorelativism of the neoconservative right, or the just-in-time logics of acceptable torture that have resulted in the USA Patriot Act, detainee suicides at Guantánamo Bay (cynically deemed publicity stunts by the Bush administration), the prisoner abuse scandal at Abu Ghraib, and the massacre of civilians by U.S. Marines in Haditha in November 2006. As a powerful piece of popular culture, however, it renders such policies and events normative. When Marilyn B. Young states that "September 11 did not change the world; but it has enabled the Bush administration to pursue, with less opposition and greater violence, policies that might otherwise have appeared too aggressive," she voices an opinion held by many who were troubled by the actions of the administration since September 11.[44] Cultural texts such as *24* suggest the striking degree to which the administration's aggressive and belligerent policies resonated with a national public keen to transform the shock of September 11 into the awe of U.S. military domination. In this transformation a reactive model of hypermasculinity belies the masquerade of family-oriented paternalism that subtends it. In the character of Jack Bauer *24* presents a figure of heroic masculinity untroubled by the old relativism of identity politics. For Bauer both the War on Terror and the market imperatives of neoliberal capital accumulation require a rearticulation of traditional forms of heroic action. What *24* offers the public, though, is not a way forward but a step backward. If September 11 was a lure for aggressive and imperialist U.S. foreign and domestic policies, shows such as *24* function as palliatives for a public that seemed to acquiesce to the erosion of its own civil liberties and personal freedoms.

As the war in Iraq dragged on, Jack Bauer—like the various, and seemingly rotating, members of the Bush administration—was able to find moral clarity and a sense of certainty and faith in his own unimpeachable actions in the face of chaos and uncertainty. The show provides us with the means to investigate the foundational assumptions that motivate the claims Bush et al. made repeatedly in our name about democracy and freedom. In a speech to troops at Fort Bragg in late 2005 Bush said, "Amid all this violence, I know Americans ask the question: 'Is the sacrifice worth it?'" "It is worth it," he answered with conviction, "and it is vital to the future security of our country."[45] The citizenry was asked, indeed required to believe in the face of a growing mountain of evidence to the contrary. What was required was trust, without question, in both methods and rationales. If people didn't quite trust George W. Bush anymore, many were willing to trust Jack Bauer. In its presentation of a reinvigorated but reactionary formation of masculine activity grounded in the affective logic of "us versus them," *24* suggests one means by which white masculinity has recouped its franchise on possibility in the contemporary United States. The lability of white masculinity has transformed and reoriented the reactionary modes of heroism that American culture has predominantly turned to after September 11.

2 FUTURE PERFECT ⤳

"Everyday Heroes" and the New Exceptionalism

We see our national character in rescuers working past exhaustion, in long lines of blood donors, in thousands of citizens who have asked to work and serve in any way possible. And we have seen our national character in eloquent acts of sacrifice.
GEORGE W. BUSH, 14 September 2001, quoted in *In the Line of Duty*

Reality and Fiction have become a tangled mess.
JEAN BAUDRILLARD, *The Spirit of Terrorism*

AFTER THE EVENTS of September 11 emergency service personnel attained an almost mythic status in the American public imaginary. Firemen in particular came to stand as exemplars of a way of life that was encoded as particularly and typically American: selfless, heroic, individually brave citizens rising in a moment of need to serve the common good.[1] The figure of the fireman as "everyday hero" has become a standard feature of American popular culture. Films, television series, novels, nonfiction accounts, memorial photo albums, commemorative television shows, custom motorcycles, New York's Major League Baseball teams, news magazines, and comic books have all commemorated this new post–September 11 hero. In 2004, for example, Touchstone Pictures released the film *Ladder 49*. In July 2004 News Corporation's FX cable channel premiered the drama series *Rescue Me*, about the life of a New York City firehouse after

September 11. Nonfiction works dealing with the lives of firemen include Zac Unger's autobiographical account *Working Fire: The Making of an Accidental Fireman* and Tom Downey's *The Last Man Out: Life on the Edge at Rescue 2 Firehouse*, both published in 2004. David Halberstam's *Firehouse* (2002) tells the story of a New York City firehouse that lost twelve men on September 11. News magazines such as *Time, Newsweek,* and *U.S. News and World Report* published commemorative issues that focused heavily on the sacrifices of New York City's emergency workers. Various publishers also released coffee-table books of photographs, such as Regan Books' *In the Line of Duty: A Tribute to New York's Finest and Bravest* (2001). Of the relationship between culture and politics John Carlos Rowe writes, "The 'new global order' endorsed repeatedly and abstractly by George H. W. Bush and now George W. Bush's regimes could not have occurred without the prior work of culture. . . . U.S. cultural production conditioned American citizens to accept the undisguised militarism and jingoistic nationalism now driving U.S. foreign policy."[2] The New York City fireman enables that militaristic nationalism by recoding masculinity within a particular framework of white ethnic and domestic manhood.

In the wake of the September 11 attacks a narrative discourse was produced in which the emergency worker as everyday hero became both victim and survivor of the attacks, and thus the exemplary U.S. citizen. Simultaneously a fracturing of narrative time produced a "time immemorial" in which the events of September 11 came to signify both an end and a new beginning for America. Often routed through a fantasy terrorist attack on the Statue of Liberty, this temporal ellipsis provided a stage on which the newly minted everyday hero could rehearse for the public a version of September 11 with a different ending. In its construction of an exemplary U.S. citizen for the post–September 11 world, this recoding of the events required and reproduced a reactionary national logic of gender and ethnic identity that coalesced around the production of an exemplary white ethnic, working-class hero, figured most completely in the image of the New York City fireman. Through the concatenation of these phenomena a recuperative national narrative was produced that inaugurated a sense of American innocence and a newly oriented exceptionalism. This new exceptionalism portrayed the experience of September 11 in traditional narratives of American innocence, allowing the Bush administration to arrogate to itself complete responsibility for producing a response fully in keeping with the purported magnitude of the event itself, to, in the words of Slavoj Žižek, " 'go back to its basics,' to reassert its basic ideological co-ordinates."[3]

While the concept of American exceptionalism has been battered in academic circles, it is a concept that still holds great value for the nation as a whole. Michael Kammen writes, "American exceptionalism is as old as the nation itself and, equally important, has played an integral part in the society's sense of its own identity."[4] Exceptionalism is often understood to result from the apparent absence of feudal struggle or class conflict in the United States. "The great advantage of the American," Tocqueville claimed in *Democracy in America*, "is that he has arrived at a state of democracy without having to endure a democratic revolution and that he is born free without having to become so."[5] As a "state of democracy" America was the city on the hill, exceptional not only because it was different, but also because it was exemplary, both a goad to the rest of the world and a model on which other nations could base their own struggles for freedom and self-determination. The majority of public and political discourse about the events of September 11 located those events within a renewed sense of the United States as an exceptional nation. As Amy Kaplan has suggested, after September 11, "a narrative of historical exceptionalism [encoded] the event to be so unique and unprecedented as to transcend time and defy comparison or historical analysis."[6] As the United States became an exceptional nation and the victim of an unprovoked and unprecedented attack, the everyday hero became that nation's exemplary citizen. David Simpson writes, "The event we call 9/11 has a past that we can rediscover, a present that we must monitor, and a future that we can project."[7] The construction of an exceptionalist master narrative of revenge and reconstitution for and from the events of September 11 relied on a reconfiguration of American manhood that restored and valorized reactionary forms of masculinist prerogative. As in *24*, post–September 11 popular culture offered up a version of traditional masculine heroism reworked for a postconsensus world.

Comic Book Patriotism

> It seems to me that whenever "heroes" are honored the question arises
> as to who needs them and why. Even in this looser sense of the term
> one can understand Bertolt Brecht's warning: "Pity the land that needs
> heroes."
> JÜRGEN HABERMAS, "Fundamentalism and Terror"

One place the phenomenon of the everyday hero found a compelling home was the comic book. Because of its long history of producing masculinist, patriotic fantasies of valor and sacrifice, the comic book industry was ideally suited to respond to the events of September 11 within the climate of patriotism the attacks produced. As members of an industry traditionally devoted to the production of juvenile fantasies of heroism and superhuman masculinity, the creators of comic books felt particularly compelled to respond to the events of September 11.[8] Despite the complex history of the industry, which underwent its own transformative moment in the late 1980s, superhero comics remain the industry's most recognizable commodity. Many of the most popular and famous comic book series, such as *Batman*, *Superman*, *Spider-Man*, and *Captain America*, dealt with the events of September 11 in single- or multiple-issue story arcs. Within a year of the attacks a number of comic book publishers had released commemorative volumes. Dark Horse Comics, Chaos! Comics, Image, and DC Comics together published the volume *9–11: Artists Respond*, DC Comics published *9–11: September 11th, 2001: The World's Finest Comic Book Writers and Artists Tell Stories to Remember*; Marvel published *Heroes* (2001) and *A Moment of Silence* (2002); and Alternative Comics published *9–11: Emergency Relief*.[9] In January 2003 *Comics Journal*, published by Fantagraphics Books, released a special issue titled "Cartoonists and Patriotism." Because the superhero is such a powerful ideological figure—Superman, after all, fights for "truth, justice, and the American way"—comic books are a particularly privileged place to examine post–September 11 constructions of heroism and masculinity.

While many of the stories in commemorative collections such as these are autobiographical and deal with writers' and artists' immediate reactions in first-person accounts, these collections also contain meditations on the value of the figure of the traditional comic book superhero at a time when heroism itself was being redefined in the national imaginary. Amy Kiste Nyberg points out the relative paucity of superhero narratives in these commemorative volumes, arguing that "the superhero narrative structure and genre conventions did not readily lend themselves to telling stories of September 11."[10] Although the industry eventually found ways to fully incorporate the events of September 11 into the preestablished ideologies of the superhero comic, many early responses spoke more to the impossibility of adequate representation.[11] As writers and artists struggled to represent the traumas of September 11 they turned to a meditation on the nature of heroism and the value of the superhero in the face of the actual heroism of New York's emergency workers. These meditations produced a complex series of responses; in some cases the superhero was portrayed as inadequate to the events; in others the superhero worked with or watched over emergency responders and ordinary citizens. As such, these comics illustrate a broader cultural working-through of the events of September 11 that were also apparent in the mainstream media's representations of the events. The cover for *9–11: Emergency Relief,* for example, echoes the covers of mainstream magazines such as *The New Yorker,* depicting a New York City fireman as a heroic figure. Such images perform important ideological work as they tie the everyday hero to the conventional models of American heroism embodied in the figure of the superhero. Constructed in the idiomatic conventions of the traditional superhero comic book, the figure of the fireman as everyday hero draws on a long and multivalent history of fantasy and wish fulfillment in American culture. Such images of heroism quickly became codified in the public imaginary. While Nyberg is correct to point out that the narrative conventions of the superhero comic were often inadequate to the task of representation, the figure of the superhero often served as a nodal point through which the heroism of September 11 was interpreted.

From the publication of the first *Superman* comic in 1938, the comic book superhero has embodied various ideals of American heroism.[12] While the history of the comic book superhero, and the ideological positions it has been called on to promote, are varied and complex, there is little doubt that for many the figure has a series of powerful meanings that neatly fit the post–September 11 masculine identity evoked in the figure of the everyday hero and the New York City fireman. In early strips Superman was a fighter for social justice and a champion of the people, beholden to the idea, rather than the letter, of the law. Much like the western gunslinger on which early comic book creators drew, the superhero existed on the margins of society but worked for the common good. Most significant, the superhero usually embodies a commitment to justice that understands that justice and law are not always the same; sometimes justice requires the superhero to step outside of the law. Thus while early *Superman* strips show the Man of Steel working within the bounds of the law, they also show him taking the law into his own hands. More often than not the comic book superhero is a vigilante figure who makes his (and only occasionally her) own justice when the judicial system seems incapable of doing so.[13] Such distinctions between justice and the law are common in American culture. As we have seen in the case of Jack Bauer and *24*, the new forms of heroism that are evoked in response to the events of September 11 are revised versions of preexisting ideological paradigms of masculine action. Like Bauer, the everyday hero is a figure who inaugurates a form of retributive justice that conforms to normative American values. Unlike Bauer, however, the everyday hero does not reside at the margins of society (while thereby constituting its core), but is placed directly at the heart of a nostalgic version of American identity. If, as Robert B. Ray explains, the outlaw and official heroes embody competing versions of individuality and communal responsibility that are reconciled in the figure of the reluctant hero, the status of the everyday hero as hero is in part a result of that figure's dichotomous position as both savior and victim.[14] Like Superman—and, indeed, because of him—the post–September 11 everyday hero stood as a paragon of moral absolutes.

By elevating the emergency service worker to the status of superhero, comic book publishers replicated a common response to the events of September 11 in which this heroic figure stood at the vanguard of a form of retributive justice. Cloaked in the patriotic mantle of the superhero, the everyday hero evokes the same notions of justice and retribution found in Bush's "Wanted: Dead or Alive" speech.[15] Randy Martin and Ella Shohat point out that narrative constructions such as this create a logic in which "an orderly and peaceful world has been subjected to arbitrary and irrational attack, and our own regenerative violence will restore the everyday order of the world 'before the fall,' a prelapsarian order for which the 'American Nation' is already nostalgic."[16] As the everyday hero offers an unimpeachable figure of masculine action that cuts through any ambiguity about the meaning of September 11, the mythic cowboy of Bush's western frontier and the vigilante superhero offer a model of behavior for any future actions. Because the everyday hero is an innocent figure of heroic action, the attacks require a form of retributive justice. The everyday hero routes that retribution through a revenge fantasy in which America has been subject to an unprovoked attack by irrational and barbaric forces that "hate our freedoms." As a vigilante figure, the superhero embodies an iron-willed certainty about right and wrong, good and evil that is taken to be unimpeachable.[17]

The figure of the comic book superhero, however, was also a source of some anxiety after September 11, and comic book publishers struggled to identify and update the value of the traditional superhero fantasy. In the story "Unreal," for example, Superman bemoans the fact that he is only a fictional character and therefore cannot actually do anything to help the United States in its hour of need. Superman need not worry, the comic suggests, because the nation already has real-life heroes and does not need his particular strengths.[18] This ambivalence about the status of the traditional superhero after September 11 does not mean, though, that superheroes do not have ideological roles to play, for by positioning Superman and others as powerless in the face of September 11, these collections also performed a palliative function: as the ordinary citizen felt powerless after the attacks, so too did the superhero. Therefore, in stories such as "Unreal," both the citizen and the superhero are asked to place their faith in the new everyday hero embodied in the figure of the fireman.

The cover of DC Comics' commemorative volume *9–11: September 11th, 2001* evidences precisely this sentiment. The cover shows Superman and Krypto the Superdog standing in awe before a mural of firemen, policemen, doctors, and other emergency service personnel. A speech bubble issues from Superman's mouth with a single word, "Wow." This cover revises a famous comic book cover from the early 1950s (reproduced in miniature on the inside cover of *9/11*) in which a small boy and his dog stood before a similar mural displaying a pantheon of superheroes. In the revision fictional superheroes are recast as spectators, watching along with the world as the new everyday hero takes their place in the hearts of Americans. Superman and his dog are humbled by the real and everyday heroism of the people commemorated on the wall in front of them. Superman's response, the cover further suggests, should also be that of the reader. Similarly one

Emergency workers and first responders replace superheroes as fantasy figures of American heroism. From *9–11: September 11, 2001* (2002).

story in *9–11: Emergency Relief* asks, "Who can we ask to help us outrun a collapsing building or a wall of smoke? Where are our Super-Heroes when we need them?" These rhetorical questions are answered in the closing panel of the page, which depicts a New York City fireman in profile against a backdrop of the Stars and Stripes, with two text blocks that read, "And then it hits me" and "They're right there."[19] Although a panel in "Unreal" shows a young boy reading a *Superman* comic as he is pulled from the wreckage, models of American heroism were renegotiated after September 11, and, without exception, the true heroes were shown to be the firemen, policemen, and other emergency service personnel who risked and gave their lives. While the relationship between the real everyday heroes of September 11 and the fictional superheroes of the comic books is complex and ambiguous, the concatenation of the two allowed for claims of innocence and calls for retribution to be uttered in the same breath without pause for thought. The everyday hero might reflect the changing contours of masculinity in the contemporary United States, but it also allowed for a return to more traditional forms of masculine action.

The most sustained response from the comic book industry to the events of September 11 and the new heroism came from Marvel Comics.[20] In addition to incorporating the events of September 11 in ongoing superhero series such as *Spider-Man* and *Captain America*, in 2002 and early 2003 Marvel published a limited-run series titled *The Call of Duty* that focused on the lives of firemen, emergency medical service personnel, and policemen, whom Marvel called "everyday" or "real-life" heroes. *The Call of Duty* is significant because it marks the most sustained effort from comic book creators to understand the heroism of September 11 through the structural and idiomatic conventions of the traditional superhero narrative. Set in September 2002 *The Call of Duty* consists of three interconnected miniseries, "The Brotherhood," "The Wagon," and "The Precinct," each of which focuses on a specific branch of emergency service work (fire, police, EMS). Published concurrently in monthly installments, each miniseries ran for between four and six issues, and the whole series was subsequently released as a two-volume paperback collection that organizes the individual comic issues in the correct temporal sequence, thereby producing a coherent narrative arc. The series was among the first sustained cultural narratives of the new exceptionalism. In a clear evocation of the ideals of heroism promulgated after September 11, Marvel's publicity materials for the series claimed that *The Call of Duty* "explores the public duties and private lives of these [real-life] heroes who face extraordinary situations every day while in the line of duty."[21] By telling the stories of America's new real-life heroes in the genre of the superhero comic, Marvel addressed the industrywide crisis over the relevance of the traditional superhero by capitalizing on the hegemonic patriotism that arose immediately following the attacks.

In its transformation of the superhero into the everyday hero *The Call of Duty* perfectly illustrates how New York City firemen came to stand as exemplars of the values and sacrifices of American citizens in the aftermath of the terrorist attacks. Marvel's real-life heroes combined commonly held notions of American individualism with the equally powerful hail of communal responsibility. The fireman became an American everyman, a figure of heroism and a paragon of the national values that were foregrounded after September 11. As a figure that flattened the complexity of the post–September 11 sociopolitical landscape, the fireman became a fulcrum around which the nation could orient its response to the event. According to Leti Volpp, "Post–September 11, there is a new national imagining as to what bodies are assumed to stand in for 'the citizen' and its new opposite, 'the terrorist.'"[22] As an all-American hero the fireman reified the new subject formations of good and evil, citizen and enemy. It is important in this regard to point out that it is the figure of the fireman particularly around which much of this ideological work takes place. Inasmuch as these reformulations of heroism and citizenship also served to recuperate a beleaguered masculine identity, the fireman is largely immune to the possible contaminating associations of the other branches of first responders. The New York City fireman inhabits a space of neutrality that the police, who run the risk of calling up images of police brutality such as the Amadou Diallo case, or the medical workers, too easily coded feminine, lack. Thus while all branches of New York's emergency service personnel were valorized after the attacks, the fireman in particular provided a powerful screen against which the nation's understanding of itself could be projected.

Such a valorization, however, required a willed amnesia in which the earlier resistance of urban fire departments to both gender- and race-based affirmative action could be forgotten. In order to function as an everyday hero and to stand for the American everyman, the figure of the firefighter needed to be divorced from the structural discrimination that enabled the FDNY to remain a bastion of homogeneous ethnic and gender identity. Nowhere is this clearer than in the valorization of Irishness found in both the FDNY and in many post–September 11 accounts of the sacrifices made by rescue workers. Such associations transform the overwhelming whiteness of the firemen from the results of resistance to affirmative action into a natural and nostalgic state of being. In the closing moments of Jules and Gideon Naudet's and James Hanlon's documentary *9/11* the song "Danny Boy," performed by the famous Irish tenor Ronan Tynan, plays as photographs of deceased firemen are displayed on screen. In their acts of sacrifice the men become heroic and structural discrimination is elided. Tynan became a fixture in New York after September 11 and made frequent appearances singing the national anthem before baseball games at Yankee Stadium.[23] Noel Ignatiev has described fire companies in the nineteenth century as a vital part of the formation of whiteness in America's major cities. This was, in large part, because of the large number of Irish immigrants who served as firemen.[24] Still today men of Irish descent make up a significant portion of the service. Of the 343 firemen who died on September 11, approximately half were of Irish descent, many of whom were members of the Emerald Society, an organization open to firemen and policemen with Irish ancestry.[25] By reformulating whiteness as a nostalgic form of ethnic identity, the more troubling associations that might exist are subordinated.

As the relationship between these new forms of heroic masculinity and long-standing ideals of American heroism already suggests, the post–September 11 moment provided the opportunity for a resuscitation or reinvigoration of traditional models of masculinity that had previously been problematized by calls for recognition and redistribution after the civil rights era. As it reorganizes the ordering imperatives of masculine action, the everyday hero produces a relationship between gender and race that cites a white ethnic identity as the unambiguously proper citizen. Of the 343 firemen who died in New York City on September 11, only twenty-four were black or Hispanic.[26] *The Call of Duty* and other representations of the fireman as everyday hero produce a white ethnic masculinity that reinaugurates a whitewashed U.S. citizenship that recodes multiculturalism as whiteness. James McDonald, the principal protagonist and narrator of *The Call of Duty*, describes himself as the perfect amalgam of different ethnic origins and masculine identity, claiming that he is "Scotch-Irish with a little German thrown in": "All I need is a little Italian and I'd spontaneously combust." White ethnic identity formations are cast here in terms of traditional understandings of masculinity and citizenship as they reference an earlier moment in the immigration history of the United States, ignoring the social and labor problems of that earlier period. In a later issue McDonald references the same white ethnic heritage after he threatens a man with an axe, saying, "If I had any Italian in me I'd be spending the rest of my life in prison." It is not the lack of Italian heritage that makes him perfectly white, but the multiethnic whiteness his Scotch Irish and German heritage connotes. He could just as easily be Scotch Irish with a little Italian thrown in. What is significant about this figure is his evocation of a melting pot version of "proper" American citizenship that consists exclusively of white ethnic identities. In this way the post–September 11 imperative to restore the relationship between masculinity, citizenship, and whiteness continues a form of masculine recuperation that was in evidence long before the attacks and should be understood to be the continuation of a preexisting cultural paradigm. The valorization of white ethnicities that *The Call of Duty* and the celebration of the New York City fireman enact must be understood in relation to these cultural transformations.

As a nostalgic figure that evokes a prior moment in the labor history of the United States, the fireman recodes contemporary citizenship by erasing difference. The place he has sworn to protect is likewise recoded. In addition to a multicultural white ethnicity, the figure of the fireman that James McDonald is an example of produces a nostalgic version of an earlier moment in the history of New York in which the city, home to both Ellis Island and the Statue of Liberty, could be symbolized as an exemplary national site.[27] In order for the attack on the World Trade Center to be understood as a national event, New York City itself needed to be reimagined as an exemplary national space. This transformation was necessary because New York City commonly stands in problematic relation to the imagined space of the nation. As Howard F. Stein points out, "The symbolism of New York [was] a crucial part of the symbolic 'healing' of America, [not least because] New York City itself had long been a projective target *within* the United States, its image alternating between idealizing goodness and demonizing badness."[28] By evoking New York's own mythic past as the gateway to America for the country's immigrant populations, this symbolic recoding ensured the city's incorporation into and ability to stand for the country as a whole, a locus of core American values. As Amy Kaplan correctly suggests, "It seems hard to imagine most Americans claiming [New York City] as part of the homeland, which has a decidedly antiurban and anticosmopolitan ring to it."[29] New York became incorporated into the homeland in part through the shift in focus from the workers killed in the World Trade Center to the valor and sacrifice of the emergency personnel who rushed to their rescue.

The almost immediate shift in focus, both in the mainstream media and the culture at large, from the overwhelming majority of victims of the attacks on the World Trade Center (office workers, custodial and service workers) to the valor and sacrifice of the emergency workers lent an identifiably American face to both a city and a building complex that might otherwise have stood outside the bounds of an easy national identification. Calling up a putatively inclusive—but always white—ethnic subject, the figure of the fireman enacts a historical amnesia that incorporated the city of New York into the space of the nation by encoding the exemplary victims and saviors of the attacks as white ethnics. No longer an extranational space onto which the nation's anxieties about multiculturalism, crime, and immigration were projected, New York was reinterpreted as a blue-collar, white ethnic bastion of normative American values of home, fraternity, and patriarchy. Nowhere was this reincorporation of the city within a traditionally gendered and domesticated national logic more apparent than in the twin focus on the site of the firehouse as an exemplary domestic space and on the widows of deceased firemen.

"A World Apart"

> Heroism feels and never reasons and is therefore always right.
> RALPH WALDO EMERSON, quoted in the Marvel Comics
> commemorative collection *Heroes*

The firehouse situates the fireman as exemplary citizen within an ideally domesticated site. The firehouse instantiates the idea that the attacks of September 11 were on the "American way of life" and constructs the "home" of "homeland security" as it miniaturizes the nation in a pseudo-domestic space of masculine affect and fraternal responsibility. The family home that is absent from September 11 is produced in the firehouse, now a site of family and fraternity and a space of traditional and time-honored patriarchal values. As a pseudo-domestic site, the firehouse is a location in which traditional patriarchy still reigns and is celebrated as the exemplary manifestation of forgotten core American values that the nation as a whole is asked to recall to itself. The firehouse and firemen are the last bastion of core values to which we are all asked to return. An exemplary masculine space that predates the erosions of white and masculine franchise is imagined as a nostalgic space of fraternal commitment, ignoring the history of raced and gendered discrimination that enabled its constitution. In *Firehouse*, his elegy to the twelve firemen from a single West Side New York firehouse who died on September 11, David Halberstam valorizes the fireman as new hero in precisely these ways. "Firemen," Halberstam claims, "live in a world apart from other civilians. The rest of the world seems to change, but the firehouses do not. This is, in fact, as close to a hermetically sealed world as you are likely to find in contemporary America."[30] The firehouse produces a spatiotemporal zone within which the traditional values and ideological beliefs of the nation are preserved. Untainted by the forces of multiculturalism, identity politics, women's liberation, or affirmative action, the firehouse stands as a last bastion of American masculinity. Its status as such, however, is seen as natural and not as the result of fierce struggles over access and discriminatory hiring and promotion practices. Like the heroic figure of the fireman, this reenfranchisement of a normative white masculine space speaks both to the needs of the new exceptionalism and to the "crisis of masculinity." The ideological work performed here is thus twofold.

The figure of the New York City fireman and the site of the firehouse produce an egalitarian space of national fraternity in which traditional values of family, home, and white ethnic heritage are reproduced as the core values of the new exceptionalism. Insisting on the overt relationships between home and work, family and firehouse, Halberstam claims, "The men not only live and eat with each other, they play sports together, go off to drink together, help repair one another's houses, and, most important, share terrifying risks; their loyalties to each other must, by the demands of the dangers they face, be instinctive and absolute." This fraternal bond between firemen is explicitly yoked to the image of the firehouse as a domestic space and fellow firefighters as brothers. "A firehouse, most firemen believe, is like a vast extended second family," Halberstam continues. In the nurturing space of the firehouse, the men "come to love one another . . . because love is a critical ingredient in the fireman's code."[31] These fraternal bonds of love cement the responsibilities of work to the pleasures of family; more than just a place of work, the firehouse is an exemplary—but masculine—domestic space.

The firehouse as home is also a persistent theme in *The Call of Duty*, which devotes considerable attention to the day-to-day functioning of the firehouse and the men who work in it, repeatedly highlighting the ways the firehouse functions as a home with all the attendant familial responsibilities. These responsibilities are presented most poignantly in the daily ritual of setting a place at the dinner table memorializing the death of the only fireman in the fictional firehouse to lose his life on September 11. Producing the deceased fireman as a lost brother by inscribing his absence at the family dinner table, *The Call of Duty* marks the relationship between firehouse and home. In texts such as *The Call of Duty* and *Firehouse* the firehouse is a para-domestic space, both beyond and beside the domestic spaces of the home and the nation. Both exceptional and exemplary, the firehouse returns the (otherwise absent) family to the events of September 11.

While the firehouse resituates the losses of September 11 in a domestic space, it is important to note that all the firefighters are men. The firehouse as a space of masculine action and fraternal sentimentality both reproduces a broader cultural generalization about the gender of firefighters and is central to the production of the fireman as everyday hero and exemplary citizen. In "Too Far Back for Comfort," an article written for *Firework* (the newsletter of the organization Women in the Fire Service), Terese M. Floren, a firefighter, points out the almost exclusive use of the term *fireman* instead of the gender-neutral *firefighter* in news accounts of September 11: " 'Fireman' is the perfect word to use when [you] want to say 'All (real) firefighters are men.' It is a deliberate rejection of the gender-neutral in order to define heroes as male. And that's exactly why these words are all over the news."[32] As Floren perceptively observes, this gender bias enables men to function as heroes while simultaneously producing women as victims. This bias permeated American popular culture in the weeks and months after September 11.

As women became victims, either of terrorists or dictatorships, men would come to their rescue. Elaine Tyler May links the events of September 11 to the cold war: "The time had arrived for an image of reinvigorated manhood. Powerful men appeared as the major players on both sides of the 'good' and 'evil' equation, while women and children seemed vulnerable, in need of protection, whether it was the widows of 9/11 firefighters or the women of Afghanistan."[33] The elevation of emergency workers to everyday heroes was accompanied by a concomitant shift in focus to the surviving widows of deceased firemen. This shift cemented the national allegory of individual sacrifice in the face of an attack on American communal values by instantiating a traditionally domesticated and gendered logic in which grieving widows highlighted the sacrifices of their husbands and boyfriends. In concert with the production of the firehouse as a domesticated site that was torn apart by the attacks of September 11, the figure of the widow transformed the attacks on the World Trade Center and the Pentagon into attacks on the American home and family and helped inaugurate the Manichaean logic of Good versus Evil that came to dominate public discourse about the motives for the attacks and an appropriate response. These traditionally coded gender logics produced a symbolic face onto which the overwhelming sense of national loss could be cathected as the nation was invited to join the grieving widow and to mourn her loss as its own.[34] As New York City came to stand for America, firemen became the nation's exemplary citizens. The heteronormative logic of gendered action and inaction evident in these beliefs produces the argument that the subsequent invasions of Afghanistan and Iraq were motivated primarily by a desire to liberate Afghan and Iraqi women from oppressive patriarchal regimes. In order to fulfill the ideological role of heroic action, however, the fireman needed to be recoded as actor as well as responder; this transformation was achieved through the symbolic placement of the Statue of Liberty in a coterminous position with the grieving widows of fallen firemen.

Guardians of Liberty

> Maybe it's time we pay less attention to people who manufacture the
> human spirit and take greater interest in those who exemplify it.
> DARWYN COOKE, "Human Values"

As the fireman became the new American hero, the Statue of Liberty came to embody everything that hero sought to protect. The commonplace understanding of the events of September 11 as an attack on American values is clearly evidenced in a semiotic relay in which the Statue of Liberty becomes the symbolic target of the attacks. Moving from the World Trade Center—often through the pseudo-militaristic symbolism of the replication of the flag raising at Iwo Jima by three New York City firemen (captured in the now famous photograph taken by Thomas E. Franklin)—to the Statue of Liberty (which these magazines show either before the attacks, dwarfed by the World Trade Center towers, or immediately after, grieving their loss), this semiotic relay effectively reorients the ideological coordinates of the events of September 11.[35] The transition produces an almost complete erasure of the concurrent attack on the Pentagon and the hijacking of United Airlines Flight 93, brought down by its passengers in a field in Pennsylvania. In this disjuncture the nascent War on Terror was divorced from a history of U.S. military and economic imperialism that might confuse the Manichaean conflict of Good versus Evil espoused by the Bush administration and became the self-defense of the American values and freedoms the Statue of Liberty symbolizes. This relay is evident both in *The Call of Duty* and in many of the news magazine commemorative editions that were published in the weeks after the attacks.

In order for the Statue of Liberty to become the symbolic face of the attacks, however, the World Trade Center—their actual target—was abstracted in a series of interesting ways. Much as New York needed to be symbolically reincorporated into the fabric of the nation, the World Trade Center required a similar ideological refitting. Unlike the city itself, however, which was filled with exemplary citizens, the World Trade Center was symbolically evacuated and flattened. As the name "Twin Towers" might suggest, the World Trade Center itself underwent significant recoding as it was memorialized in the aftermath of September 11 and emptied of almost all of its prior meanings. Marita Sturken has pointed out, "Standing untouched, the World Trade Center had been invested with many meanings in its duration of almost thirty years—the folly of oversized public building projects, the banal glass towers of modernity's fading years, the symbol of New York tourism, and, later, the arrogance of American capital. Yet, once fallen, their absence spoke more profoundly than their presence ever could."[36] The Statue of Liberty replaces the World Trade Center as target while also becoming the symbolic inhabitant of the Twin Towers.

This symbolic transition was reproduced in almost every news magazine's commemorative issue. The front cover of *Time*, for example, shows a moment just after the impact of the second plane into the World Trade Center and the back cover shows the Statue of Liberty foregrounded against a haze of smoke and debris, marking the absence of the Twin Towers. The inside back cover is taken up by a full-page photograph showing the flag being raised by the firemen in the foreground, with the remains of one wall of the World Trade Center in the background. The front cover of *People Weekly* is a photograph of a moment just prior to the impact of the second plane, and a picture of the Statue of Liberty appears on the second page. While it is shot from exactly the same location as the photograph in *Time*, the *People* photograph is a stock image, taken before September 11, accompanied by the caption "A Portrait of What Was. As the day began, New Yorkers had no idea that in a matter of moments their city and their lives would be changed forever."[37] In this conjoining of text and image the Statue of Liberty is represented as an inhabitant of New York. Like the grieving widows portrayed in the media, the Statue is the symbolic face of the nation that must be protected from further threats to her national security by rogue terrorists and whose losses must be avenged. And the fireman, paradoxically, ensured that revenge would take place.

As New York's emergency workers became the guardians of Liberty (both the Statue itself and the values it embodies), their role was codified through the replication of the flag raising at Iwo Jima captured in Franklin's photograph. This photograph (and others like it) appeared in countless newspapers and magazines after its original publication in *The Record*. For example, the image was also reproduced as a postage stamp and served as the source for a proposed memorial to the firefighters who lost their lives on September 11.[38] An almost identical photograph appeared on the final page of *People Weekly*, accompanied by the caption "A Banner Yet Waves. In an echo of Iwo Jima, firefighters, at day's end, raise the flag."[39] While these photographs have been presented as unmediated and spontaneous, their symbolic value should not be underestimated. Even the most seemingly spontaneous photograph is enframed, as Susan Sontag argues, in an overdetermined array of meanings that belie its status as the representation of reality.[40] The "echo of Iwo Jima" explicitly evoked by *People* points to the symbolic link that joined the firefighters to the triumphs and heroism of the Second World War—the last "good war"—and lent them a martial air. Moreover as these photographs evoke the memory of the war in the Pacific they link the events of September 11 to the Japanese attack on Pearl Harbor that inaugurated America's entry into the war.[41]

In these photographs the firemen become more than just emergency workers; as the country's new heroes, they were at the vanguard of the War on Terror. Liam Kennedy suggests that in many of the photographs depicting the actions of emergency workers "is a story of individuals acting heroically by doing their civic duty and of a nation united in grief and a resolve to regenerate its core values and dreams."[42] Still civilians and not properly part of the armed forces, these firemen helped foster the understanding that any response to the attacks would be an act of self-defense rather than an act of aggression. Situated as the proper moral center of the country's response to the attacks, New York emergency personnel were both exemplary victims and survivors; their status ensured that any critique of that response had to be seen as a critique of the valor of those who sacrificed their lives for others in New York on September 11.[43]

As the attack on the World Trade Center is reimagined as a potential attack on the Statue of Liberty, it becomes an attack on a set of absolute values. Unlike the World Trade Center or the Pentagon, the Statue of Liberty stands for a set of values that are understood to be universal and unimpeachable: liberty, freedom, democracy, and justice. The Statue of Liberty becomes the symbolic face of a fantasy that, like the figure of the fireman, reimagines New York and the nation as pluralistic and multicultural (if solely inhabited by white ethnics) and incorporates the events of September 11 into the standard range of U.S. national narratives.[44] Once the attack on the World Trade Center became an attack on the "nation of immigrants" it became an attack on the world and, more significantly, an attack on the universal values the United States claims to embody. This rhetorical and symbolic transformation is evidenced most clearly in Marvel's *The Call of Duty* when the Statue of Liberty itself comes under terrorist attack on September 11, 2003. The Statue is displayed in a two-page spread at precisely the moment it is destroyed by terrorists. Echoing and revising the now iconic images of the falling Twin Towers, this image literalizes the ideological transformation of the attack to one on American

The Statue of Liberty comes under attack in a revisionist fantasy of September 11. From *Call of Duty*, Marvel Comics (2002).

values. The innocence embodied in the Statue is further enhanced by the image of a young girl with her father, walking toward the Statue, late for a meeting with her mother and two brothers, who are already climbing the interior steps. As the rockets approach, the girl's mother calls her on a cell phone to say that she is "only half way up," and the girl watches as her family members are murdered in the attack.

As the personification of a series of abstracted universal values, the Statue of Liberty also contributed to the deconstitution of September 11 as an event in history; as the Statue of Liberty and the fireman came to inhabit a fantasy space of national incorporation, they also came to inhabit a temporal space in which the events of September 11 were open to further recuperative reinterpretation. In the national fantasy of revenge and reclamation the Statue of Liberty is not only gendered as female and produced as a victim, but also comes to stand for both the future and the heroic past of the nation. As such, the attack on the Statue of Liberty at the heart of this national fantasy becomes both an attack on "universal" American values and an attack on the memory of September 11. Because the Statue serves as the cathectic face of mourning after September 11, the horror embodied in the fantasy of her destruction in a future attack is doubled. As an attack on the unimpeachable memory of September 11, this fantasy exploits the traumatic nature of the very events it claims to memorialize. In a discussion of trauma and memory Cathy Caruth points out that, "Not having been fully integrated as it occurred, the [traumatic] event cannot become, as [Pierre] Janet says, a 'narrative memory' that is integrated into a completed story of the past." Seemingly inassimilable to lived experience, the traumatic event remains outside of narrative memory; it is "a history that literally *has no place*, neither in the past, in which it was not fully experienced, nor in the present, in which its precise images and enactments are not fully understood."[45] Temporally incoherent, the traumatic event stands outside of history. Inhabiting the structural temporality of an inassimilable event, September 11 was immediately narrativized *as* a traumatic event, and the logic of trauma was mobilized to recast September 11 as an exceptional event, standing outside of history.

Time Immemorial

> What is terrible about "September 11," what remains "infinite" in this wound, is that we do not *know* what it is and so do not know how to describe, identify, or even name it.
>
> JACQUES DERRIDA, "Autoimmunity: Real and Symbolic Suicides"

The transformation of the attacks on the Pentagon and the World Trade Center into an attack on a universalized set of American values required an almost willful historical amnesia wherein the attacks were unique, unequaled in magnitude, and unprecedented in the history of the world. In addition to providing a symbolic reorientation for the events of September 11, the semiotic relay from the World Trade Center to the Statue of Liberty participates in this temporal reconfiguration as a recuperative temporality is constructed that substantiates the exceptional nature of the event. If, as Judith Butler has suggested, "the enormous trauma [of September 11] undermines narrative capacity," the fantasy of an attack on the Statue of Liberty constructs a recuperative narrative that both overcomes and manipulates the trauma of the event.[46]

The sense of September 11 as a missed event standing outside of historic or narrative time is a central aspect of the overall plot and narrative structure of *The Call of Duty*. This is evidenced most clearly in the proliferation of September 11s in the series: the actual September 11, 2001; a fictional September 11, 2001; a September 11, 2002, that is the present time of the comic's action; and a September 11, 2003, in which a terrorist attack on the Statue of Liberty occurs. The references to September 11, 2001 (both real and fictional), in "The Brotherhood" come immediately after the depiction of the attack on the Statue of Liberty. The first comes in the form of a quote from Lieutenant Richard Smith of the Brooklyn Fire Department: "September 11 was an off-day and we were out playing golf. That probably saved my life." This quote is set in white type against a black background in a page-wide panel. It is immediately duplicated in the plot of the comic as the panel below it shows James McDonald, lying on a couch, ruminating about the loss of one of his fellow firemen on September 11, 2001. A sequence of nonspeech narrative boxes say, "On September 10th I went to bed early. . . . Bunch of us had been planning a golf game for about a month. . . . We had an early tee time the next morning. . . . We lost one of my best friends that day. . . . He wasn't a golfer." This sequence, which takes up six page-wide panels over two pages, ends with the depiction of an empty place-setting left at the dinner table in the firehouse to commemorate the lost fireman. This sequence links the real to the fictional and links both to the fantasy of a future attack. Each of these narratives describes an absence and tells how the speaker missed the events of September 11. To be able to talk of September 11 means one has survived it. Lieutenant Richard Smith and James McDonald are both describing the trauma of survival. The real trauma of September 11 is shown here to reside in its status as a missed event. Speaking of September 11, Fredric Jameson points out, "It is important to remember that historical events are never really punctual—despite the appearance of this one and the abruptness of its violence—but extend into a before and an after of historical time that only gradually unfold, to disclose the full dimensions of the historicity of the event."[47] The multiplication of September 11s in the narrative space of *The Call of Duty* functions as a traumatic narrative and continually offers up the event for interpretation and reinscription. The fantasy attack on the Statue of Liberty becomes an event that literally cannot be missed. As Caruth points out, "The crisis at the core of many traumatic narratives . . . often emerges, indeed, as an urgent question: is the trauma the encounter with death, or the ongoing experience of having survived it?"[48] What *The Call of Duty* goes on to produce is an event that will not be missed and in which the tragedy of September 11, 2001, is overcome.

The transition from September 11, 2001, to a future perfect for a vigilant national body is literalized in *The Call of Duty*, as the future attack on the Statue of Liberty is both represented and prevented and the fireman as everyday hero becomes the nation's savior.[49] Throughout the early issues of the series a young girl repeatedly appears at the scene of fires, crimes, and accidents, warning people, "Everyone in New York is going to die." The reader eventually discovers that the girl has been sent back to September 11, 2002, from September 11, 2003, by her father to warn "someone in uniform" about a terrorist attack on the Statue of Liberty, in which her mother and two younger brothers have been killed. Transmitted telepathically by the young girl to a fireman who has just regained consciousness after being badly burned, the representation of the attack on the Statue of Liberty is in many ways the climactic moment in *The Call of Duty*. However, because the event that is described on the page has not yet happened in the narrative sequence of the plot, it is a climax that has not yet happened. The September 11, 2003, described in *The Call of Duty* inhabits an elliptical space, outside the comic's narrative and outside of history; it is an event from the young girl's past but the fireman's future. It is precisely in the space of this temporal ellipsis that the exceptionalist narrative of national recuperation replaces the trauma of September 11. In the space between the traumatic past of September 11, 2001, and the future perfect of September 11, 2003, the event is prevented.

By substituting an exception that stands both outside of history and beyond it for the traumatic temporality of the missed—but yet too present and real—event, the new national fantasy links the traumatic temporality of September 11 to the gendered heroism of the everyday hero. Turning the trauma of September 11 against itself, the new exceptionalism evidenced in these popular texts cynically replaces the inability to narrate the traumatic event with a new national fantasy. Attending to the relationship between the temporality of September 11 and the political fantasies of the Bush administration, Donald E. Pease writes, "Inherently nonsynchronous, September 11 calls for a time to come."[50] The figure of the everyday hero inhabits that time to come and stands as the guardian of the American values that the attacks of September 11 sought to destroy. The ideological fantasy of the fireman as guardian of liberty reinscribes American exceptionalism by producing a counternarrative that reorients the ideological beliefs of and about America. Substituting a fantasy attack on the State of Liberty for the traumatic memory of the attacks on the World Trade Center and the Pentagon, *The Call of Duty* constitutes a recuperative narrative of redemption that was a central facet of the post–September 11 national fantasy of revenge and reclamation. The proper prehistories of September 11 are lost in the insistent claim that the attacks were unprecedented in history. As a result of this symbolic accretion September 11 comes almost instantly to stand outside of historical time as both a traumatic and an unprecedented event. Through the collation of these two notions of the eventness of September 11—trauma and exception—the very real trauma is transformed into a national narrative in which the trauma becomes the loss of the prior innocence inherent in American exceptionalism. In the substitution of a future attack on the Statue of Liberty for the prior attack on the World Trade Center, what Butler calls "a decentering of the narrative 'I'" is forestalled.[51] No longer a victimized figure, the American male is able once again to control events rather than suffer from them. As the everyday hero protects the nation from the forces of evil that threaten Lady Liberty, the structuring ideologies of possessive individualism and masculine action regain their position as active agents.

In the everyday hero the United States found a powerful figure through which the nation could flatten the complex terrain of the post–September 11 world into a prelapsarian state of exception. History, Kaja Silverman writes, "sometimes manages to *interrupt* or even *deconstitute* what a society assumes to be its master narratives."[52] As the epigraph from George W. Bush at the beginning of this chapter illustrates, however, the United States was soon able to incorporate the events of September 11 into a series of preexisting national narratives about America's character. In the immediate aftermath of September 11 the state was able to reorient and forestall the deconstitution or interruption of American master narratives by transforming the inassimilable into the exceptional. As the events ruptured the time of the nation, the new national fantasy of revenge and recuperation healed the narcissistic wound inflicted by the attacks and inaugurated a fantasy future perfect in which the United States would not fail to act. At the center of this fantasy narrative of revenge and recuperation stood the figure of the everyday hero. Like the melodramatic heroism of *24*, the everyday hero substitutes old for new under the guise of a transformed national destiny. That the nation's new heroes had so much in common with its old ones should come as no surprise. If, as Žižek suggests, the September 11 attacks allowed the Bush administration to "go back to basics," they afforded white masculinity the same opportunity. The everyday hero was constituted in direct relation to the powerful preexisting paradigms of heroism and masculine action that animate many discourses about America's national character. By casting the needs of the nation after September 11 in the affective structures of martial masculinity, white masculinity was able to reclaim its status as the proper location of decisive action and communal responsibility.

Whiteness, Class, and
the Postindustrial Subject

3 Automotive Television Programming and Contemporary Working-Class Masculinities

[*American Chopper*'s] popularity is demonstrable, if resolutely inexplicable.
DAVID CHATER, *The Times* (London)

These guys are highly volatile.
STEVE NIGG, producer of *American Chopper*

AMERICANS HAVE OF LATE (and perhaps again) developed an infatuation with blue-collar labor. To take professional sports as an example, in 2004 the champions in each of the country's three major sports leagues (the NBA, the NFL, and Major League Baseball) all claimed solidarity with the American working man. The NFL's New England Patriots secured their third Super Bowl in five years despite a much-heralded lack of superstars. The Detroit Pistons of the NBA took pride in their self-proclaimed status as a team of "blue-collar workers" who brought their "lunch pails" to every game. During their run to the World Series the Boston Red Sox rallied around the nickname "the idiots" and claimed to be a team of hardworking individuals who reflected the blue-collar heritage of Boston—this despite a team payroll in excess of $121 million (second only to their archrivals the New York Yankees) and individual salaries of as much as $19.8 million (with twenty players earning over $1.5 million each).[1] Since the 1970s, however, globalization and the postindustrial service economy have produced marked transformations in the landscape of American labor that simultaneously belie and account for the realities behind this infatuation. As a result of these transformations, Donald M. Lowe suggests, "the labor force as a whole is being polarized into a mildly expanding top echelon, a shrinking middle, and an enlarged bottom."[2] As traditional forms of industrial work and blue-collar manual labor have been replaced by the knowledge and service work of the new economy, the blue-collar laborer valorized by the millionaire athletes of the Patriots, Pistons, and Red Sox has all but vanished. The recent cycle of automotive programming on cable television is a response to such contemporary discourses of masculinity at the level of cultural representation. In particular, the Discovery Channel's highly successful television show, *American Chopper*, stands at the vanguard of a number of popular reality-based automotive programs that have appeared in the past few years.[3] In addition to *American Chopper*, for example, the Discovery Channel also airs *Monster Garage*, *Motorcycle Mania*, *American Hotrod*, and *Biker Build-Off*. Popular automotive shows on other channels include MTV's *Pimp My Ride*, Spike TV's *Ride with Funkmaster Flex*, TLC's *Overhauling*, and the Speed Channel's *Tuner Transformation*, *Build or Bust*, and *Dream Car Garage*.

American Chopper premiered as a two-episode pilot in September 2002, emerging as a fully fledged series in March 2003. In over one hundred episodes having aired to date, the show follows the day-to-day trials and tribulations of the father-and-son team Paul Teutul Sr. (Senior) and Paul Teutul Jr. (Paulie), the owners of Orange County Choppers (OCC), a custom motorcycle shop located in Upstate New York. Other central characters in the show include Mikey Teutul, Senior's youngest son, and OCC employees Vinnie Dimartino, Cody Connelly, and Rick Petko. The show consistently attracts over three million viewers a week and is among the highest rated nonsports shows on cable television.[4] A typical episode follows the Teutuls and their employees as they design and build a custom motorcycle based on a specific theme. Episodes have seen the Teutuls build bikes for companies such as Snap-on Tools, Gillette, Nike, Trim Spa (a diet product company), NAPA, and Caterpillar. They have also built bikes for individuals, such as the golfer Davis Love III, the *Tonight Show* host and motorcycle enthusiast Jay Leno, and the actor Will Smith (as a tie-in for the film *I, Robot*). In addition to commissioned bikes they have also built commemorative theme bikes saluting U.S. veterans of the Vietnam War, the American worker, and the New York City firemen who lost their lives on September 11, 2001.[5]

While *American Chopper*'s phenomenal success can be attributed in part to its position in the broader cycle of reality-based television that has recently saturated network and cable television, the show's central appeal derives from its presentation of men at work and its production of a masculine family melodrama.[6] The combative relationship between Senior and Paulie is a central focus of the show, and their onscreen arguments are highlighted in the show's advertising. I situate *American Chopper* within the broader cultural paradigm of white male injury and examine how the show produces a recuperation of the prerogatives of patriarchal authority. If, as Hill suggests, "the encroachments of capital upon the patriarchal family unsettle masculinity," capital also has the capacity—and the motive—to restore masculine authority.[7] *American Chopper* produces a recuperative blue-collar masculinity that attenuates the putative losses suffered by working-class men under the postindustrial service economy of the contemporary United States. White masculinity, DiPiero suggests, should be understood not as a fixed identity position, but "as a symptomatic reply to cultural demands."[8] In its presentation of the Teutuls as authentically blue-collar the show valorizes a form of working-class manual labor at precisely the moment when such labor has all but disappeared in the United States.[9]

"A Very Patriotic Theme": Myths of Mobility and Blue-Collar Celebrity

> I worked for everything in my life. I never got anything given to me.
> PAUL TEUTUL SR.

> We have some of the most affluent audience in the history of the network, it's not downmarket in the least.
> CLARK BUNTING, Discovery Channel general manager

Central to the allure of *American Chopper* is the mythic status of the custom motorcycle and the outlaw biker lifestyle in American culture. The custom motorcycle embodies a powerful set of symbols that integrate the outlaw lifestyle of the biker gang with the myth of the American frontier that still maintains a powerful hold on the American psyche. Riding a chopper, Senior tells the viewer in one episode, is "kind of a real freedom feeling." Like the western gunslinger, the outlaw biker is a figure of fantasy wish fulfillment. Symbolizing freedom from the constraints of society, the chopper and the outlaw biker evoke a series of potent American myths about civilization, individuality, and social responsibility. Mythologized in films such as *The Wild One* (1954), starring Marlon Brando, outlaw motorcycle clubs and the motorcycle subculture arose in the United States in the immediate aftermath of the Second World War. GIs returning from Europe brought back army surplus motorbikes and began riding, racing, and customizing them for recreation. The outlaw chopper culture of Southern California that grew out of these clubs, most notoriously depicted in Hunter S. Thompson's *Hell's Angels: The Strange and Terrifying Saga of the Outlaw Motorcycle Gang* (1966), became a powerful symbol of youthful rebellion and of the counterculture movements of the 1960s. The chopper's status as a sign of countercultural rebellion was codified in Dennis Hopper's and Peter Fonda's classic antiestablishment film *Easy Rider* (1969).[10]

In the current nostalgia boom fueled by the purchasing power of the newly affluent baby boomer generation, the custom motorcycle has become a nostalgic symbol of youthful rebellion and individuality co-opted (apparently without irony) to display middle-class affluence. The motorcycle's countercultural symbolism has made it a potent icon for the members of the baby boomer generation who "finally [have] the time and money to buy the choppers they could only long for in their youth."[11] For the middle-class consumer of the motorcycle, the mutual imbrications of these two symbolic functions are a much-desired aspect of the motorcycle's commodity function as economic affluence provides them with the freedom to rebel, albeit only symbolically. As the baby boomer generation has moved up the socioeconomic ladder and come to command an increasingly large percentage of the nation's purchasing power, popular culture has undergone a series of transformations that reflect the values of that generation and a nostalgic longing for the popular youth cultures of the 1950s and 1960s. Following David Harvey's work on postindustrial modes of flexible accumulation, Lowe suggests that "the new pattern [of capital accumulation] favors the production and consumption of a variety of rapidly changing, specialized products targeted at specific market segments."[12] *American Chopper* illustrates the degree to which the outlaw biker and the blue-collar worker have become commoditized identities made available for middle-class consumption. While the show valorizes a particularly working-class form of manual labor, it does so for a predominantly middle-class audience. As the success of shows such as *American Chopper* and the renewed popularity of the Harley-Davidson motorcycle as a symbol of economic success might suggest, the counterculture has gone mainstream; the motorcycle has gone from being a countercultural symbol of dissatisfaction with the traditional values of bourgeois American nationalism to embracing those same values. As the asking price of a new Harley-Davidson is in excess of $20,000 and an OCC chopper is upwards of $50,000, only the truly affluent can afford to be rebels in contemporary America.[13]

The Teutuls' upward economic mobility is as significant to the success of *American Chopper* as the outlaw status of the motorcycles they build, and while the show celebrates the Teutuls as genuine blue-collar workers, it also betrays a slavish attention to the economic success the show has brought them. As such, *American Chopper* evidences an often contradictory set of impulses that nevertheless replicate traditional American beliefs about the interrelationships between individuality, community, and social responsibility. The voice-over narration for the second *American Chopper* pilot calls OCC "an American Dream built on blood, sweat, and steel," and since the show first aired OCC has grown into a multimillion-dollar enterprise. The Teutuls have become icons of a rejuvenated working-class masculinity at precisely the moment they transcend it. In each season of *American Chopper* OCC has moved into ever more spacious accommodations and the Teutuls' increasing economic affluence has been put on display for the viewer: new homes, expensive cars, and extravagant gifts such as custom Harley-Davidsons have all featured prominently. The Teutuls have also been transformed by their celebrity status and have become frequent guests of the late-night television hosts Jay Leno and David Letterman. The massive popularity of the show and its stars has significantly increased the asking price for the Teutuls' bikes. While the cost of a basic OCC chopper starts at about $50,000, theme bikes built on the show have cost as much as $250,000.

Because of the increasing popularity of the show, the celebrity status of the Teutuls, and the marketability of OCC as a recognizable brand, the relationship between the show's stars, the bikes they build, and the corporations who commission them has become increasingly complex. In addition to direct endorsement by the Teutuls and on-air product placement, the creation of theme bikes for corporate clients is a central aspect of the show. When a company such as Gillette commissions a bike from OCC, it is purchasing not only the bike itself but also—on the episodes in which the bike is built—a one- or two-hour-long advertisement for their product and the implicit endorsement of the Teutuls. Advertisements for Gillette razors, for example, prominently bookended each segment of two episodes during which the Teutuls built a bike for Gillette based on the style and colors of the company's new Mach III razor. The first episode began with the Teutuls taking a tour of Gillette's headquarters in Boston and using the company's products. In addition the Discovery Channel names each individual episode after the company or product around which the bike is being built (e.g., "Gillette Bike," "Caterpillar Bike," "NAPA Bike"). The Teutuls have also been hired to advertise and endorse companies such as AOL, 7-Eleven, and NAPA Auto Parts (for whom they built a theme bike over two episodes of the show). As Senior observed, "We're so marketable, we could sell ice to the Eskimos."[14]

While episodes of *American Chopper* that feature the building of bikes for corporate clients clearly indicate the increasingly entwined connections between cultural production and consumer capital, the show also relies on an affective nationalist discourse that cites consumption as the proper location for patriotic citizenship. Early in the second season, for example, the Teutuls were commissioned by Miller Electric (a company that manufactures welding equipment) to build a bike commemorating the company's seventy-fifth anniversary. Rather than seeing the bike as a commissioned project for a corporate client, however, the Teutuls considered it, in the words of Paulie, a "tribute to the American worker." The "Miller Electric Bike" episode constructs a fantasy of American masculine labor in which the blue-collar worker is cast in a nostalgic position of anteriority and is abstracted to a series of beliefs about American national identity. In its discourse of commensurate affect, *American Chopper* produces a form of blue-collar patriotism that situates the American worker as a nostalgic figure, and the Teutuls' celebration of working-class masculinity should be understood as a response to the declining labor opportunities in the postindustrial economy of the late twentieth century.[15] John Hartigan Jr. has suggested that references to white trash, redneck culture, and "downmarket chic" have surged in concert with the "dramatic changes of the post–civil rights era and the rise of postindustrialization in the United States."[16] *American Chopper* betrays a similar fascination with the laboring body as it recuperates a form of working-class patriotism from the wasteland of traditional labor forms.

The affective logic of working-class masculinity evinced in the "Miller Electric Bike" episode is codified through a series of explicitly patriotic cross-identifications in which comparisons are made between blue-collar labor and patriotism. Commenting on the bike's red, white, and blue color scheme, Vinnie Dimartino, an OCC mechanic, makes this connection explicit for the viewer when he proudly observes, "Everything about this bike definitely screams 'Made in America.'" During the bike's unveiling in front of an audience of workers at the Miller Electric plant, Paulie claims that the bike "really is a tribute to the American worker," and Miller Electric vice president Jeff Rappold echoes Vinnie's earlier observation when he emphatically proclaims, "Make no bones about it, this is a 'Made in USA' bike." The final words of the episode belong to Senior, who claims, "It's all about the red, white, and blue and to me, you know, this is a special project for us." The relationship that is evoked in these statements between American patriotism and traditional labor practices produces a form of working-class nationalism that turns on the celebration of core American values.

Many of *American Chopper*'s early episodes feature similarly patriotic themes. In the first pilot episode, for example, Paulie builds a "jet bike," modeled on a U.S. military aircraft, that he describes as a "very patriotic theme [that] people are just going to eat . . . up." Other episodes from the first two seasons see the Teutuls build a "liberty bike," plated in copper reclaimed from the Statue of Liberty after a refurbishment project, and a "Comanche bike," modeled after a top-secret U.S. Army helicopter. Commemorative projects such as these concatenate the show's idealization of working-class identity with traditional American values such as liberty and freedom and a form of militaristic patriotism that codify the affective engagements with working-class labor evinced in the Miller Electric bike. Arjun Appadurai argues that "late industrial consumption relies on a peculiar tension between fantasy and nostalgia that gives substance (and sustenance) to consumer uncertainty about commodities, money, and the relationship between work and leisure."[17] *American Chopper* negotiates that tension by constructing a fantasy of blue-collar labor in the present that is predicated on a nostalgic form of exemplary citizenship. The Teutuls literally embody the interrelationship between nostalgia and fantasy.

In the "Miller Electric Bike" episode the link between the working-class male body and the tools of its trade are sentimentalized as the bike becomes an opportunity to celebrate Senior's own labor history. During the build Senior recalls his own humble beginnings as a freelance welder and explains the personal significance of the bike. "I'm kind of excited about this project," he says, "because, you know, for the past thirty-five years these tools and whatnot have been a pretty big part of my life. . . . In a way, you can say that they made me what I am today, and I think that it's great that OCC is getting an opportunity to pay tribute to that. . . . I think that, you know, it's special that, you know, you're able to build this bike for the people that build the product that allows you to build the bike for them." As an opportunity for Senior to celebrate his own working-class roots the bike pays tribute to an abstract notion of working-class identity based on the patriotic cross-identification signified in the statement "Made in America" and explicitly signifies the working-class origins of Senior's own economic success. If Stanley Aronowitz is correct and globalization is "capital's counterattack against the constraints on its power won by labor movements throughout the world, including the United States," then the transformation of actual physical labor into commodity spectacle obfuscates the lived effects of capital's assault on opportunity.[18]

In its celebration of Senior's own humble beginnings *American Chopper* concatenates the mythic figure of the outlaw biker and the sentimentalized figure of the blue-collar laborer. An overbearing and physically imposing giant of a man, Senior is presented as a hardworking and industrious individual who, before he started OCC, single-handedly built another multimillion-dollar company (Orange County Ironworks) from a single welding machine and a secondhand truck. Paulie says of his father, "He built himself an empire from a pickup truck, so he has earned anything that he wants to do." Paulie's choice of the word *earned* situates his father within a clearly definable frame of American individualism and condones his success: coming from nothing he is entitled to everything. Senior is portrayed as the apotheosis of the nostalgic logic of blue-collar labor, a man who has achieved the American Dream through hard work and sacrifice and who is now able to reap the benefits. "It was really cool watching my father drive the bike in, you know," says Paulie. "He started in business thirty years ago and he's come such a long way since then." As the bike is unveiled for the Miller Electric workforce Senior is likewise placed on display as an example of the opportunity available to hardworking Americans. His celebrity, as much as his economic prosperity, is a reward for his hard work. Despite the show's focus on labor, Paulie's description of his father's journey involves more than just his business success.

Despite Senior's business acumen and resulting success, during the early years of the ironworks his personal life was a shambles as he struggled with alcohol and drug addiction. In the second episode he admits, "Most of my life I was involved in drugs and alcohol"; he describes a cycle of depression, addiction, and destructive behavior that ultimately led to the breakdown of his marriage. In the same episode Paulie describes the effect his father's problems had on him when he was a child: "With alcoholism he wasn't always there, so there was a lot of bitterness." Despite being a talented athlete and a member of his high school football team, Paulie followed Senior into an early adulthood of alcoholism and unmet expectations. "It got really bad and I actually, like, experienced a nervous breakdown," Paulie explains. Having hit bottom, Senior "got involved in programs and . . . got sober." Paulie likewise was saved when he discovered religion; he is shown attending church while a voice-over describes his battle to overcome his addictions.[19]

In *American Chopper* recovery is a sign of masculine strength; the show portrays the Teutuls' problems with addiction within a narrative arc that replicates their socioeconomic ascendance. Senior cites the time when he overcame his addictions as the hardest period of his life, but he also points out that it was the period when he was able to properly focus on his business. Similarly Paulie says, "It wasn't until I got cleaned up that I was able to function properly and really get creative on the level that we're at now." By presenting the Teutuls as recovered addicts *American Chopper* mobilizes a logic of recovery and self-help in which both men are ultimately strong enough to help themselves and do not require the intervention of the state. By yoking its discourse of recovery to the American Dream of economic and social mobility *American Chopper* mobilizes what Lauren Berlant calls an "antipolitical politics [of] national sentimentality" in which the home and the family have become the appropriate sites for individual action.[20] As such, the Teutuls produce a powerful corrective to the ills of the welfare state. The proper recipients of the opportunities offered by America, the Teutuls are exemplars of both the promise and the reward of the American Dream, proof that hard work and native know-how are all you need to get ahead in America. In this way they are both a corrective to the welfare state—strong-willed individuals able to fix themselves—and examples of the ills of affirmative action and other civil rights labor programs.

Although the Teutuls' talk of addiction and recovery seems to run contrary to the rugged individualism of the outlaw lifestyle and blue-collar masculinity the show ostensibly valorizes, it seamlessly fits into the show's sentimental logic of masculine affect and neoliberal citizenship. Thus when Senior says that he "never got anything given to [him]," he is talking about both his economic success and his recovery from drug and alcohol addiction. Hardworking, independent, highly motivated, and patriotic, the Teutuls are presented as exemplary citizens who want nothing given to them and have earned everything they have. The show evinces what Berlant recognizes as a "conservative ideology" that "has convinced a citizenry that the core context of politics should be the sphere of private life."[21] Inasmuch as recovery is a sign of masculine strength, individual responsibility that eschews the welfare state is the proper way to deal with addiction. The example of Senior's and Paulie's self-help situates the privatization of public life under neoliberalism at the heart of the American Dream. The father-and-son team also rehearses a series of debates about the relationship between leisure and labor that revolves around the nostalgic vision of labor and lost opportunity the show produces.

"Nothing You Do Motivates Me": Family Melodrama and the Cultural Politics of Visible Labor

> His failure as a son is your failure as a father.
> MIKEY TEUTUL

> We're from two different schools.
> PAUL TEUTUL JR.

As much as *American Chopper* draws on the cultural resonances evoked by nostalgic blue-collar labor and the outlaw biker lifestyle, conjoined in the custom motorcycle, the show also trades on a complex set of beliefs about the nature of work in America. The show devotes considerable attention to a long-running series of arguments between Senior and Paulie that are a central aspect of its popularity. These arguments are often about the nature of real work and reproduce a commonplace series of cultural dichotomies: public/private, production/consumption, masculine/feminine, physical/ mental, work/leisure. In the distribution of labor at OCC (at least as it is presented on *American Chopper*) Senior is a self-made businessman and Paulie is an artist. The value of Paulie's artistic labor to the success of the business is a common subject in the arguments between the two men. However much Senior may enjoy the fruits of Paulie's artistic labor, he doesn't quite trust it. When Paulie is able to show concrete progress on a build (the fabrication and welding of a gas tank, for example) his father is happy, but when Paulie is engaged in the mental labor of artistic and conceptual work (during which he may spend an hour or a whole work-day staring at a bare motorcycle frame as he comes up with design ideas) his father inevitably appears and an argument ensues. During the course of these arguments Senior accuses Paulie of being lazy, self-absorbed, and unaware of the significance of deadlines. "Here we are, already behind schedule," quips Senior in one memorable incident, "and Picasso is chang-ing his mind about what he wants on this bike." By derisively referring to Paulie as "Picasso," Senior is equating his son's work with leisure and a type of luxury he believes he cannot afford. This dynamic relies on common-place beliefs about the relationship between manual and mental labor and is largely a product of Senior's inability (or unwillingness) to recognize mental labor as work.

Senior's inability to recognize Paulie's labor as such is hardly surpris-ing. Despite the real economic benefits he derives from it, what Senior sees when he watches Paulie is not what he expects work to look like. The distinctions between labor and leisure that motivate Senior's distrust of Paulie's work ethic also reflect trenchant beliefs about the relationship be-tween gender and work in American culture. As Michael Denning notes, "Culture is seen as the equivalent of leisure, not labor."[22] If Senior's view of labor (as something tangible and quantifiable) is trenchantly masculine and working class, Paulie's labor (intangible and unquantifiable) is both feminine and bourgeois.

Because of his experience running Orange County Ironworks, Senior is used to being able to measure and reward the output of his employees, and his status as the signer of weekly paychecks is often raised as a threat to Paulie and other workers whom Senior believes to be slacking on the job. As its name might suggest, Orange County Ironworks functions under the traditional logics of capitalist accumulation. Raw materials come in, finished products go out; each employee has a function in a chain of tasks that must be completed, and their value to the company can be clearly assessed. Under such a system the value of each individual worker and his corresponding remuneration is clearly quantifiable. As Paul Willis points out in *Learning to Labour*, "The productivity of capital is the liberated productivity of labour power given not as a quantity but as a capacity."[24] Indeed this is one of the grounding assumptions of wage labor, and Senior fully expects OCC and its employees to manifest just such a recognizable relationship between labor and production. Paulie's mental labor is thus untrustworthy because it isn't visible or quantifiable labor; it is not measurable in the form of a weekly pay packet.[23]

Senior also believes that Paulie's ineffective work habits are linked to time ("Here we are, already behind schedule"), and the producers of the show rely on this link for much of the show's narrative tension. Because almost every episode of *American Chopper* revolves around a tightly scheduled bike build, the issue of time and its relationship to labor is invested with great significance. " 'Time is money,' " Willis writes, "but the real measure which connects the two is abstract labour."[24] Indeed from Senior's perspective the deadlines that seem to constantly plague OCC are imbued with an almost moral weight. The conflation of domestic melodrama with labor dispute is a central aspect of the show's appeal. As Senior himself says, "It's a family show. And people have the same struggles we do, and they identify with it."[25] To the considerable degree that Senior believes that Paulie is always behind schedule, he finds his son's tardiness to be a moral failure and a sign of his lack of commitment both to the company and to him. To measure the passage of time (and to ensure that time is being *spent* wisely), Senior is always looking for recognizable signs that Paulie is working; when he cannot find them he gets angry. "You don't get involved in anything that you gotta get your hands dirty with," he says in one episode. Because his own labor history is such a significant part of his self-identity, Senior views Paulie's seeming rejection of his values as a personal attack. Paulie, for whom their arguments are about the value

Senior and Paulie argue about work, family, and responsibility. Stills reproduced in *American Chopper: At Full Throttle* (2004).

of artistic expression, often complains that his father doesn't understand the artistic process and that his continual interference only causes further delays. During one such argument Paulie tries to explain to his father the nature of artistic labor and its different relationship to time: "There was a lot of staring at this bike that just needed to be done to figure out what had to be done. Even when there was time that we were here working there was still a lot of figuring, you know what I mean?" Clearly Senior doesn't know what Paulie means. For Senior, Paulie's attention to artistic detail at the expense of visible progress marks him as a member of a generation that has forgotten the value of hard work. Thus while Paulie is the artistic member of the partnership, Senior is presented and self-identifies as "old school."[26] For Senior the term signifies authenticity, tradition, and the value of hard work and manual labor.[27]

The valorization of manual over mental labor in Senior's championing of old-school ways upholds a gendered division of labor that complements traditional capitalist modes of production. As Willis suggests,

"Manual labour is associated with the social superiority of masculinity, and mental labour with the social inferiority of femininity. In particular manual labour is imbued with a masculine tone and nature which renders it positively expressive of more than its intrinsic focus in work." The reversal of the manual/mental dichotomy functions hegemonically as it assures capitalist production of a willing workforce, in part because manual labor becomes tied to assumptions about masculinity and the relationship between work and the body. And this, perhaps, is why Senior's response to people's mistaking Orange County, New York, for Orange County, California, is to get a large "OCC New York" tattoo inked on his left bicep (a process that is shown on air). However, as Willis also points out, "in the capitalist mobilization of the mental/manual distinction it is conventionally, and according to the dominant ideology, the mental labourers who have the legitimized right to superior material and cultural conditions. Mental work is held to be more exacting and therefore to justify higher rewards."[28] Thus while Senior believes that his work habits are authentic and old school, it is Paulie who is more in step with the realities of the contemporary neoliberal guise of commodity capitalism. If, as Appadurai suggests, "consumption has . . . become the driving force of industrial society," *American Chopper* turns industry into a form of consumption (and vice versa).[29] The arguments between Senior and Paulie about the nature of real work are in many ways a dramatization of the transformation to neoliberal modes of capitalist production and consumption.

"Like Martha Stewart on a Motorcycle": Gender, Class, and the Laboring Body

> They get way too much play for cake decorators.
>
> BILL DODGE, West Coast Choppers

The issue of authenticity is a central aspect of debates about *American Chopper*; the Teutuls' celebrity has made them problematic figures, signifying countercultural rebellion and working-class authenticity for some and bourgeois co-optation for others.[30] Like the arguments between Senior and Paulie about the nature of real work, the debates about authenticity often break down along a common fault line of class- and gender-based assumptions. As the epigraph from Bill Dodge (an employee of

West Coast Choppers, an OCC competitor) suggests, their fellow bikers often deride the very aspects of the Teutuls' bikes that make them popular with a mainstream audience. That derision is regularly produced as an issue of gender inauthenticity. As "cake decorators" the Teutuls are situated in the domestic sphere of family, leisure, and femininity. Deemed to be insufficiently masculine, the Teutuls do not warrant the respect of hard-core bikers. Because they build choppers for corporate clients and, according to some, do little more than assemble their bikes from prefabricated parts, they have lost touch (if they ever had it) with the authentic roots of the biker community. Many other chopper builders actively work to distance themselves from the media-fueled celebrity of builders such as the Teutuls. Scott Long of Central Coast Choppers, for example, says, "People tell me [my bike] doesn't look like the choppers they see on TV, and that's about the biggest compliment I can get." Yoshi Hannya of Rodeo Motorcycles echoes Bill Dodge's complaints about the overly decorative bikes the Teutuls build: "I don't think a chopper should have any parts on it that don't make it go faster or look better. Original choppers were basically just frames, motors, and a few parts for style—that's all."[31] Because their design aesthetic more often relies on the embellishment than the paring down of the motorcycle's basic components the Teutuls' choppers signify leisure, feminized domesticity, consumption, and the inauthentic for bikers such as Hannya and Dodge.

Authentic masculinity is derived from a blend of skill and dedication that has become diluted by culture, leisure, and consumption. Mike Seate claims in his book *Outlaw Choppers*, "Riding and managing not to crash a radical chopper *back in the day* labeled the rider a hard man amongst men, the sort of guy who chases his tequila with Jack Daniels."[32] Warren Fuller, the creator of a biker lifestyle website, highlights the relationship between consumption and authenticity that grounds such beliefs when he claims that the Teutuls do not truly represent the chopper community. "These guys are pulling a $25,000 motor out of a box," he says. "What's so special about that?"[33] Because they can afford to buy an expensive motor the Teutuls evidence a form of consumerism that holds little value for the biker community, which places more value in abilities, such as bartering, that are driven by economic necessity. Such comments reflect a twofold complaint about the Teutuls' work and, implicitly, their celebrity status that further highlights the relationship between gender and socioeconomics.

While *American Chopper* presents the Teutuls as authentic examples of both the outlaw biker and the blue-collar worker, they do not function as such equally for everyone. The Teutuls are deemed to be inauthentic because of both the feminized nature of their work and their newfound socioeconomic standing.

The problematic status of the Teutuls is also an issue for *American Chopper*'s fans. The relationship between consumption, class, and authenticity arises most clearly in arguments about the relationships between the Teutuls and OCC employees such as Vinnie Dimartino and Rick Petko. These debates, which take place on online discussion boards devoted to the show (such as the one hosted by the Discovery Channel on its website), focus on whether the Teutuls give their employees enough respect and acknowledgment for their contributions to the success of OCC.[34] Vinnie and Rick perform the real work at OCC and possess the real mechanical skills, the argument goes, and without them the Teutuls would be exposed for the fakes they really are; Senior and Paulie have gained a financial success that is incommensurate with their mechanical ability, while highly skilled mechanics such as Vinnie do the real work. Such debates take place in three locations: between Senior and Paulie on the show, between other builders in the industry, and among viewers. In each of these locations the question is the same: Who is actually working? In this the show becomes a place where serious issues about labor and opportunity in the contemporary United States get worked through. While viewers often debate whether OCC's employees are given enough credit for their contributions to the Teutuls' success, this question seems doubly relevant in the case of the invisible workers who produce the OCC-branded merchandise that accounts for a large percentage of the economic windfall the Teutuls have realized since the show has been on the air.

A significant portion of *American Chopper*'s success results from the show's validation of a world of blue-collar manual labor that, coded through the Teutuls' laboring bodies, is both masculine and definitively male, but the economic mobility the Teutuls have gained comes in large part from the labor of others who are rendered invisible in the show's making. Fans of *American Chopper* and OCC who are unable to afford the astronomical price of an OCC chopper but who still wish to buy into the show's performative masculinities can buy *American Chopper*– and OCC-themed merchandise such as T-shirts and baseball caps.[35] The Teutuls, who have attained celebrity because of their status as (and claimed solidarity with) blue-collar workers, benefit economically from the hidden labor of others; the solidarity they espouse for the American worker does not seem to extend to the laborers, many of them women of color, of the garment industry. This is in part because the forms of solidarity with working-class labor the show valorizes have been transformed into the elective choices of postindustrial consumer society. "Mass culture has won," says Denning. "All culture is mass culture under capitalism." As such, "there is no working-class culture that is not saturated with mass culture."[36] *American Chopper* contextualizes consumption as a form of labor that attenuates the real issues of class, gender, and racial inequality produced under neoliberalism. Therefore, despite the actual losses suffered by women under the neoliberal service economy of contemporary America, such workers are not visible in the show's index of authentic labor. Despite the comparison of the Teutuls to cake decorators and the show's reliance on the affective structures of family melodrama, the forms of worthwhile labor *American Chopper* can imagine are all coded as masculine.

In disputes about their authenticity the Teutuls are often compared to Jesse James, the owner of West Coast Choppers, the subject of the Discovery Channel special *Motorcycle Mania*, and the host of the channel's other hit automotive reality show, *Monster Garage*. James is presented as a far more rebellious figure than the Teutuls. While the Teutuls are "cake decorators," Jesse James is "an artist and people see the dignity in the way [he] makes his living."[37] While *American Chopper* focuses on family relations, in *Motorcycle Mania* James is portrayed as a loner and an outlaw. He claims to be a descendant of the Jesse James of American frontier mythology (the stylized chambers of a pair of six-shooters embellish many of his motorcycles), and the show presents him as the last of a dying breed of real men. As with *American Chopper*, *Motorcycle Mania* also conjoins the iconography of the biker with blue-collar labor and devotes much attention to James's considerable skills as a metalworker. He is portrayed as an artisan who pays tribute to the workers who have come before him and to the old-fashioned and traditional ways of working with metal that have been rendered obsolete in the contemporary world of automated manufacturing. He is repeatedly hailed—not without hyperbole—as the last worker of his kind in the world. By positioning James as the last of a dying breed *Motorcycle Mania* also constructs a nostalgic view of manual labor. As an artisan James is the embodiment of an authentic manual labor that makes a space for culture by coding artistic labor as artisanship and craft. Moreover, as the show charts the arc from custom builder to artisanal welder, the fordist system of assembly line labor is completely removed. The show moves from pre- to postfordism without lingering in the middle. Moving directly from the consumerist present to a nostalgic artisanal past, the show displaces the history of the American motorcycle industry as an industry and reconstitutes the motorcycle as a consumerist object available only to the most affluent. Thus there is no lost American motorcycle industry to be mourned, no closed factories, no unemployed workers, just exemplars of a nostalgic model of individual labor to be celebrated.[38]

Over the course of the three *Motorcycle Mania* specials the viewer sees James construct a gas tank from scratch out of sheet metal, use an obsolete metal rolling tool he salvaged from an abandoned factory to smooth out sheets of steel, and take a pilgrimage to learn how to work with copper from one of the last skilled copper workers in the country. The viewer also sees James's scarred and bloody hands, proof that he does the work himself and a sign of his dedication to the old ways.[39] The motorcycles he builds embody an aura of authenticity that they gain from their status as custom-made, hand-built machines. Like the Teutuls, however, James also builds bikes for corporations (such as R. J. Reynolds and AOL), and the asking price for his motorbikes (which begin at $40,000) places them out of the reach of the average consumer. Indeed much like OCC, West Coast Choppers has become an identifiable brand name, and because of the visibility brought on by *Motorcycle Mania* and *Monster Garage*, an addition to the company's buildings in Long Beach shown in the third special includes a storefront for the sale of WCC merchandise. James also has an extensive celebrity client list that includes the basketball player Shaquille O'Neal, the wrestler Bill Goldberg, the rock star Kid Rock, and the male supermodel Tyson Beckford. Despite the differences in representation between the Teutuls and James, in both shows the original status of the custom chopper as a signifier of countercultural rebellion sometimes conflicts with its newfound position as a consumable object of bourgeois fantasy identification.

"From the Heart": The Affective Production
of Male Sentimentality

> This project had more than mechanical aptitude and ability; it had
> deep, deep meaning.
> DAN DAVINCI, DaVinci Performance

> Watching *Chopper*, you learn a little about bikes and a lot about how
> men express love with outbursts and power tools.
> JAMES PONIEWOZIK, *Time*

American Chopper's affective discourse of working-class sacrifice and commemoration achieved its most potent expression in a bike the Teutuls
built to commemorate the New York City firemen who lost their lives
on September 11, 2001. The single most popular OCC creation and a significant reason for the overall success of the show, the "fire bike" was built
over the course of three episodes that first aired in April and June 2003.
The fire bike distills *American Chopper*'s affective logic of working-class
masculinity in the figure of the New York City fireman. The elevation of
firemen to everyday heroes after September 11 produced a potent affective
logic of unimpeachable masculine sacrifice that the fire bike successfully
feeds into.[40] As the Teutuls celebrate the fallen firemen of September 11
they situate those heroic figures within a realm of working-class masculine
sacrifice and domesticity, and the valor and heroism for which the fallen
firemen are being celebrated signal the value of working-class masculinity in general. The affective commemoration of New York City firemen
becomes a celebration of the white ethnic working-class masculine identity the Teutuls themselves embody for the audience of *American Chopper*.
Through a series of cross-identifications, the "Fire Bike" episodes situate
the Teutuls within the same representational space as the fallen firemen.

The relationship between the Teutuls and the firemen is rendered both
explicitly and implicitly. While Paulie is designing the bike he and Mikey
visit a firehouse in the Bronx where Mikey's best friend, Al Ronaldson, is a
junior fireman. They help the firemen cook dinner and, replicating a task
he is often seen performing at OCC, Mikey takes out the trash. The two
brothers also eat with the firemen and follow them when they go out on a
call that interrupts the meal. After the visit Paulie claims, "Ever since I was

younger I've always admired firemen. . . . Getting a chance to spend some time with these guys really helped me to see a little more into the meaning of the project other than just building a bike." The finished bike is later unveiled at the same firehouse for an audience of New York City firefighters. The connections between the Teutuls' authentic blue-collar roots and the figure of the fireman are also produced in more implicit ways, most clearly in the presentation of Paulie as an exemplary citizen.

If the "Miller Electric Bike" episodes cited Senior as the proper locus of blue-collar commemoration, the "Fire Bike" episodes situate Paulie in a similar logic of affective engagement. During the course of one "Fire Bike" episode Paulie shows a visiting group of high school students around OCC and the ironworks. Hosting the students is a significant nostalgic moment for Paulie because they attend a BOCES (Board of Cooperative Educational Services, an institution offering continuing education and high school equivalency) in New York State that Paulie himself attended.[41] Much like the focus on Senior's humble beginnings in the "Miller Electric Bike" episodes, the inclusion of the students' visit to OCC during the "Fire Bike" episodes situates Paulie as an example of the possibilities available to all hardworking Americans. As one student says when asked about the trip, "I never thought that someone who was in a program like me could succeed like this." The success of Paulie and OCC in the eyes of the BOCES students codifies the affective value *American Chopper* gives to blue-collar labor because it highlights the rags-to-riches transformation of the American Dream while still valuing manual labor as a bona fide origin point for economic success. This gesture also replicates traditional sentiments about the intrinsic value of manual labor. Seeing someone like Paulie succeed is good for the students, the BOCES instructor tells the viewer, because it shows them that "anything they do with their hands is worth doing well." The placement of this encounter during the fire bike build is significant because the viewer is encouraged to view Paulie's success as the result of sacrifice and hard work that mirrors, albeit with starkly different results, the sacrifice of the firemen. Manifesting a commensurate logic of affective production, Paulie's authentic blue-collar identity is being celebrated alongside that of the firemen.

The "Fire Bike" episodes also create a masculine sentimentality in which each of the principal builders involved in the creation of the bike professes the emotional effect his involvement in the project has had on him personally. Paulie lays out the emotional stakes of the project at the very beginning, claiming, "Ever since 9/11 I think that, you know, it's been in my heart to do something for the firemen, you know, just to pay tribute." "These guys are true heroes," he says later, "there's just no question about that. I just hope I could create a bike that will honor them in the way they deserve to be honored." Many of the men involved in the build believe that working on the fire bike changed them. Paulie himself claims, "I don't know what it is about this particular bike, but it's really affected me in a way that no other bike has." In a proclamation about the significance of the bike that must have thrown his father into conniptions, he tells the viewer, "This bike is more important than any deadline." Paulie's statement interrupts the show's normal narrative logic by producing a transparency that ostensibly transcends the artifice of television. Because of the solemnity of the bike's commemorative subject matter, both the show's normal rules of operation and the Teutuls' disputes are to be put on hold during the course of the build.

Working on the fire bike is also a significant experience for the vendors occ contracts during the build. Justin Barnes, the bike's painter, explains the effect the bike has had on him: "I've never worked on anything that has affected me quite like this bike. . . . There were a couple of times when we were working on it that the whole meaning of the bike really hit me hard, especially when we started doing the '343' . . . what that number represents."[42] The builders of the gas tank and wheels each claim that they "put a lot of heart and soul into this one." A representative of DaVinci Performance, which manufactured a custom carburetor in the shape of a fire hydrant, made a similar comment about the pride the company's workers felt being able to participate in the project. Such statements highlight the investment in physical labor as a form of feeling in which, as it was in the Miller Electric bike, affect is routed through the relationship between the body and the machine. The sentimental burden of commemoration is transformed into the expenditure of manual labor. The fire bike reinserts *tears* in the "blood, sweat, and *steel*" of *American Chopper's* American Dream; both steel and tears become products of emotion and the correct response to American valor and sacrifice. This affective transformation is further brought to the fore in the pages of the tie-in volume, *American Chopper: At Full Throttle*, in which the viewer as consumer is able to participate in the emotional economy in which the fire bike

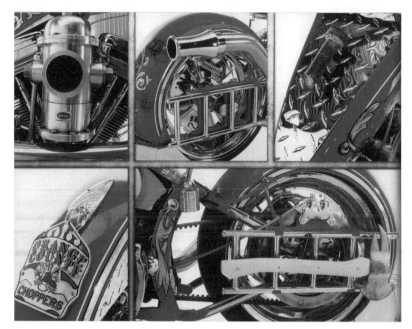

Detail shots of the fire bike, showing the piece of steel reclaimed from the World Trade Center (top right image). From *American Chopper: At Full Throttle* (2004).

circulates by becoming intimate with the world in which it is created. The volume thus serves as a supplement to the television show's already strong affective economy of masculinist emotional embrace and disavowal.

At Full Throttle is published by the Discovery Channel in partnership with Meredith Corporation, a media and marketing company and the publisher of popular magazines such as *Ladies' Home Journal, Fitness*, and *Better Homes and Gardens*. The lavish volume is intended to draw the reader into the world of OCC and to allow a more intimate engagement with the bikes and their makers than the show itself allows. It contains episode-by-episode multipage features of the bikes produced during the show's first season. Along with quotations from the episodes, interviews with the Teutuls and their employees, technical details of the bikes, and backstage gossip, the book provides detailed photographs of the various custom bikes. In the pages devoted to the fire bike a full-page collage of close-up images of the bike highlights not only the craft of the individual vendors but also the seriousness of the project. Alongside detailed photographs of the DaVinci carb, the custom wheels, and the immaculate paint job, a photograph of the top of the bike's gas tank shows the steel bolt salvaged from the wreckage of the World Trade Center that the Teutuls mounted on the bike at an unveiling before New York City firefighters. As they are while viewing the episode, readers are drawn in to the exacting detail of the bike makers' commemoration of the fallen firefighters. In the affective economy of manual labor evidenced in *American Chopper* the bike's builders channel their emotions through a proper conduit, and the affective discourse of commemoration is located in an inanimate—and overtly masculinized—object. As much as the Miller Electric bike, the fire bike is a concrete expression of the exhortation "Buy American." Because that object—the custom motorcycle—has become a signifier of bourgeois success, consumption is presented as a proper means of emotive expression.

American Chopper presents an idealized realm of masculine interaction that reproduces traditionally coded divisions of public and private, masculine and feminine, and labor and leisure, while updating those divisions in the face of the corrosive pressures of the neoliberal service economy. Collapsing the separate spheres of public and private, work and home into the pseudo-domestic world of fraternity and labor that is the OCC workshop, *American Chopper* relocates the franchise of masculinity. If, as Robyn Wiegman has argued, the white male subject in contemporary American culture "is cast not only as a minority identity but as one injured by the denial of public representation," then automotive television programs such as *American Chopper* situate the white male laboring body at the heart of a nostalgic construction of authentic citizenship.[43] As it elides the transformations of labor that have devastated the manufacturing landscape of the United States *American Chopper* produces a fantasy figure of blue-collar celebrity that valorizes the transition from production to consumption that characterizes contemporary neoliberalism.

In its presentation of a world of masculine labor and fraternal affect *American Chopper* constructs a nostalgic world of blue-collar work in which the skilled manual laborer—always understood to be male—still reigns supreme, untroubled by the supposed defeats suffered by hegemonic masculinity in the post–civil rights era and by the labor losses of neoliberalism. By celebrating neoliberal consumer capital and the traditional consumption of the American Dream as coterminous discourses of celebrity identity, the show ignores the increasingly vast gaps in opportunity and remuneration that separate the haves and the have nots in the contemporary United States. As Vinnie Dimartino, OCC head mechanic and *American Chopper*'s moral center, says, "It's just the way you do something, and then the way it's shown on TV."[44] What *American Chopper* shows on TV every Monday night is a world of fraternity and male bonding that rehabilitates blue-collar labor by presenting the world of work as an emotionally fulfilling habitat in which men are still free to be men and masculine identity is produced as consumer choice. Through the example of the Teutuls and their employees *American Chopper* constitutes a patriarchal form of normative citizenship predicated on modes of consumption that ameliorate the real losses suffered by both men and women under neoliberalism. Moreover by collating the Teutuls' American Dream and the privatized neoliberal consumer subject the show incorporates the very losses it elides into the structures of possibility it celebrates. Searching for the exemplary neoliberal citizen, *American Chopper* finds him at the heart of the American Dream.

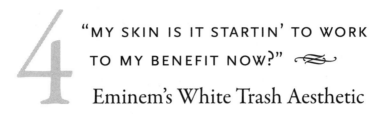

"MY SKIN IS IT STARTIN' TO WORK TO MY BENEFIT NOW?" ⤳
Eminem's White Trash Aesthetic

White people find it very difficult to live in an environment they don't control.—COLEMAN YOUNG, mayor of Detroit 1974–1993, quoted in Clemens, *Made in Detroit*

I'm 'bout as normal as Norman Bates, with deformative traits,
A premature birth that was four minutes late.
EMINEM, "Role Model"

IN THE OPENING LINES of "Cleanin' Out My Closet," the second single from his best-selling and Grammy Award–winning CD *The Eminem Show* (2002), the white rapper Eminem asks, "Have you ever been hated or discriminated against? I have." These lines, and the sentiment behind them, provide an example of the appeal to injury or claim of disproportionate representation that grounds the sociocultural transformations this book examines. Like Chuck Palahniuk in the example discussed in the introduction, Eminem mobilizes the discourse of injury in order to account for his attention to the subject position of white masculinity; like Palahniuk, he believes the transformations of civil rights have adversely and predominantly affected white men. Eminem typically narrativizes this appeal to injury in relation to his status as, on the one hand, a marginal figure of white disgust and, on the other, an influential celebrity figure who speaks back to the establishment voices who seek to marginalize and reject him. He represents himself as a marginal white trash figure who has attained fame and fortune by "speaking to suburban kids" who embrace his rejection of the bourgeois values of mainstream America. In his embodiment of race and gender Eminem offers another aspect of the contemporary lability of white masculinity.[1] Over the course of five full-length CD releases and one "best of" compilation CD he has developed a coherent constellation of personas that draw in equal parts on the tropes of hip-hop and commonly held stereotypes about white trash.[2] He blends white and black cultural forms in order to manufacture a coherent marginalized subject. At the same time he draws on commonly held beliefs about socioeconomic mobility that allow him to cast his success within the ideological orbit of possessive individualism that undergirds American exceptionalism.[3] What does it mean that Eminem, a successful artist and prominent celebrity figure, can call himself a victim of discrimination? What cultural work does this perform? What cultural work does his self-presentation as a marginalized figure of debased white ethnicity perform? If the celebrity figures of *American Chopper* represent a nostalgic blue-collar worker grounded in the transformations of American celebrity culture, Eminem mobilizes a different figure of white socioeconomic disenfranchisement to strikingly similar ends.[4]

Routed through the idioms and tropes of contemporary black urban culture, Eminem's self-presentation as white trash produces a celebratory figure of white disempowerment that enables him to transcend his origins. Reveling in his status as both white trash outcast and co-opter of black American culture, he presents himself as a liminal figure, able to cross cultural divides and as such to trouble the boundaries of bourgeois white middle-class sensibility.[5] Eminem has been able to reap the benefits of the cultural transformations of which he is an exemplar and to move into the mainstream. When Rabbit, the character he plays in *8 Mile*, boasts, "I'm a piece of fuckin' white trash and I'll say it proudly," he is transforming the term from an insult into a valorized identity. At the same time he is hyperaware of his status as a white performer in a predominantly black American field of cultural expression and frequently charts the responsibility bestowed on him by that status.[6] He mobilizes the multiple discourses of authenticity, especially in relation to ethnicity, that prevail in hip-hop.[7] The mobilization of white trash as a form of marginal subjectivity allows whiteness to be recast as a minoritized but celebrated identity; performing class becomes a means of performing whiteness without apology. Saul Williams, a slam poet and hip-hop artist, says, "Eminem . . . is still unapologetically white. He is himself and he is dope as hell and talented, but it's clear that Eminem is white and that was part of the attraction."[8] While Eminem has adopted and adapted a mode of black urban expression, he has not done so in order to reject or overcome his whiteness, but in order to manage the ways whiteness is understood.

Eminem's self-presentation as white trash marks a significant shift in the term's sociocultural meanings. White trash is more often used to describe and ostracize others than to represent oneself. White trash names and marginalizes, and as such serves as a boundary-policing term. As John Hartigan Jr. suggests, "*White trash* is primarily a distancing technique before it is an identity."[9] Matt Wray points out likewise that "for much of its long history, *white trash* has been used by Americans of all colors to humiliate and shame, to insult and dishonor, to demean and stigmatize." Linking white skin color to economic deprivation, white trash names a class-based subject that is so debased as to become racialized. To be white trash is to be less than white. The term therefore disrupts typical understandings of the isomorphic relationship between whiteness and privilege; it suggests that whiteness is as much an economic as a racial category. As Wray says, "*White trash* also speaks to another tension, that between what have for too long been competing categories of social analysis: race and class."[10] White trash names a form of whiteness from which the privilege of skin color has been all but erased, in which whiteness has been transformed from a normative position into a marginalized identity. Hartigan suggests that "the term's boundary maintenance work allows little room for valorized self-identification."[11] It is a subject position used to define a norm against, rather than one used to define the self. As Eminem asks in the song "Role Model," "How can I be white? I don't even exist." He uncouples white trash from shame and humiliation by celebrating the stereotypes of social marginalization that the term typically names. He turns shame into celebrity, thereby reworking the privileges of white masculinity. Whiteness becomes, to use Diane Negra's term, "enriched" as white trash names a form of white legitimacy manufactured from the raw materials of class-based oppression that affects the poor across racial lines.[12] To own the term as a class-based identity formation is to own whiteness while simultaneously recoding that whiteness as a minority identity of which one *can* be proud. He is not a "white" performer in a "black" world, but a white trash performer, ostensibly endowed with a completely different relationship to the privileges of whiteness. Through this act of self-marginalization Eminem is able to achieve a form of authenticity that might be denied him otherwise. He has been able to overcome the complaints about authenticity that plagued an earlier white rapper, Vanilla Ice. While, as Tricia Rose explains, Vanilla Ice used the ghetto as a "source of fabricated white authenticity" that was soon exposed, Eminem has more successfully positioned himself in relation to the presumed realities of black urban living and, in spite of his skin color, is often perceived to be authentic.[13] As one young African American argues, "He's rapping about life—you know, stuff that we go through out here. Some of it's a goof, but some of it's real, and it sounds like it comes from the heart, you know. A lot of us can relate to that."[14] However, Eminem's valorization of white trash serves ultimately to enable his escape from it. He transforms white trash into a valedictory identity in order to transcend it; he attains the privileges of being white by denying that he is.

"Mom, I Love You But This Trailer Has Got to Go": From White Trash to Black Gold

Eminem's rap lyrics are often (pseudo-) autobiographical, and many of them describe his childhood growing up on the socioeconomic margins of society. His raps often portray him in a debased and degraded light, telling tales of substance abuse, sexual degeneracy, child and spousal abuse, domestic disturbances, and bodily excess, presenting an image of Eminem as a grotesque white trash figure. He has become a touchstone for vulgarity and bodily excess. In an *Entertainment Weekly* article in which he likens the rapper to Elvis Presley, Owen Gleiberman describes him as a "feral, small-framed man with the stare of Timothy McVeigh [and] the daydreams of Leatherface."[15] Likening the rapper to both the Oklahoma City bomber and the villain of the cult horror movie *The Texas Chainsaw Massacre*, Gleiberman locates him within a pantheon of debased figures of white trash excess and criminality. Calling him "feral" and "small-framed," he finds evidence for personality disorders in the rapper's physiognomy. Barely human, the rapper is described as an animal, subhuman and lacking in recognizably human characteristics, either physical or psychological. With such a description Gleiberman locates Eminem in a eugenicist discourse of white marginality that dates back to the nineteenth century.[16] In a very different context Sander L. Gilman evokes Eminem's "sick art" in the introduction to an article on health, sickness, and race in the nineteenth century.[17] These two examples suggest how powerful and wide-ranging the image of Eminem as a touchstone of white bodily excess has become. In both *Entertainment Weekly* and *Opera Quarterly* he is a recognizable symbol of debasement and immorality. This is an image that the rapper both revels in and attempts to contextualize: on the one hand he explicitly sets out to shock and disgust; on the other he offers a coherent series of explanatory narratives for his own excesses and his subsequent success that are typical of the gangsta rap genre. It is in the interrelationship between excess and explanation that Eminem recasts the meanings of his debasement.

In *The Slim Shady LP* (1999, Aftermath Entertainment/Interscope Records), his first full-length release, Eminem foregrounds his white trash origins by reproducing various stereotypes of white trash. In "If I Had" he complains about the deprivations of living hand-to-mouth as a child:

> I'm tired of being white trash, broke and always poor
> I'm tired of taking pop bottles back to the party store
> I'm tired of not having a phone
> Tired of not having a home to have one in if I did have it on

In these lines Eminem mobilizes a series of common tropes of white trash: poverty, alcoholism, social and economic marginalization. As he bemoans the experiences of his childhood, however, he also understands that those experiences have formed the character that has allowed him to achieve success. Thus, while in songs such as "Guilty Conscience" and "Brain Damage" he presents himself as morally and genetically disturbed, he also sees his stupidity as more than just a disability. Claiming to be "too stupid to know any better" is a rhetorical strategy he employs with great frequency. In "Role Model" he links the stupidity of his youth to his negotiations of early celebrity when he claims, "I'm dumb enough to walk in a store and steal / So I'm dumb enough to ask for a date with Lauryn Hill." Here the "moral unworthiness of poor whites" is transformed into a go-getting spirit that doesn't understand—and is therefore not constrained by—the limits being placed on his rights to equal opportunity.[18] Troubling the boundaries of acceptable behavior, Eminem succeeds by valorizing his own inability to understand what he can and cannot do. He refuses, in short, to conform to the social expectations established by society.

Eminem's insider's guide to social marginality takes a darker turn in the revenge fantasy raps in which he fantasizes about killing his ex-wife, Kim. In "'97 Bonnie and Clyde," a song addressed to his daughter, Hailie, he describes a scene in which he disposes of the body of his ex-wife after he has murdered her following an argument. In this song the immorality of the white trash subject is presented at its most extreme as a domestic dispute leads to spousal abuse and then murder. In songs such as these Eminem replicates stereotypes about the inability of the white trash subject to resolve conflict without recourse to violence. Such stereotypes are a staple of daytime television programs such as *The Jerry Springer Show* and sensationalist tabloid stories such as the case of Lorena Bobbitt. At the same time as they situate Eminem as a morally deprived individual, such songs present habitat as the primary constraint on opportunity. In this way Eminem's lyrical content, extreme though it may seem, can be related to the nature versus nurture debates that ground nineteenth-century American social realism. In "'97 Bonnie and Clyde," for example, he tells his daughter that he had to murder her mother: "'Cause Momma's got a new husband and a stepson / And you don't want a brother do ya?" In other songs, such as "Cleanin' Out My Closet," Eminem's own mother inhabits the position of constraint as he asks listeners if they can imagine what it was like growing up with a mother who did more drugs than he did. There is a gendered aspect to these narratives; Eminem repeatedly accuses his ex-wife and his mother of limiting his opportunities for personal and career development. The only female who gets off without complaint is his daughter, whom he repeatedly discusses in reference to his own responsibilities as a father.

In these ways Eminem's raps have much in common with one of the genres from which they clearly derive: gangsta rap. Eithne Quinn explains, "The power and pleasure of the gangsta phenomenon—aside from its seductive music—stemmed from its dramatization of immediate and shocking characters, coupled paradoxically with its equally compelling impulse towards reflecting on and explaining such characterizations." The metatextual representation of "shocking characters" within complex and often contradictory explanatory narratives is a hallmark of Eminem's work. That Eminem would be heavily influenced by gangsta rap is no surprise. Not only was it one of the most popular forms of rap during his formative years, but his mentor, Dr. Dre, was one of the genre's principal practitioners. Dr. Dre has worked closely with Eminem throughout much of his career, producing hit songs such as "My Name Is" and "The Real Slim Shady." A member of the seminal gangsta rap outfit N.W.A. (Niggaz with Attitude), Dr. Dre achieved his greatest acclaim with the solo album *The Chronic* (1992, Death Row Records). The album sold over three million copies and was widely credited with popularizing—if not originating—the G-funk (gangsta-funk) style of rap. The formula for G-funk, Quinn says, was "vulgar topics coupled with highly produced and highly commercial beats."[19] This description could serve equally for Eminem, who has substituted the vulgar topics of white trash for those of the West Coast hood. In substituting a fantasy narrative of white trash existence for the equally fantastical narratives of black urban living that make up the lyrical content of gangsta rap, Eminem is still offering up a fantasy of marginal existence for the young white middle-class suburban males that predominantly make up the audience for mainstream rap music. He has replaced one surface fantasy with another, but has done so within the generic and thematic confines of the original.

The visual content of the liner booklets for Eminem's CDs provides a visual supplement to the lyrical and musical content of the songs and charts the stages of his transition from white trash to celebrity. The cover of the CD booklet for *The Slim Shady LP* illustrates a scene from the song "'97 Bonnie and Clyde." The picture shows Eminem with his daughter standing on the end of a pier; in the foreground the body of his wife can be seen hanging out of the trunk of a car. This image provides a visual representation of the revenge fantasy that figures repeatedly in Eminem's lyrics. It conjures the image of domestic abuse, an image that is further enforced by the picture from the back cover, which shows Eminem, dressed in a blood-splattered white T-shirt, standing against a cartoon image of a window with a flower on the windowsill. The images inside the booklet depart from the violent fantasy represented on the covers, offering instead another stereotype of white trash: the uncontrolled and libidinous body. The center spread features a two-page cartoon of a trailer home with rust and dirt dripping from the windows, mutant magic mushrooms growing

Slim Shady's trailer trash fantasies. Liner image from *The Slim Shady LP* (Aftermath Entertainment/Interscope Records, 1999)

on the roof, and "Free Slim Shady" spray-painted on the back wall. A bandage-wrapped zombie figure, glowing green, runs away from the trailer, having been caught in the act of spraying graffiti by two under-dressed and overweight white women. On the CD itself is a cartoon of an anthropomorphized Vicodin pill, and the image inside the back cover of the CD jewel case shows the zombie from the center spread, with hypodermic needles hanging from its body, being chased and consumed by pills.

As with his lyrical references to drug use, HIV infection, and sexually transmitted diseases, these images situate Eminem within a milieu of substance abuse, deviancy, and dependency that reproduce various stereotypical beliefs about social marginalization that cite the white trash body as abject. Hartigan suggests, "The perception and ascription of white trash hinges on bodily sensibilities; it involves a reaction to bodily conditions and behaviors that offend certain class decorums."[20] This abject body becomes a site to which the excess remainder of middle-class sensibilities can be annexed. By celebrating these bodily irruptions Eminem is fashioning himself as a threat to the moral and social order. He understands that this dangerous marginality is a primary aspect of his appeal to a white middle-class youth audience, and in *The Slim Shady LP* he foregrounds his status as a debased and marginal figure, outside the bounds of acceptable middle-class decency and self-regulation. The lyrical content and the supporting CD cover art not only represent a debased white trash existence, but also disrupt and satirize the bourgeois middle-class home life such images typically serve to protect. Thus while he situates himself firmly within one milieu, he has his sights set on gaining access to another.

Even at this early stage in his career Eminem's self-presentation betrays his desire to transcend his white trash origins, to "free Slim Shady" from the confines of his preordained existence. Eminem's fantasy of a successful escape from the white trash existence he otherwise chooses to celebrate suggests the ambivalence inherent in this valorization. For Eminem, to celebrate white trash is a means of transcending it. That the zombie is attempting to escape from the women and pills, each symbols of white trash debasement, that are consuming him is significant for just this reason. The predatory deviant of the revenge fantasy of "'97 Bonnie and Clyde" is transformed in these images into a victim. Not only representations of bodily excess and social marginalization, these images also suggest a fantasy of escape. As in the fantasy of escape from his wife, the desire to escape from substance abuse and promiscuous women is about overcoming the inevitability of white trash. Eminem achieves this through the production of a traditional narrative of self-sufficiency grounded in the ideologies of possessive individualism and resulting in the acquisition of a compensatory form of celebrity identity. His celebratory self-marginalization reproduces as much as it disrupts traditional narratives of socioeconomic self-making.

Eminem's narrative of socioeconomic transcendence ultimately rests on a series of commonly held beliefs about possessive individualism in American society. The CD booklet for *The Marshall Mathers LP* (2000, Interscope Records) clearly develops this dialectic of celebration and disavowal as it charts the beginning of Eminem's transformation from white trash to properly consuming subject. The cover art contains a sepia photograph of Eminem as a homeless vagrant, sleeping outside a warehouse loading dock.[21] The images inside the booklet are of two distinct types: actual photographs of Marshall Mathers as a child and fictional representations of the adult Marshall Mathers working in the kitchen of a fast-food restaurant or diner. In this second group of pictures he is dressed in kitchen scrubs, a dirty white apron, and a baseball cap worn backward and is taking out kitchen trash. These pictures continue the rags-to-riches narrative of Eminem's transformation from white trash to hip-hop superstar that began with *The Slim Shady LP*. In these images the transition from welfare to work ethic is clearly delineated. He has a job—it might not be a good one, but it's still a job—and is not a burden on the welfare state. On the back cover he is shown composing rap lyrics. Humble his status may be, but a work ethic is clearly visible. While in the cover art that accompanies the first CD Eminem is a white trash figure, in the art from the second he is represented as a member of the white working poor.

Eminem's narrative of self-empowerment reaches a celebratory conclusion in the CD booklet for *The Eminem Show* (2002, Aftermath Records), which takes the rapper out of the hand-to-mouth existence he describes in his first two CDs and situates him firmly within a bourgeois middle-class milieu of conspicuous consumption. In a series of images that reflect back on and update the scenes of menial labor presented in the booklet for *The Marshall Mathers LP* Eminem is shown, again, taking out the trash. In these images, however, he is no longer working but is at home, wearing a dressing gown with a sleeping mask propped on his forehead and taking out his own trash. No longer a laboring body, he has become a member of the leisure classes. This image of bourgeois domesticity is further developed in a series of pictures showing him in various domestic scenes: in an indoor swimming pool with Hailie, collecting the mail, hanging out with his posse in a large living room, and pulling a jacket from its hanger in a large walk-in closet. In these images Eminem is situated as both a middle-class consumer and homeowner and a celebrity subject. All of these photographs are presented as still images from security or surveillance cameras: the trappings of celebrity come at the expense of privacy and personal independence. He may no longer be representing himself as white trash, but he still understands himself to be a victim; no longer trapped in a white trash existence, he is now trapped by the pressures of celebrity. In the same way as the purchasers of his earlier CDs were encouraged to position themselves as either voyeurs or inhabitants of the social conditions Eminem presented, the purchaser of *The Eminem Show* is situated as a voyeuristic figure.

The presentation of these images as surveillance shots transforms the family album–style center spread of *The Marshall Mathers LP* into something altogether more sinister. Eminem's transcendence of his white trash existence and his entry into middle-class stability are linked to the privations of the celebrity status and success that have enabled this transformation. In one image he sits, dressed in black suit pants, a white dress shirt, and tie, reading the stock reports in the newspaper. On the wall beside him a bank of TV monitors show images of paparazzi staked outside his house with cameras equipped with large telephoto lenses. The booklet's back cover shows the control room for the surveillance cameras that have produced the images. The threat comes from both inside and outside; domestic space must be surveilled to prevent intrusion, but venturing outside places the surveiller in the position of the surveilled. That the CD departs from the nomenclature of the previous two releases—it is a "show" and not an "LP"—further suggests that Eminem's status as a celebrity has overshadowed his status as a hip-hop artist.[22] While an LP—anachronistic as the name may be in the digital age—is a finite object, a show has no definitive scope or duration. As a celebrity, the realm of his performance transcends the duration of a single CD. The issue of naming is particularly relevant because, while they are each different, the titles of each of Eminem's first three full-length CD releases are eponymous: *The Slim Shady LP*, *The Marshall Mathers LP*, *The Eminem Show*. The progression from the earlier pseudonym to the latter, via the artist's real name, logically culminates in the citation of "Eminem" as the proper name of the celebrity subject that Slim Shady has become; if Slim Shady is white trash, Eminem is a celebrity. Marshall Mathers—as persona if not real identity—occupies a liminal space between the two, through which he manages his twin personas. Eminem's transformational tale of possessive individualism is supplemented by a series of songs in which he mobilizes a confessional model of bourgeois sentimentality grounded in alternative depictions of family and celebrity life. Using the discourses of self-help, these songs firmly position him within the orbit of the privatization of social responsibility under neoliberal modes of governance.

"I'm Sorry Momma": The Epistemologies of Eminem's Closet

The tales of white trash debasement and domestic abuse that are so prevalent in Eminem's lyrics sit alongside other songs in which he employs a sentimentalized self-confessional form. While the confessional mode employed in these songs could be likened to the public display of excessive emotion in *The Jerry Springer Show* and the presumed inability of white trash subjects to engage in appropriate disclosure, it can be linked more accurately to the confessional mode of postmodern autobiography in books such as *Prozac Nation* and *Girl, Interrupted* and in the sentimental turn in bourgeois culture. The lyrical content of songs such as "Cleanin' Out My Closet" and "Stan" transforms the revenge fantasies in which Eminem kills his ex-wife or publicly criticizes his mother and the voyeuristic narratives of self-abuse and deviancy into sentimental songs in which he describes the psychological toll the deprivations of his childhood have taken, the responsibilities of being a good father, and the burden of being a role model for his fans. This second genre of songs, which might at first seem to be incongruous with the tales of murder and deprivation already discussed, actually supplements them in interesting ways as it transforms the debasement of white trash into a sentimentalized possessive individualism that is congruent with the bourgeois sensibilities of affirmative self-help, the flip-side of white trash bodily excess. If " '97 Bonnie and Clyde" is *The Jerry Springer Show*, songs such as "Stan" are *Dr. Phil*.

The song "Stan" from *The Marshall Mathers LP* uses an epistolary form to narrate the disillusionment of a young fan who sends an increasingly frustrated series of letters to his idol, Slim Shady. The song opens with a long sample from the first verse of "Thank You," an overly sentimental love song by the English pop singer Dido.[23] The sample is repeated as the chorus. Over the sound of rain splashing against a window and a looping bass line, Dido is heard singing:

> My tea's gone cold, I'm
> Wondering why I got out of bed at all.
> The morning rain clouds up my window and I can't see at all.
> And even if I could it would all be grey,
> But your picture on my wall
> It reminds me that it's not so bad, it's not so bad.

In the context of the original song, these opening lines describe the ennui of a rainy Monday morning as the narrator thanks her lover for making the day-to-day boredom of her life bearable. "Stan" takes that context and changes the romantic relationship between two lovers into the relationship between a celebrity and a fan. The picture on the wall is transformed from the photograph of a lover into a young fan's poster of a rap idol. "I got a room full of your posters and your pictures, man," Stan boasts to Slim.[24] The song thus transforms the sentimental tropes of the love song into the possessive demands of a fan, and romantic love is recast as the overidentification of a young fan with the object of his adulation. In each of the letters that Stan writes to Slim the weight of that responsibility is made clear.

> See, I'm just like you in a way.
> I never knew my father neither.
> He used to always cheat on my mom and beat her.
> I can relate to what you're saying in your songs.
> So when I have a shitty day, I drift away and put 'em on.
> 'Cause I don't really got shit else, so that shit helps when I'm depressed.
> I even got a tattoo with your name across my chest.

In these lines Eminem suggests that the lyrical content of his earlier songs—broken homes, abusive parents, neglect—do more than just present a grotesque picture of white trash existence. By relating tales of his own experience he is offering a means of self-expression to his similarly disenfranchised fans. His grotesque and debased lyrical content is transformed into a form of self-help. The tattoo across the chest, which suggests the problematic confusion of romantic love and celebrity fandom, signals an overidentification that further highlights the weight of responsibility Eminem describes. This overidentification is then related to self-mutilation; in the following lines the fandom epitomized by a room full of posters and an encyclopedic knowledge of the artist's discography turns darker and more psychologically complicated. Stan writes:

> Sometimes I even cut myself to see how much it bleeds.
> It's like adrenaline. The pain is such a sudden rush for me.
> See, everything you say is real, and I respect you 'cause you tell it.

The confession of self-mutilation recalls Eminem's recollections in his earlier songs of the debasements and psychological problems of his own youth. When Stan's cry for help is not heard, he replicates Eminem's revenge fantasies and kills his pregnant girlfriend and himself by driving his car off a bridge. This scene reproduces the imagery from the cover of *The Slim Shady LP* and the violent fantasies of songs such as "'97 Bonnie and

Clyde." As such, Eminem situates the young fan's cries for help within the history of his own career, thereby transforming, if only subtly, the original meanings of such songs.

In the song's final verse the narrative voice shifts from Stan to Slim as he replies to Stan in a letter written, as he realizes at the end of the song, too late. In this letter he apologizes for the tardiness of his reply and offers Stan advice:

> And what's this shit you said about you like to cut your wrists too?
> I say that shit just clownin', dog, c'mon, how fucked up is you?
> You got some issues, Stan, I think you need some counselin.'
> To help your ass from bouncin' off the walls when you get down

The overidentification of a young fan is here a form of misrecognition in which Stan cannot distinguish between Eminem's real life and the fantasies of his various personas. Eminem's "just clownin'" has been taken seriously by his young fan, who, like the artist's conservative critics, cannot distinguish between the real and representation. Misrecognition or not, Eminem does not dismiss Stan or tell him to get his shit together, but suggests that he get some counseling, thereby replicating the neoliberal forms of governance predicated on the erosions of the welfare state and the privatization of citizen responsibility. This seeming incongruity suggests the degree to which the transformations of white masculinist experience have come to orient themselves around the requirements of neoliberal capital accumulation. Stan is not pilloried by his idol, but encouraged to delve deeper into himself, to uncover the root cause of his problems. What Eminem is suggesting to Stan is that he engage in the form of self-help and self-regulation that is so central to the organizing rubrics of neoliberal subjectivity. As in the case of Senior and Paulie Teutul, self-help is understood to be an acceptable activity for men.[25] Moreover as it replaces the welfare dependency of the white trash subject it constitutes a conservative politics of privatized responsibility in which men's emotions are placed at center stage. This foregrounding of masculinist emotion is prominent in many of Eminem's raps in which he airs the intimate details of his private life—or fantasies thereof—for his fans. In "Cleanin' Out My Closet," for example, he describes both the pressures of celebrity and the deprivations of his childhood.

"Cleanin' Out My Closet" uses a structure similar to "Stan," in which the song's verses present a vitriolic narrative of misunderstanding and disappointment while the chorus provides a sentimental counterpoint. In the first verse Eminem describes the public response to his earlier work:

Have you ever been hated or discriminated against?
I have.
I've been protested and demonstrated against,
Picket signs for my wicked rhymes,
Look at the times.

In these lines, as I have already suggested, he casts his public reception in terms of minority discrimination and the discourse of identity politics. In the lines that follow, however, his attention turns from the public response to his lyrics to his personal motivation for writing them. "Sick is the mind of the motherfuckin' kid that's behind all this commotion," he raps. "Emotions run deep as oceans explodin'. Tempers flarin' from parents." From here on, the lyrics describe the "skeletons in [his] closet," describing what it was like growing up in a broken home with a pill-popping mother who only wanted his money. By linking the pressures of his status as a reviled public figure to the privations of his childhood, Eminem links the negative reaction his songs' subject matter produces to the experiences he relates in them. In this way he explains conservative reactions against him as a form of intolerance to minority difference. Lacking the privilege of a middle-class bourgeois upbringing, he positions himself as a product of his environment and cites minority difference as the reality of his experience. That the minority subjected to this prejudice is white trash is elided in the focus on form over content. "Picket signs for my wicked rhymes," Eminem sings, highlighting his verbal dexterity and rapping skill. *Wicked* has a double connotation here, evoking both evil and exemplarity, and expresses the fact that Eminem has mastered a black American musical form to describe white minority discontent. Foregrounding the fact that he is a product of public housing and the welfare state, Eminem locates difference in the structural inequalities of a class-based oppression that he likens to racism. These inequalities are then recast within the frame of a sentimentalized narrative of familial dysfunction that he had to overcome. In the song's chorus he locates the thematic content of its verses within a sentimentalized discourse of familial responsibility and failed expectations. After a closing line in which he tells his mother that he is going to "make [her] look so ridiculous now," Eminem sings—not raps—the chorus for the final time:

> I'm sorry mama, I never meant to hurt you,
> I never meant to make you cry,
> But tonight I'm cleanin' out my closet.

These lines speak to a resignation born of the long experience of failed expectations that have been spelled out in the song's verses: "This is my life; I'd like to welcome you all to the Eminem show." While the chorus presents a discourse of sentimentality that seems to contradict the content of the verses, the song's music links them together. The lyrics are rapped over a percussive rhythm driven by a sampled snare drum, and the chorus is sung over a guitar lick that echoes the AOR sound of bands such as Aerosmith, Lynyrd Skynyrd, and Alabama that were fixtures on FM radio in the 1970s and that Eminem evokes in his descriptions of his broken childhood.

The use of samples and quotations from typically white musical genres such as country and hard rock are a staple of Eminem's songs. "Sing for the Moment," also from *The Eminem Show*, contains a sample from the Aerosmith song "Dream On" (1973) in the chorus.[26] Using samples of Steven Tyler's lyrics and the guitar solo of Joe Perry, the song evokes the sentimental form of the rock "power ballad" for which Aerosmith is famous and locates Eminem's confessional belligerence within a form of masculine sentimentality that is explicitly racialized as white. The power ballad was a staple of rock albums in the late 1970s and 1980s. Often taking the form of a love song, these ballads were more sentimental in their lyrical themes and musical format than the more overtly aggressive songs of sex, drugs, and rock 'n' roll that are characteristic of the hard rock genre.[27] Like the custom motorcycle of *American Chopper*, the guitar solo–driven sentimentality of the power ballad provides a conduit for masculine affectivity. Moreover the lyrical content of these songs provides a way for men to describe the loss of security and the erosions of patriarchal and paternal authority that are common in the postindustrial masculine experience. It is these resonances that Eminem hears as he locates his own tunes within this sentimentalized musical discourse. The lyrics from the song he employs for his chorus are "Sing with me, Sing for the year / Sing for the laughter, sing for the tears / Sing with me, if it's just for today / Maybe tomorrow, the good Lord will take you away." These lines bridge the gap between the young fan who survives his days by listening to Eminem and Eminem himself. In the first verse Eminem begins by describing the fears of middle-class parents whose children identify with his music. "These ideas are nightmares to white parents," he raps, "whose worst fear is a child with dyed hair and who likes earrings." The child rails against a hostile world and expresses himself through the use of the black vernacular born of oppression: "His thoughts are whacked, he's mad so he's talkin' back / Talkin' black, brainwashed from rock and rap." Eminem understands that his lyrics provide narratives to which his young fan can relate, enabling him to survive.[28]

Eminem's quotation from and sampling of rock music from the 1970s and 1980s further link his tale of personal disenfranchisement to a white minority discourse that is tied to both the postindustrial North and the post–civil rights rural South of the contemporary United States.[29] Anthemic southern rock songs such as Lynyrd Skynyrd's "Freebird" and "Sweet Home Alabama" evoke nostalgic images of the South that obfuscate the realities of postreconstruction racial tensions as they portray the South as a shelter from the pressures of contemporary society and responsibility. In "Sweet Home Alabama," for example, the South is a place of family and civility:

Big wheels keep on turning
Carry me home to see my kin
Singing songs about the Southland
I miss Alabamy once again.

. . .

In Birmingham they love the Governor
Now we all did what we could do
Now Watergate does not bother me
Does your conscience bother you?
Tell the truth.
Sweet home Alabama
Where the skies are blue

Sweet home Alabama
Lord, I'm coming home to you.

Referencing both the Watergate scandal and the controversial governor
George Wallace, the song explicitly contrasts the political and urban North
to the civil and rural South and finds the North wanting. In the context of
a sentimentalized and pastoral South, the history of racism and the more
recent transformations of the post–civil rights era are elided in a masculinist discourse of benign paternalism. In his referencing of traditionally
white musical forms such as southern rock and hard rock Eminem provides a musical link between the generic conventions of hip-hop and the
discourse surrounding the crisis of masculinity that participates in the
transformation of white masculinist concerns into the identity discourses
of the politics of representation and recognition. Explicitly evoking the
mainstream white rock music of the 1970s and 1980s, these songs situate the pressures of disenfranchised youth within the broader history of
masculinist disenfranchisement. That he is a white performer working in
a predominantly black mode of cultural expression endows Eminem with
an aura of authenticity that positions him as a troubling figure able to
work across class- and race-based expectations.

In "White America," a song explicitly addressed to a white audience
(and to the parents of his young fans), Eminem suggests that his skin color
has enabled his career:

Look at these eyes, baby blue, baby—just like yourself.
If they were brown Shady lose, Shady sit on the shelf.
But Shady's cute, Shady knew Shady's dimples would help—
Make ladies swoon baby—ooh baby!—look at my sales.
Let's do the math—if I was black I woulda sold half.

While he acknowledges the benefits of his skin color, he also understands
that spectral similitude ("eyes, baby blue, baby—*just like yourself*") to be a
misrecognition. He understands that the threat he poses to the establishment is the threat of socioeconomic transgression, in which race is a meta-
phor for class-based social mores. The transgression of class boundaries
from white trash to the white middle-class is also a transgression of racial
boundaries. "Hip hop," he points out, "was never a problem in Harlem,
only in Boston / After it bothered the fathers of daughters startin' to blos-

som." It is the proximate relationship between Eminem and his audience that is so troubling to these overprotective white parents. If middle-class white culture's libidinal investment in black American culture is motivated by the displacement of desire onto an other, Eminem brings that desire home:

> See the problem is, I speak to suburban kids
> Who otherwise never woulda knew these words exist;
> Whose moms probably woulda never gave two squirts of piss
> 'Til I created so much motherfuckin' turbulence.

Not only has he been able to move out of white trash and into whiteness, but he has also infected middle-class white society with the very thing he has sought to transcend.[30] "So to the parents of America," he spits, "I am the Derringer aimed at little Erica to attack her character."

> Fuck you Ms. Cheney! Fuck you Tipper Gore![31]
> Fuck you with the free-est of speech
> This Divided States of Embarrassment will allow me to have.
> Fuck you!

When Tipper Gore and Lynne Cheney bemoan the state of contemporary American culture and cite Eminem as an example of its slide into the gutter, they fail to recognize just how completely he epitomizes the very conservative values they embrace. As Eminem reassures listeners in the last line of the vitriolic "White America," "I'm just kidding America, you know I love you." And how could he not? It has made him what he is today. Throughout his career Eminem has successfully cultivated a model of possessive individualism that has been central to his transformation of white trash abjection into bourgeois celebrity. This transformation into whiteness and his capitulation to a conservative mode of possessive individualism reach an apotheosis in *8 Mile*.

Detroit Confidential: *8 Mile* and the Racialization of Class

Released in the United States in 2002, *8 Mile* marked the culmination of an extraordinarily successful year for Eminem. The Grammy award–winning *The Eminem Show* was the best-selling album of the year, "Cleanin' Out My Closet" reached number four in the Billboard Hot

One Hundred, and on the weekend of the film's release "Lose Yourself" (an original song from the film's soundtrack for which Eminem won an Academy Award) was number one in the Billboard Hot One Hundred.[32] Produced for less than $41 million, *8 Mile* grossed $51.2 million in its opening weekend, marking the fourth best opening weekend in the history of Universal Studios (behind *The Lost World*, *The Mummy Returns*, and *How the Grinch Stole Christmas*). The film's final domestic gross was $116.7 million, a figure supplemented by foreign box office receipts of $126 million and Region One DVD sales of over $130 million.[33] The film's box office success was accompanied by generally good reviews that applauded Eminem's performance and the gripping nature of the plot. Writing for *Time*, Richard Shickel lauded Eminem's acting: "[He] has the potential to draw in, even enchant people to whom hip-hop has been just a scary blare of rage emanating from the car drawn up next to them at a stop sign."[34] In *The Village Voice* J. Hoberman wrote, "[Eminem] imbues [his character] with charismatic stoicism."[35] Elvis Mitchell likened the rapper to Elvis: "[When] Rabbit starts hollering or rapping, he does indeed give off the explosion of vitality that Presley had while singing in his very early movies."[36]

Unfolding over the course of a single week in 1995, *8 Mile* tells the story of Jimmy Smith Jr. (who goes by the moniker "Bunny Rabbit"), a young white wannabe emcee from inner-city Detroit. The story is loosely based on Eminem's own experience growing up in Detroit and attempting to achieve success in a predominantly black cultural world. Despite its pseudo-autobiographical status, however, the story of *8 Mile* is an old one, told innumerable times by Hollywood: through hard work and sacrifice a young man overcomes the limitations of his humble origins and achieves success. Rabbit has recently broken up with his longtime girlfriend (Taryn Manning), and the opening of the film finds him moving back in to the mobile home his mother (played by Kim Basinger) shares with her young daughter. Recently fired from a job working at a pizza joint, Rabbit has found employment at one of the last vestiges of Detroit's moribund automotive industry, a steel works called New Detroit Stamping. He hangs out with his multiracial crew, half-heartedly pursues a relationship with an aspiring model, Alex, and engages in street battles, both verbal and physical, with the members of a rival crew, The Free World, and their leader, Papa Doc (Anthony Mackie). The action of the film serves primarily to provide narrative content for the final scene, in which Rabbit achieves the success he has been seeking and wins a rap battle. Rabbit is betrayed by Alex (Brittany Murphy), who sleeps with his erstwhile friend, Wink (Eugene Byrd); he falls out with his best friend, Future (Mekhi Phifer), argues with his mother, engages in fistfights with his mother's boyfriend, a high school contemporary of his, and learns that, if he is to succeed, he must take responsibility for his own future.

The film's racial shell game is evidenced most clearly in the relationship between Rabbit's enabling self-identification as white trash and the film's capitulation to this traditional American narrative of possessive individualism. In *8 Mile* the reorientation of white male privilege can be most clearly seen when reading the film's narrative teleology against the grain of its conflated politics of white agency and disavowal. The film's fictional protagonist mobilizes a cross-racial identitarian politics of class affiliation in order to overcome forms of social disenfranchisement. The narrative resolution relies on a putatively progressive form of cross-racial, class-based coalition building that promises to move beyond an essentialized understanding of racial difference but that in reality does anything but. For all its seeming progressivism, *8 Mile*'s coalitional politics of difference—in which class trumps race—merely enables a traditional tale of white male empowerment. Like Eminem, Bunny Rabbit marshals the strategies of identity politics in order to reenfranchise white masculinist privilege. At its core, *8 Mile* is a film about the ideology of possessive individualism, and as such it epitomizes the love of the underdog and faith in the American Dream of economic and social mobility. In both plot and thematic content the film follows the generic conventions of the sports film and has as much in common with Sylvester Stallone's *Rocky* as it does with *Purple Rain*. I foreground the traditionalism of the film's plot here because I wish to emphasize how it is through precisely the sleight of hand of its postidentitarian politics of difference that the film recuperates white privilege.

8 Mile opens and closes with scenes in which Rabbit competes in rap battles hosted by his friend Future at a grimy downtown Detroit club called The Shelter. In these battle scenes the film's racial politics come most visibly to the fore. It is giving nothing away to say that Rabbit loses the first of these battles—because of stage fright he is barely able to reach the stage and is actually unable to compete—and triumphantly wins the second. While the traditionalism of the film's plot requires Rabbit to earn the right to succeed by accepting responsibility for his own future, the transformation from choke artist to verbal assassin that characterizes the difference between the battle scene that opens the film and the one that closes it requires something different. To win a rap battle the successful combatant must display a verbal dexterity and wit that allow him to verbally destroy his opponent. Rabbit's transformation is staged as a question of racial authenticity. In the opening battle he is defeated both by his own lack of self-confidence and by his opponent's use of race against him. Highlighting Rabbit's whiteness (and thus his purported inauthenticity), the rapper tells him, "They don't laugh because you're whack, they laugh 'cause you're white with a mic"; he accuses Rabbit of being "faker than a psychic with caller ID," a "tourist," and tells him, "[You] don't belong." "This here Detroit," the opponent concludes his assault. "Sixty mile road is that-a-way." By situating himself as authentically from inner-city Detroit and Rabbit as a tourist from across "sixty mile road," the opposing rapper evidences a spatialized understanding of raced identity that is central to the film. If you are from inner-city Detroit, you are black; if you live across Eight Mile Road, and thus in greater Detroit rather than the city proper, you are white.

The discontent of white masculinity in the era of neoliberalism finds particular resonance in the story of Detroit's decline and fall in the aftermath of the failures of the American automotive industry. With a boom-time population of over 2 million in the 1950s, the city has dwindled to around 822,000. The white population hovers at around 10 percent, having dropped by over a million and a half during the same period.[37] White flight hit Detroit harder than almost any other city in the United States. These facts make Detroit unique and help account for the city's unusual race relations. Paul Clemens describes his experience growing up in Detroit during the 1970s and 1980s: "There was, too, the disconnect of being white in a society in which this is seen as an 'entitled' status but having been born and raised in late-twentieth-century Detroit, where whiteness entitled one to nothing at all." The transformation of Detroit from a predominantly white to a predominantly black city arose as a result of the declining availability of traditional forms of blue-collar employment. As the automotive industry moved manufacturing overseas, the city's whites fled to the suburbs. Those who stayed faced the sorts of limits to their expectations that Faludi explores in *Stiffed*. A year younger than Eminem, Clemens provides an interesting point of comparison with Eminem's tales of white trash existence:

> This was that hard-bellied stratum of white America where, to borrow from Heller in *Catch-22*, the men were possessed of a variety of useful, necessary skills that would keep them in a low-income group all their lives. There was nothing these men couldn't build, nothing they couldn't fix, no problem they couldn't solve—and it would never do them a damn bit of good economically. They could fix other people's cars, but such work couldn't be relied on to provide enough money for them to fix their own, let alone trade up to a nicer one. Though largely uneducated, they were skilled enough to go into business for themselves, running towing services, bump shops, and pinstriping places, only to find that being self-employed meant long hours, huge headaches, a lack of health insurance, and—when one's clientele is also working-class—being entirely at the whim of an economy in which very little ever trickles down.

Clemens's family avoided being white trash because his father was always employed and because he was Catholic. "As Catholics" he writes, "we weren't white trash; we were working class." This despite his father's revving his muscle car to full throttle early in the morning, an activity that "situates itself at white trashdom's essential core."[38] To be poor and white in Detroit is to be figured as marginal, always on the verge of tipping the scales from white to white trash. It is in this context that Eminem, who grew up on the other side of Eight Mile in Warren, a Detroit suburb, situates his own marginalized identity. Socioeconomic privilege is understood here in terms of racial identity and space. The experience inscribed in that space relies on a racialized understanding of authentic urban experience.[39]

Unable in the film's opening battle to offer an alternative reading of his whiteness and therefore unable to cast whiteness as anything other than privilege, Rabbit has no recourse but to accept the truth of his opponent's assertion that he does not belong and leave the stage in humiliated defeat. In order to win the final battle Rabbit must "flip the script" and make himself an authentic and legitimate combatant. Between the first battle and the finale Rabbit is provided with the wherewithal to make this transformation; he is given both the ammunition to defeat his black opponents and the strength of character to ensure that he does.

Rabbit's success is achieved in two ways. First he is able to manifest the verbal and linguistic virtuosity to blow away his competitors. Fueled by a confidence born of self-sufficiency, his raps finally flow as he proves himself to be a verbally dexterous and scathing opponent who has mastered the form of the battle. He gains this confidence by becoming a wholly self-sufficient member of society who does not rely on help or handouts from others.[40] He must earn his success. Central to the film's moral logic is his decision to go it alone, without his crew, and his transformation at work from someone who repeatedly complains "It wasn't my fault" to someone who humbly responds "It won't happen again." After he has defeated Papa Doc in the final battle his newfound work ethic prompts him to return to work to complete the overtime shift he has recently been awarded.

Second, Rabbit is able to perform whiteness as a form of class rather than racial identity in which authenticity resides somewhere other than at the specular level of racial embodiment. He is able to develop a persona in which where he lives becomes more important than his race. As the opposing rapper's references to the trailer park, the bourgeois family life of the 1950s, and the patriarchal traditionalism of *Leave It to Beaver* suggest, race and class are inextricably intertwined in the minds of The Shelter's audience, and whiteness carries with it an assumption of privilege and domestic security. Although his own experiences have more in common with those of the audience than with Beaver Cleaver, Rabbit is unable to make those similarities legible. What he needs to be able to do in order to win the final battle is extricate class from race and thereby alter the meanings of both. He is able to do this in part by evoking a spatial rather than a racial logic of identity in which authenticity resides somewhere other than skin color. From its title on, *8 Mile* is preoccupied with questions of space and place that are also central to hip-hop. Hip-hop has manifested a profoundly spatial logic since the early days of the culture and, whether through tagging and graffiti or collective sound systems, has constituted itself as a spatial art. Locations, real or imagined, such as the ghetto, the hood, and the East or West Coast feature prominently in the language, narratives, and styles of hip-hop. Murray Forman argues that the "overlapping practices and methods of constructing place-based identities, and of inscribing and enunciating individual and collective presence, created the

Bunny Rabbit challenges the audience in the final battle scene. From *8 Mile* (2002).

bonds upon which affiliations were forged within specific social geographies."[41] Tied to notions of authenticity and forms of collective solidarity, location dictates not only where hip-hop plays but also what hip-hop means. As such, the issue of authenticity that dominates the battle scenes in *8 Mile* revolves around both racial identity and lived experience. Rabbit is able to win over the audience at The Shelter by making location more important than race.

While Rabbit's newfound confidence and mastery of the battle form allows him to negate the ammunition Papa Doc uses against him—"This guy ain't no motherfucking M C, I know everything he's got to say against me," he quips at the beginning of the contest—he is also able to show that Papa Doc is inauthentic because his own class bona fides are suspect. "But I know something about you," Rabbit taunts his opponent. "You went to Cranbrook and that's a private school." Having learned from a friend that Papa Doc is from a wealthy suburb of Detroit and does not reside within the city limits, Rabbit is able to out Papa Doc as a fake. "This guy's not a gangster," he tells the audience, "his real name's Clarence and Clarence lives at home with both parents." In this rap Rabbit de-emphasizes Papa Doc's blackness and highlights his middle-class affluence. Both his education—Cranbrook is an exclusive private school in suburban Detroit with annual tuition fees of $23,000—and his settled home life mark Papa Doc as outside the presumed realm of the African American experience within the limits of Eight Mile Road.[42] Calling on the audience to join him as he chants the Detroit area code—"Everybody from the 313"—Rabbit humiliates Papa Doc while forging his own ties of affinity. Denied the authenticity he believes his racial identity confers on him, Clarence is shown to be more *Leave It to Beaver* than Rabbit will ever be. Thus while Rabbit can close his rap with a triumphant and belligerent boast—"I'm a piece of fucking white trash and I'll say it proudly"—Papa Doc is left where Rabbit started, an inauthentic choke artist. "What's the matter, dog," Rabbit baits him, "you embarrassed?" As he cites Papa Doc as inauthentic, Rabbit uses his own status as white trash to produce an experiential similitude between himself and The Shelter's predominantly black audience and is thus able to disavow race as the primary index of lived experience.

As Rabbit is able to produce class as the principal signifier of lived experience, however, his body, explicitly raced as white, comes increasingly to the fore. And this fact in many ways provides the key to the film's double logic of white disavowal and elevation. By mobilizing an indexical series of racial tropes, *8 Mile* produces a logic of racial embodiment that is coterminous with the spatial economies of class and urban identity that, despite its putative move beyond race, only the film's white protagonist is finally able to transcend. In the battle scene that opens the film Rabbit is dressed in a baggy hooded sweatshirt with a watch cap pulled down low over his forehead. His body is covered and, with the exception of a sliver of his face, is hidden from view. In the final battle at The Shelter, however, his body is explicitly put on display and becomes a referential indicator of his class-based disenfranchisement. In his rebuttal of an opponent's character assassination in the penultimate round, for example, Rabbit pulls his pants down and moons his opponent and the audience as he rhymes that he is going to "walk [his] white ass back over Eight Mile." Here he owns the whiteness that he was unable to overcome in the first battle, where his opponent was able to defeat him with almost the same words he now uses. Rabbit performs race by making his body visible on stage, but he transforms that body's significance in the process. In the final round in which he defeats Papa Doc to become champion, he sheds his sweatshirt and appears on stage in a sleeveless vest. Like the moon of the preceding round, the body the vest places on display not only highlights Rabbit's whiteness but also performs that whiteness as a marker of minority affiliation by transforming the embodiment of race into the embodiment of class. "Fuck you all if you doubt me," Rabbit spits at the audience. "I'm a piece of fucking white trash and I'll say it proudly." As *white* becomes *white trash* it loses the stigma of privilege it has previously held. Unabashedly claiming his social status as white trash and the racialized form of white identity that accompanies it, Rabbit produces whiteness as both embodiment and culture.

Flipping the script in a confessional mode liberates Rabbit, as it does Eminem, from the confines of undifferentiated whiteness. That *8 Mile* leaves its black characters behind while its white protagonist, having found success, crosses Eight Mile Road, presumably heading not for the trailer park but the city's exclusive suburbs, home to both Cranbrook School and Marshall Mathers, should give us pause. Historians of the white working class such as Michael Denning, Eric Lott, and David Roediger have persuasively shown that in the history of American labor and social justice movements racial difference has often been used as a wedge to divide groups with other natural affinities.[43] That mainstream culture now uses white working poor identities to shore up rather than to criticize the excesses of white privilege suggests the extent to which the political strategies of progressive identitarian politics have been co-opted in the contemporary United States.

Family Melodrama and
the Fictions of State

5

Ethnic Whiteness
and *Million Dollar Baby*

Protect yourself at all times.
FRANKIE DUNN, in *Million Dollar Baby*

Everyone's life is a long series of miraculous escapes.
JOHN BUTLER YEATS (father of W. B. Yeats), quoted in
W. B. Yeats, *Autobiographies*

IN CLINT EASTWOOD's critically acclaimed and
Oscar-winning film, *Million Dollar Baby* (2004),
Irishness functions as a recuperative form of ethnic
identity that transforms a problematic white patriarchy into something altogether more benign.[1] The
film produces a relationship between Irishness, a
positive form of white minority identity, and white
trash, a negative form. Despite the ostensible plot
of female empowerment the film is primarily concerned with the recuperation of white patriarchy, a
recuperation that the film casts in the affective structures of melodrama. It manufactures a space for the
reenfranchisement of white patriarchal authority
through its transformation of the white trash body
into an exemplary white female body, virginal and
Irish, that requires protection. I suggest that Irishness recuperates not only whiteness, but also masculinity by transforming white patriarchy into a form
of benign Irish paternalism. Such examinations of
identity, which take place within the film, cannot be

fully understood without also considering them in relation to the celebrity persona of Eastwood himself.

In *Million Dollar Baby* white trash and Irishness are opposite points on a spectrum of classed, raced, and gendered bodies. Unlike Eminem and *8 Mile*, Eastwood and his film find nothing to celebrate or valorize in white trash and much to be overcome. While white trash itself offers a form of particularity (as I discussed in the previous chapter), it is one that the film's protagonists do not want. In *Million Dollar Baby* white trash is something to be avoided at all costs. In current beliefs about race and ethnicity in American culture Irishness is often used to substitute an acceptable ethnic identity for a problematic notion of monolithic whiteness. As Diane Negra suggests about the emergence of Irishness as an idealized identity, ethnic white identities offer a form of "enriched whiteness" that allows for the celebration of whiteness by casting it as something other than privilege.[2] In popular culture the conception of Irishness as "enriched whiteness" relies on an understanding of the history of the Irish in the United States in which the travel into whiteness from minority status is brought to the fore. In the terms of this study, Irishness ethnicizes whiteness and provides a means by which whiteness can particularize itself; it offers, as with the figure of the firefighter discussed in chapter 2, a way of owning and celebrating white identity in the wake of multiculturalism and identity politics by transforming the symbolic power of whiteness into a minoritized identity. *Million Dollar Baby* participates in this transformation while using the particularization of Irish ethnic whiteness as a tool for the concomitant recuperation of patriarchal white masculinity.

Set in present-day Los Angeles, *Million Dollar Baby* tells the story of Frankie Dunn (Clint Eastwood), an aging fight trainer, cut man, and gym owner, and Maggie Fitzgerald (Hilary Swank), a thirty-one-year-old waitress and would-be boxer from rural Missouri whom Frankie reluctantly agrees to train. *Million Dollar Baby* was adapted for the screen by Paul Haggis from two short stories, "Million Dollar Baby" and "Frozen Water," by Jerry Boyd (under the pseudonym F. X. Toole), a longtime cut man and aspiring writer. *Rope Burns: Stories from the Corner*, the collection from which the stories were drawn, was Boyd's first published work; he died shortly after its publication at the age of seventy-two. The story is narrated in an off-screen voice-over by Eddie "Scrap-Iron" Dupris (Morgan

Freeman), a longtime friend of Dunn's who is an ex-boxer and the janitor at Frankie's gym, the Hit Pit. The plot traces Maggie's journey from waitress to world title contender under Frankie's tutelage. In a dramatic turn three-quarters of the way through the film, however, Maggie's ascension comes to an abrupt halt when she is left paralyzed from the neck down after being sucker-punched by Billie "the Blue Bear," her opponent in the internationally televised title fight. The remainder of the film is devoted to Maggie's decline and Frankie's response to it. Confined to her hospital bed, Maggie deteriorates rapidly and, unable to endure the gradual disintegration of her body, asks Frankie to help her commit suicide. After much anguished soul-searching Frankie accedes; the film ends with her death at his hands and Frankie's subsequent disappearance. While the plot of *Million Dollar Baby* describes Maggie's rise and fall, the principal affective investment of its story is, unsurprisingly, in Eastwood's character.[3] Frankie Dunn, the audience discovers early on, is a man left alone with a troubled past. Still attempting to train fighters in his seventies he is unable to commit himself and for three years has been turning down offers for a title fight challenge for "Big" Willie Little (Mike Colter), his sole remaining fighter. He lives alone and is estranged from a daughter to whom he nevertheless writes letters every week. The letters, however, are always returned; in a bizarre instance of product placement, he dutifully files them away in a Nike shoebox. While the audience learns nothing of Frankie's daughter but her name and the fact that she was an athletic child, his problems of family and paternal responsibility are a central concern of the film. More than anything else *Million Dollar Baby* is about the sacrifices and redemption of Frankie Dunn.

What Maggie Knew: White Trash and Social Recycling

In the voice-over narration that introduces Maggie Fitzgerald to the audience, Scrap opines that she grew up "somewhere between nowhere and goodbye . . . knowing one thing: she was trash." The audience soon learns that Maggie is from rural Missouri and, now thirty-one, has been waitressing since she was thirteen. Boxing, Scrap tells the audience, is about respect, and respect is what Maggie wants. For Maggie Fitzgerald, boxing is a way of escaping the socioeconomic confines of her white trash identity. Her desire to become a prizefighter is a desire to escape the confines of a sociocultural demarcation that limits the horizons of her future possibilities. As it does in *8 Mile*, white trash denotes here a class identity so vilified in the United States that it signifies a shift in both class and racial status. To be white trash is barely to be white at all. Frankie Dunn, *Million Dollar Baby* suggests, is Maggie's only opportunity to overcome, or at least disavow, what Scrap says she knows. If Maggie's function as a recuperative object for Frankie is central to the film, as his surrogate daughter, platonic lover, and the primary vehicle of his redemption, Maggie must also be transformed: she must become someone who is worthy of Frankie's final sacrifice. In order to achieve this she is transformed from white trash into Irish. There is thus a double process of recuperation at work here. In order to save himself, Frankie must save Maggie twice, first by turning her into a fighter and transforming her from trash to Irish, second by killing her. It is only when Maggie becomes Irish that she becomes worthy of being killed, worthy, that is, of the sacrifice Frankie is willing to make on her behalf.

The film charts Maggie's transition from white trash to Irish in a number of ways, most particularly in the regulation and transformation of her body and her libidinal impulses. Maggie's status as white trash is encoded in the film primarily in relation to the body and to consumption along stereotypical lines. Her body (and what goes in it and on it) is a central fascination of the early scenes. As Hartigan explains, the common perception of white trash "involves a reaction to bodily conditions and behaviors that offend certain class decorums."[4] Maggie in fact understands her own socioeconomic status in just such a fashion. If Frankie won't train her, she tells him early in the film, she may as well "find a used trailer, buy a deep-fryer and some Oreos." The members of her family—the most villainous and certainly the most simplistically stereotyped characters in the film—all inhabit monstrous bodies. Her mother, Maggie tells us, weighs three hundred pounds. Her brother is incarcerated and covered in tattoos. Her sister is perpetually pregnant and claims welfare checks in the name of a dead baby. Small wonder Maggie spends so much time in the gym. Scrap's earlier description of Maggie—"she was trash"—explicitly links her marginal social standing to consumption through the trope of food. Scrap's observation accompanies a sequence during which she takes a half-eaten steak from the plate of a customer in the diner where she works, tells her boss that it's for her dog, and then takes it home and eats it while counting out the loose change that constitutes her tips for the night. In another early incident Frankie challenges Maggie about the provenance of the "homemade" lemon meringue pie sold at the diner, telling her that he doesn't want the "kind with the canned filling crap." "Big can, yay size, says homemade on the label," Maggie responds, already aware of just how far she can push the increasingly affable Dunn.[5] Bad food and poor eating habits (junk and table scraps more fit for a dog), improper consumption, and the excessive or improper consuming body all signify social marginality, and Maggie must learn to treat her body and her consuming self with respect. If, as Stanley Aronowitz suggests, "the main criterion for middle-class membership is one's participation in the huge consumer celebration," then Maggie is required not to stop consuming, but to learn how to consume properly.[6] This in part is what Frankie teaches her. Maggie's movement away from her minoritized status as white trash is defined by her growing ability to consume in socially acceptable ways.

If the white trash body is always a problematic body, Maggie's transformation from trash to Irish requires her to harness her body's impulses, to control its urges. The properly regulated body requires a process of self-governance that Julian B. Carter, following Matthew Frye Jacobson, claims lies at the center of white self-authorship.[7] Therefore, while Maggie's transformation from white trash orphan to Irish daughter is signaled in a variety of ways, her corporeal metamorphosis is central. If the fact that her body is transformed is of paramount importance, that she is the author of her own bodily transformation is doubly significant. Her sociological transformation is produced at the level of the body; as she develops as a fighter her body becomes both properly inhabitable and available for consumption. Thus while Frankie turns her into a fighter, he also teaches her how to transform her body into one that is legible to and eligible for the sympathetic attentions of the audience (both of the film and of her fights). This transformation is signaled in a number of ways, most notably in the way Maggie's body changes as she gains control of and learns to regulate her impulses and desires.

A genre requirement of the boxing film is the training montage, wherein the protagonist goes from hopeful neophyte to world title contender. *Million Dollar Baby* does not disappoint. In a montage sequence following Frankie's agreement to train Maggie, the audience watches her undergo this protean transformation. This sequence highlights the passage of time through a rapidly edited series of shots of her training. Over the course of the two-minute-long sequence Maggie is transformed, in Frankie's words, from a girl into a fighter as her newfound ability to regulate her body is displayed on screen. Frankie first criticizes the immobility of her feet in relation to the wild flailing of her arms; he teaches her how to control her body by grounding her action in the proper use of her feet. As she learns the footwork necessary to withstand the force of her opponent's punches and to marshal the available power behind her own, she is fashioned into a professional athlete. Inasmuch as her bodily metamorphosis is largely symbolic of such a transformation, that transformation is not only physical but also mental. She is, Scrap tells the audience early on, a girl with a great deal of heart.[8] She badgers Frankie until he reluctantly agrees to take her on and seems to spend every nonworking waking hour in the gym. She is, though, untrained, and her method displays more energy and enthusiasm than technique. Untutored, Maggie throws punches that are more likely to cause her injury than to halt an opponent. Unlike her family and unlike "Danger" Barch, the Hit Pit's other white trash transplant, Maggie is successfully able to learn how to regulate her body, to manage it effectively, because she is committed. This process of maturation involves her departure from the dead-end world of waitressing and her subsequent arrival in the world of professional sports.

What goes into the body is a central concern of the film's early scenes, but what goes on it is of equal importance. The fitter Maggie becomes, the better and more appropriate her clothes. At the beginning of the training montage Maggie is clothed almost in rags: old T-shirts, gray cut-off sweatpants, camouflage-patterned undershirts. She ends the sequence dressed in form-fitting leggings and a sports bra. On one level, of course, this is merely a practical necessity of the film's production schedule: the transition from baggy gray cotton sweats to Lycra sports bra and glistening flesh allows the development of Maggie's body while hiding Hilary Swank's, which presumably began the production as fit as Maggie's needed to become. The focus on clothing during this metamorphosis, though, also suggests Maggie's social transformation. As she becomes the fighter Frankie now believes her to be, she transcends her marginal status as white trash by becoming properly incorporated and, as her correct clothing decisions suggest, capable of middle-class consumer choice. The fitter Maggie becomes during the course of this training montage, the more her newly proper body is revealed to the audience. As she regulates her bodily movements, hers becomes a body worth looking at. In short, her body gains the normality that Carter describes as "a specifically modern, indicatively white combination of erotic and emotional sensitivity and self-government."[9] This healthy body is then unveiled for the consumption of the viewer.[10] Having watched the transformation of her body and her mind into those of a world title contender, the audience understands and *feels* the horror of the later disintegration of her body. In order for her assisted death to be acceptable to the audience, the depths of Maggie's fall must be clearly legible. That she later has the determination and the willpower to attempt suicide even though she is paralyzed only confirms how far she has come.[11] By learning to control and harness her body Maggie is able to cast off the negative bodily associations evoked by her white trash family.

As in *8 Mile*, a blue-collar work ethic is central to the subject's ability to achieve the benefits offered by the ideology of possessive individualism and what we might call liberal personhood. Robyn Wiegman defines "liberal personhood" as the "formation of social subjects within a modern state that recognizes and confers personhood on the basis of contractual relations. . . . These domains of contract obligation—of citizen, spouse, and laborer-owner—have operated historically as powerful technologies for the production and excision of proper national subjects, mediating the relationship between the seemingly private world of personal affect, intimacy, and reproduction and the public realm of social exchange, itself evinced by the birth certificate, the voting card, the draft card, and the marriage license."[12] Having cast off the improper modes of consumption that adhere to the white trash body, Maggie begins to enjoy the benefits of consumer citizenship and liberal personhood almost immediately. As he makes the preparations for Maggie's title fight in Las Vegas, Frankie offers her the choice of flying or driving. Giddy with the excitement of consumer choice, Maggie refuses to deny herself either option and decides that they will fly there and drive back. Her entry into the middle-class world of purchasing power places her at odds with the welfare dependency of her family. A major source of conflict between Maggie and her family involves a house she buys for her mother from the money she has saved from her winnings. Her mother fears the government will find out about the house and stop her welfare checks. After her accident, when her family comes to Los Angeles to divest her of any remaining assets, Maggie rejects her mother's advances, and because her mother failed to carry out the bureaucratic formalities necessary for the house to be transferred to her, she is forced to leave with nothing after Maggie threatens to take it away from her. "You're so worried about your welfare you never signed those house papers like you were supposed to," Maggie tells her mother, "so anytime I feel like it, I can sell that house from under your fat lazy hill-billy ass, and if you ever come back, that's exactly what I'll do." Unlike Frankie, who counsels Maggie to purchase property, her mother does not understand the relationship between property ownership and possessive individualism.

By learning the self-control and self-governance that her family is seemingly incapable of, Maggie attains a form of citizenship that is symbolized in the associational shift from trash to Irish that Frankie is able—and now willing—to manufacture for her. Before Maggie's first international fight, which takes place in London, Frankie gives her an emerald green warm-up robe with a gold harp and the Gaelic inscription "Mo Cuishle" stitched on the back. This inscription holds deep significance for Frankie, but he refuses to tell Maggie what it means.[13] The meaning is not disclosed—to either Maggie or the audience—until the final scene. *Mo cuishle* nevertheless becomes a battle cry, and the spectators at Maggie's fights take to chanting it in support of her. Enrobed in Frankie's gift, Maggie is transformed: the Kelly green robe, the golden harp, the Gaelic inscription all name her as Irish. She has claimed no Irish heritage herself, and aside from her surname the film has previously given no indication that she has any Irish blood. It is not uncommon for white boxers in the United States to strongly identify, often falsely, with a national origin that codes them as something more than just white. Eoin Cannon writes, "Boxers have long been understood to represent their ethnic background, and have often drawn their strongest support from fans who identify with it."[14] Maggie's newly avowed Irishness is thus both a fiction of Frankie's and a commonplace in the world of professional boxing. By enrobing Maggie in the tropes of Irishness Frankie is providing her not only with a legible ethnic identity for her boxing persona, but also with a legible history of the transit into U.S. citizenship that elides her own white trash origins. Irishness functions here as what Negra has called, in another context, "a crucial dis-

Maggie Fitzgerald is reborn as Irish. From *Million Dollar Baby* (2004).

cursive platform for articulating white working-class legitimacy and innocence."[15] By becoming Irish Maggie gains access to the lower rungs of the
ladder of economic and social mobility that structures consumer citizenship and that she will now attempt to climb. This transformation from
one particularized white ethnic identity to another provides her with the
key to her own success by eliding the structural effects of white supremacy and by foregrounding the working-class work ethos of her newfound
Irishness. If, as the film proposes, white trash subjects are southern, rural,
and racist, the Irish are northern, urban, and ethnic. Maggie's transformation is explicitly cast in terms of ethnic and sexual purity such that the
problematic associations of the white trash body as a burden on the state
are rewritten.

As Irish, Maggie symbolizes a virginal innocence that belies the libidinal excesses of her earlier incarnation as white trash. In the introduction
to the fight in which she breaks her neck, Maggie is accompanied into the
arena by a phalanx of Irish pipers, resplendent in kilts and sporrans. Throwing off her green robe, she stands resplendent in white boxing shorts with
her name stitched in gold and green on the high waistband. The perspective shifts to an overhead crane shot in which her dazzling white form is
surrounded by the pristine white of the canvas. Enrobed in the whitening
power of Irishness, Maggie is transformed, and the fight serves as a coro-
nation in which she appears before the world as pure, virginal, and white.
Her opponent, by contrast, is accompanied into the arena by a phalanx

of muscular men dressed in gray military-style trousers and tight black shirts. Her dark-blue robe and metallic-blue corset-like top contrast with Maggie's virginal and innocent whiteness. Here the racial politics that the film otherwise attempts to disavow come to the fore: Maggie's opponent is not only a former prostitute from the formerly communist East Germany, but also a light-skinned black woman. Discussing other films with Irish themes, such as Alan Parker's *The Commitments* (1991), Hazel Carby has pointed out that "black bodies are instant referents for carrying the history of oppression."[16] In *Million Dollar Baby* that referentiality is displaced by an insistence on the threat posed by the black to the white body. Here Irishness is not linked to any history of oppression that might find common cause with people of color, but names a purity that is both beyond and firmly entrenched (however blindly) in questions of race that are recast as the sentimental bonds of kinship.

The film's conception of Irishness as enriching or otherwise transforming whiteness in positive ways is, of course, the exact opposite of earlier conceptions of the Irish in American culture as debased and negatively racialized. For the English and, later, for Americans, the Irish have long been problematic because as both white and native they disrupt common categories of racial and colonial discourse. As Luke Gibbons suggests, the "'otherness' and alien character of Irish experience was all the more disconcerting precisely because it did not lend itself to visible racial divisions." Gibbons quotes the famous remark of Charles Kingsley, who opined of the Irish, "To see a white chimpanzee is dreadful; if they were black, one would not feel it so much, but their skins, except where tanned by exposure, are as white as ours."[17] In the context of the United States the trajectory of the Irish from racial other to white citizen has been well documented. Noel Ignatiev describes the situation of the Irish in the nineteenth century:

> To Irish laborers, to become white meant at first that they could compete for jobs in all spheres instead of being confined to certain work; to Irish entrepreneurs, it meant that they could function outside of a segregated market. To both of these groups it meant that they were citizens of a democratic republic with a right to elect and be elected, to be tried by a jury of their peers, to live wherever they could afford, and to spend, without racially imposed restrictions, whatever money

they managed to acquire. In becoming white the Irish ceased to be green.[18]

If, as Ignatiev suggests, the Irish only *became* white in America during the nineteenth century, Irishness currently embodies a particular ethnic valence that makes it both more than and less than properly white; it is this valence that *Million Dollar Baby* underscores. Rather than the ascendancy of the not-yet-white of the new immigrant populations Ignatiev describes, however, this new form of liminal whiteness encoded as Irish offers a route away from rather than toward hegemonic whiteness. As Maggie's transformation becomes the vehicle for Frankie's redemption, the film's logics of white ethnic racial innocence gain a gendered component that cannot be overlooked.

When Irish Eyes Are Crying:
Melodrama and the National Racial Scene

As Maggie's transformation from white trash to Irish enables her own self-fulfillment, it is also central to the recuperation of Frankie, who rewards Maggie for her hard work by making her his own. *Mo cuishle* names Maggie as Irish, but it also names her as Frankie's. Frankie tells Maggie the inscription's meaning only at the moment he takes her life. Immediately prior to injecting her with a lethal dose of adrenalin, he leans in and, kissing her on the lips, tells her that *mo cuishle* means "my darling, my blood." Frankie's term of endearment names not only an object of affection, but also that object's possession: *my* darling, *my* blood. The possessive pronoun cites a familiar and indeed familial relationship that Frankie wishes to bestow on Maggie. Moreover, because Frankie originally presents his gift just after he has jokingly told Maggie that he will propose to her if she wins the fight, the gift also signals the ceremonial exchange of marriage vows. His gift marks her as his—both daughter and platonic lover—and his refusal to tell her what the inscription means only confirms this. He is claiming possession of her meaning in the various circuits of exchange— familial, sporting, ethnic—in which the two protagonists move. As Frankie's daughter, lover, and wife, the newly enriched Maggie transforms Frankie in a similarly sentimental way, for her rise and fall are only half the story *Million Dollar Baby* seeks to tell. Maggie performs a recuperative function for Frankie as she enables him to rewrite his own prior history, for it is the embodiment, quite literally, of Irishness that opens up a space for masculinist self-expression within the film.

In addition to his penchant for Gaelic terms of endearment and Kelly green warm-up robes, Frankie is also fond of quoting Yeats. He reads from Yeats at two significant moments in *Million Dollar Baby*: first in a hospital waiting room after Maggie's nose is broken in a fight and again in her hospital room after she becomes paralyzed. The first instance is only really significant because of the second; indeed it sets it up. When Maggie is taken to see the emergency room doctor after breaking her nose she asks Frankie (who is holding a small book) what he is reading. "It's Yeats," he replies. "How you doing?" Scrap asks him, as if the mere fact that he is reading is enough to suggest the possibility of serious emotional trauma.[19] Always the literalist—despite Yeats—Frankie points out that he wasn't the one who got hurt. While this exchange highlights Frankie's refusal to consider emotional hurt an affliction from which he might suffer, it also, despite his self-presentation, names Yeats as a source of comfort, something to which he turns during times of need. Unable to communicate his own feelings Frankie inhabits the words of someone else. Much like the transformation of Maggie into an Irish virgin, the mythic Ireland of Yeats situates Frankie as the author of his own destiny. Yeats's poetry becomes a lingua franca of masculine emotion steeped in a nostalgic vision of Ireland. When Frankie reads Yeats again, this time aloud to Maggie, the poet need not be named. Yeats has become, for Frankie and for the audience, familiar.

When Maggie is paralyzed Frankie turns once more to Yeats for comfort and deliverance. As she lies in her hospital bed he reads aloud to her from Yeats's well-known poem "The Lake Isle of Innisfree." Familiar to all Irish schoolchildren, the poem describes a domestic scene of masculine self-empowerment in the nostalgic images of a mythic Ireland and stands as an example of the Irish Renaissance, in which Yeats was a key figure:[20]

> I will arise and go now, and go to Innisfree,
> And a small cabin build there, of clay and wattles made:
> Nine bean-rows will I have there, a hive for the honey-bee,
> And live alone in the bee-loud glade.

And I shall have some peace there, for peace comes dropping slow,
Dropping from the veils of the morning to where the cricket sings;
There midnight's all a glimmer, and noon a purple glow,
And evening full of the linnet's wings.

I will arise and go now, for always night and day
I hear lake water lapping with low sounds by the shore;
While I stand on the roadway, or on the pavements grey,
I hear it in the deep heart's core.

C. Stuart Hunter writes, "The speaker's return to Innisfree is a journey in search of poetic wisdom and spiritual peace, a wisdom and peace that can be realized through a poetic and spiritual grasp of the parity that exists between the legendary past of Ireland and the present day."[21] The location of the poem's setting had important resonances both in Celtic folklore and for Yeats himself, who used to visit the area as a child. In his autobiography he describes the genesis of the poem and links the location of its setting to the particularly American context of Henry David Thoreau's *On Walden Pond*: "I had still the ambition, formed in Sligo in my teens, of living in imitation of Thoreau on Innisfree, a little island in Lough Gill, and when walking through Fleet Street very homesick I heard a little tinkle of water and saw a fountain in a shop-window which balanced a little ball upon its jet, and began to remember lake water. From the sudden remembrance came my poem *Innisfree*, my first lyric with anything in its rhythm of my own music."[22] Yeats's association of Innisfree with Thoreau's Walden Pond is of great importance, for an understanding of the poem itself and of its significance in *Million Dollar Baby*, because it locates the poet's nostalgia for a Celtic past within the orbit of possessive individualism that grounds the tropes of American manhood Thoreau (and Frankie Dunn) sought to codify. As Hunter explains, "Familiar with Thoreau's work, the young Yeats was also familiar with the way in which Thoreau saw the retreat to a childhood-visited rural setting and the occupation of oneself in gardening as tropes for the poetic retreat in search of wisdom."[23] For Frankie Dunn, the poem signifies just such a retreat.

Maggie, unfortunately, shares Frankie's love of the literal. "Are you goin' to build a cabin, boss?" she asks him when he has finished reading the poem to her, "because I could see you there real easily, with your books and your lemon pie." "I could learn to bake," she concludes, assuming she will be going with him; for her the poem constitutes a domestic fantasy of the recovery she knows will never come and not, as the poem's thematic content clearly suggests, Frankie's fantasy alone. The poem symbolizes for Frankie a retreat into a mythic Irish past that is both an escape and a homecoming, a reward for the sacrifices he has made on Maggie's behalf. Having saved Maggie, Frankie is rewarded with the solitude he so strongly desires. In *Million Dollar Baby* a nostalgic vision of rural Ireland replaces the American West of Eastwood's earlier oeuvre as a repository of masculinist fantasies of freedom and mobility. In this exchange the "used trailer" and Oreos of Maggie's limited white trash horizons become the "small cabin" and "lemon pie" of Frankie's own Irish redemption. It's a shame that the film cannot imagine that redemption coming at anything other than the cost of Maggie's life. If the mythic frontier of the Hollywood western is no longer a place where the white man can quit the pressures of civilization, then perhaps Ireland is—in the nostalgic version being evoked here, at least, for Frankie's Ireland is no Celtic Tiger.

Despite his love of Yeats (who was a Protestant) and the fact that the priest at his church considers him to be a "fucking pagan," Frankie is a devout if troubled Catholic who prays every evening and has attended mass every day for twenty-five years. When Maggie asks him to help her die, to do for her what her "daddy did for Axel," the old family dog her father shot and buried in the woods shortly before his own death from cancer, Frankie turns to the Catholic Church for advice and asks Father Horvak what he should do. "If you do this thing," the priest tells him, "you will be lost . . . somewhere so deep you'll never find yourself again." Frankie does it anyway, and he is not lost. In fact the act confirms his salvation. In part the focus on Catholicism is a holdover from Boyd's original stories, but it is also significant inasmuch as its discourse of repentance, penitence, and absolution underscores the film's focus on white male recuperation. The film understands Frankie's actions to be the ultimate form of self-sacrifice, for he stands to lose as much as he ultimately gains. In the act of arrogating to himself the responsibility for Maggie's life, Frankie's beleaguered white patriarchy becomes an unimpeachable and trouble-free Irish paternalism. The end of the film leaves Eastwood's character in a familiar place: alone and outside the bounds of community and family. Frankie is redeemed by the sacrifice of his soul, by the strength of his love and commitment, both to Maggie and to his estranged daughter, for whom Maggie serves as a surrogate. By killing Maggie he has proven that he is capable of making such sacrifices and is thus free to leave the pressures of home, family, and community behind; he is free to retreat into the fantasy of Celtic nostalgia offered him by Yeats and Gaelic.

In its turn to the affective structures of the family romance *Million Dollar Baby* suggests that melodrama remains a paradigmatic site for the recuperation of white patriarchy. Locating its solutions to the perceived problem of white male self-worth in the contemporary United States in a story of sacrifice, redemption, and salvation, the film asks the audience to respond to the travails of its male protagonist affectively. Frankie Dunn is a deeply troubled man, unable to let go of a past he cannot fully comprehend, and therefore unwilling to allow himself a future. In typical fashion Maggie's ministrations transform the gruff and unreachable Dunn into a caring man who, though he is still unable to express his emotions, is almost willing to admit he has them. The film is a melodrama of loss and self-sacrifice that turns on the affective production of sentiment for much of its pathos (and narrative logic). As one reviewer lamented, "Near the end of [the film] Clint Eastwood breaks down and cries. It's disturbing to say the least."[24] The affective structures of melodrama the film employs revolve around the production of an ennobling and transformative form of mythic Irishness in which Frankie is recuperated through not only his recuperation of Maggie but also his own self-transformation.

The final sequence of the film clearly illustrates its turn to the affective structures of melodrama. After stating that Frankie never returned to the gym on the night of Maggie's death and that he has neither seen nor heard from him since, Scrap concludes his voice-over: "I hoped he'd gone to find you, somewhere between nowhere and goodbye." The concluding shot of the film shows Frankie, sitting in a diner in the woods that he had previously visited with Maggie, eating a slice of lemon pie. As Scrap had hoped, Frankie has found a place that refashions the "between nowhere and goodbye" of Maggie's white trash existence and makes it home for a resurgent white patriarchy absolved of the sin of its past and no longer required to account for the actions of its present. The audience does not know whether this final image is fact or fantasy. But whatever the case, Frankie has found his home, alone. "I thought you should know," Scrap concludes his voice-over, "what kind of man your father really was." The *you* and *your* of this final line transform the film's off-screen narrative into a letter from Scrap to Frankie's estranged daughter. By naming the daughter as the proper recipient of Scrap's elegiac missive, the film places the viewer, its actual recipient, in a position of filial responsibility. As such, the viewer becomes the one who caused "return to sender" to be stamped on all those letters. It's a cheap trick. The film's affective structure comes full circle, and the audience is required to applaud Frankie's actions, to understand the depths of his sacrifices, while being held responsible for his failures.

As much as the film is concerned with a white patriarchy it transforms into an innocent and benign Irish paternalism, it is also obsessed with white racial guilt, and the recuperation Maggie affords Frankie must also be understood in the context of American race relations after the civil rights era. If Frankie is being forgiven for his failures in the domestic spheres of home and family, he is also being divested of responsibility for the structural and societal racism that has long ensured white masculinity's franchise on opportunity in American society. In addition to his family problems Frankie is haunted by another event from his past that recasts the film's concerns with familial responsibility in a national frame. As the cut man working the corner during Scrap Iron Dupris's final (and hundredth) professional fight in the late 1950s, Frankie watched as his friend was beaten so badly that he lost the sight in one eye. While he was neither Scrap's manager nor his trainer, and thus had no authority over the fight, Frankie holds himself responsible for Scrap's fate and, as Scrap suggests in his voice-over, has never been able to forgive himself. By casting this horrific event in terms of white self-forgiveness, the film miniaturizes and sentimentalizes the structural racism of the Jim Crow years. Casting the relationship between Frankie and Scrap as one of deep attachment and sentimental affiliation born of a half-century of friendship, the film refuses to countenance the possibility that the two men's histories have been profoundly marked by racial difference. Frankie's guilt, his inability to forgive himself, is offered as evidence of a lack of personal culpability for Scrap's misfortune that the film is unable to cast within a broader, more realistic discourse about race. The differences between Frankie's and Scrap's fortunes are understood solely at the level of individualism and are divorced from the broader history of race relations and the legacies of plantation slavery.

If Maggie knows she is trash, Scrap is also well aware of his own marginal social standing. As the off-screen narrator of the film and a central character, Scrap is both testifier of and testament to Frankie's character. Because the events of Frankie's past are left so vague, the audience is reliant on the opinions of Scrap for their insights into his character. As Tania Modleski points out, because the audience does not know anything about Frankie's relationship with his daughter or about his past more generally, they are kept from judging him: "How can we condemn the man when we don't even know what he's done?" Moreover the film cannot imagine any other sympathetic characters of color. As Robert Sklar points out in his discussion of the film, "*Million Dollar Baby* presents Scrap the sidekick as the film's only black figure who is other than disloyal, treacherous, or cruel."[25] Hollywood has a long history of using black characters to testify to (or enable) the innate goodness of their white friends and colleagues. Morgan Freeman has himself played such characters on a number of occasions, most notably in *Driving Miss Daisy* (1989) and *The Shawshank Redemption* (1994), and has recently played a similar role alongside Jack Nicholson in the interracial buddy film, *The Bucket List* (2007); it is impossible to see him in Eastwood's film without feeling the resonances of those earlier performances.[26] That Scrap absolves Frankie of any responsibility for his own misfortunes leaves the audience in no position to respond in any other way. The structural racism of American society is recast as the character deficits of a few rural racists and consigned to a position in the nation's historical past. The film even offers Scrap the opportunity to reclaim his self-worth and complete his hundredth fight when he steps into the ring at the Hit Pit and saves Danger Barch from a vicious beating he is being given by Shawrelle Berry, one of the gym's African American patrons.[27] Scrap single-handedly (literally: he puts on only one boxing glove) knocks out Berry, a man less than half his age, and tells him "Get a job, punk" as he lies prostrate, spitting out teeth, on the canvas. That Scrap is redeemed by saving a rural white southerner from a brutal beating at the hands of a young African American from the inner city further highlights the film's warped racial politics. Older white men such as Frankie are absolved from responsibility for the historical mistreatment of people of color; younger white men such as Danger are protected from the threatening specter of black male brutality. It is therefore significant that it is Scrap—and not Frankie—who rescues Danger from his attacker.

If black-on-white violence is a feature of the film's present, white-on-black violence is effectively confined to the past.

The Trouble with (Dirty) Harry: Rescuing Frankie Dunn, Recuperating Clint Eastwood

There is, of course, an extratextual white elephant in all of this: the figure of Clint Eastwood himself, as actor and director. Eastwood is one of Hollywood's last remaining auteurs (at least some use that term), and *Million Dollar Baby* must also be read as a significant contribution to the revisionist recuperation of Eastwood or, more accurately, his oeuvre. Reviews of the film in the American mainstream media were overwhelmingly positive and suggest that reviewers were keenly aware of the relationship between the film, its characters and plot, and Eastwood's own star persona. Jonathan Rosenbaum of the *Chicago Reader*, Roger Ebert of the *Chicago Sun-Times*, Ty Burr of the *Boston Globe*, A. O. Scott of the *New York Times*, Kenneth Turan of the *Los Angeles Times*, and David Denby of *The New Yorker* (to name but the most influential) all gave the film glowing reviews.[28] Significantly each of these reviewers devoted as much attention to Eastwood as they did to the film itself. Turan called the film Eastwood's "most touching, most elegiac work yet" and called Eastwood's performance "the most nakedly emotional of his 50-year career."[29] Scott called the film "the best movie released by a major Hollywood studio this year" and "a work of utter mastery." He suggested that Eastwood had become "more fully and complicatedly himself as he grows older," that, as a director, his "innate toughness has mellowed into a sinewy grace," and as an actor, "his limitations have become a source of strength."[30] Ty Burr wrote, "Eastwood makes Frankie a close-cropped silver fox."[31] Denby added the film to the "honor list of great fight films" and said that Eastwood "doles out his feelings slowly, parsimoniously, with powerful restraint." He wrote that the film had "a beautifully modulated sadness that's almost musical" and "the smoothly melancholic tones of Coleman Hawkins at his greatest."[32] In their descriptions of Eastwood's acting and directing each of these reviewers juxtaposes terms such as *economy*, *strength*, *toughness*, and *sinews* with *grace*, *elegy*, *mellowness*, and *restraint*. While strength is tempered by mellowness and sinews by grace, they are not erased entirely. The purported strength of Eastwood's performance and the attention given to his body by these reviewers suggests that the film articulates the ongoing debates about the status of white masculinity in American culture in powerful ways. What Eastwood embodies for these reviewers is a form of rugged masculinity that has learned how to restrain its impulses and control its urges. Like Maggie, Eastwood is exemplary of a model liberal personhood. Unlike Maggie, Eastwood is allowed to hold on to his personhood and to benefit from it.

Such responses to the film and to Eastwood, as both actor and director, are hardly surprising. Since the release of *Unforgiven* (1992), and arguably much earlier, he has embodied a revisionist masculinity that, for many critics, works through and redeems the western gunfighters and rogue cops of his early career. Christopher Frayling argues that since the mid-1970s "there is certainly a new mellowness, and a humanity, about Clint Eastwood's best films," that "the characters he plays within them tend to be capable of an uncharacteristic gentleness and sociability."[33] In more recent films, such as *Unforgiven, The Bridges of Madison County* (1995), *Blood Work* (2002), and *Mystic River* (2003), Eastwood has been reworking his own legacy as both actor and director. *Million Dollar Baby* contributes to this revisionist project by offering him a vehicle for the continuing project of his own masculinist recuperation. These reviews illustrate the ongoing anxiety in American culture about the form of masculinity Eastwood embodies precisely in their heralding of it. Richard Dyer writes that movie stars not only "articulate . . . ideas of personhood," but also "at times [register] the doubts and anxieties attendant on it."[34] Anxieties about white masculinist personhood are clearly articulated in the focus in these reviews on Eastwood's body and on his performance through that body. His "sinewy grace" and "powerful restraint" recast the film's melodramatic plot devices and overall mood within the bounds of a trenchantly masculinist bodily control.

If, as Frankie warns Maggie early in the film, "tough ain't enough," a certain masculine stoicism is still a central aspect of the appeal of Eastwood and his brand of filmmaking. *Million Dollar Baby* enshrines that masculine stoicism in Eastwood's body. What critics seem to be impressed by is his ability, in his mid-seventies, to still *embody* masculinity—and not its dissolution. In a discussion of the actor's body and its relation to the performances that he gives (as opposed to the characters that he plays), Paul Smith writes of Eastwood's younger self that the "body that Eastwood builds for his most typical performances is a body that . . . is destined to disappear in the end, and yet it must submit itself along the way to the harsh regimes of the action. It is a body that must at least *appear* to be both powerful enough to be indestructible and experienced and at the same time ordinary enough to disappear." The body's disappearance, what Smith refers to as its "resolutory hypostasis," is something that *Million Dollar Baby* achieves in two complementary ways: in the surrogate hypostasis of Maggie's body which disappears so that Frankie's doesn't have to, and in Frankie's own disappearance into the cabin in the woods to which Scrap consigns him at the film's end. Unable or unwilling to put Eastwood's aging body through the sorts of trials endured by characters he portrayed in his past, if not precisely his youth, the film consigns that responsibility to Maggie, whose body literally disappears before the audience's eyes as she is first paralyzed and then loses a leg to gangrene.[35] Frankie, unlike Maggie, is left intact at the end of the film and is able, like so many Eastwood characters before him, to leave society behind, having ensured its survival. Folding Maggie's literal bodily fragmentation into Frankie's symbolic disappearance, the film performs yet another sleight of hand. As the viewer becomes responsible for Frankie's failures (by refusing to understand him and therefore to answer his letters), it is the film's primary female character who must be lost in order that its male protagonist can be found. Still trim and endowed with the "sinewy grace" that Scott applauds, Eastwood embodies a benign white patriarchy that is left to stand because of, rather than in spite of, the reactionary masculinities of his past performances.

The reviews of *Million Dollar Baby* in the mainstream press leaned heavily on Eastwood's own star persona and celebrity identity, as did many of the mainstream critical reviews of *Gran Torino* (2008), the most recent film in which Eastwood serves as both lead actor and director. *Gran Torino* has been widely reported to be the last film in which Eastwood will act (he currently has at least two directorial efforts in production); thus it deserves some attention in the current discussion. Released in mid-December 2008 (making it eligible for that year's Oscars), *Gran Torino* also demands consideration here because it so fully realizes the interconnection between actor and character that underscores Eastwood's celebrity and through which many attendant discussions of masculinity are routed. The film tells the tale of a retired Detroit autoworker, Walt Kowalski (Eastwood), who is one of the last white citizens remaining in a suburban Detroit neighborhood that has become populated by Hmong immigrants. Kowalski is an embittered racist who has just buried his wife, who died following a long illness. His racism is repeatedly linked to his service during the Korean War and to his belief in the values of possessive individualism that undergird his ideology of self-respect and individual empowerment grounded in a (vanishing) blue-collar work ethic. The plot of the film revolves around Kowalski's relationship with a Hmong woman and her two teenage children, who have recently moved in next-door to him. He grudgingly comes to respect and hold affection for the two teenage children, Thao (Bee Vang) and Sue (Ahney Her), and intervenes when a Hmong gang tries to recruit Thao as a member. In the sequence that gives the film its name, Walt interrupts Thao's late-night attempt to steal his prized 1972 Ford Gran Torino coupe. From this improbable start Walt is given the opportunity to transform himself, as Eastwood's character does in *Million Dollar Baby*, by transforming Thao. In the earlier film Eastwood's character was required to turn a white trash "girlie" into a professional boxer; in the later film he must turn an effeminate Asian boy into an American man. Thao is consistently feminized in the film's early sequences, where he is shown doing the washing up during a family gathering and gardening while his sister watches.[36] Walt, the film suggests, must learn to respect difference in order to survive in the multicultural world in which he belatedly comes to realize that he lives. He achieves this transformation in part by teaching Thao how to be a man. More important, however, is Walt's *failure* to undergo any such transformation and, as a result, the necessity for him to die at the close of the film. In the film's final scenes he confronts the gang members who have raped Sue. In a violent showdown he allows himself to be killed by the gang, thereby assuring that they will be punished—for his death, if not for Sue's rape.

The combination of Eastwood in what many believed would be his last starring role and the prerelease buzz surrounding the film (when it was widely rumored to be a sixth and final installment in the *Dirty Harry* franchise, and the first since *The Dead Pool* [1988]) secured a large audience for *Gran Torino*.[37] Domestic gross box office receipts totaled $148 million ($48 million more than *Million Dollar Baby*), foreign box office receipts just over $115 million. Produced on a budget of $33 million, the film was a resounding financial success for Warner Bros., the primary producer.[38] The film was not only a commercial but also a critical success. For many critics, the film was rescued from its melodramatic and simplistic plot and its clunky and overly telegraphic dialogue by Eastwood's performance and by his character's resonances with previous Eastwood heroes. In a manner typical of many reviews of the film in the mainstream media, Peter Travers wrote in *Rolling Stone* that what one sees on the screen when one looks at Eastwood's character in *Gran Torino* "isn't just Walt," but all of the characters Eastwood's presence on screen conjures up: "It's the Man with No Name taking aim in those spaghetti Westerns. It's Dirty Harry Callahan asking, 'Do you feel lucky, punk?' It's William Munny, from *Unforgiven*, digging deep to note, 'It's a hell of a thing, killing a man. You take away all he's got and all he's ever gonna have.' It's even Frankie Dunn, the fight manager from *Million Dollar Baby*, who knows 'tough ain't enough.'" "Tough has never been enough for Eastwood," Travers concludes. "A lifetime in movies runs through this prime vintage Eastwood performance. You can't take your eyes off him. The no-frills, no-bull *Gran Torino* made my day."[39] For Manohla Dargis of the *New York Times*, "these spectral figures [of Eastwood's past heroes], totems of masculinity and mementos from a heroic cinematic age, are what make this unassuming film—small in scale if not in the scope of its ideas—more than just a vendetta flick or an entertainment about a crazy coot and the exotic strangers next door." Dargis also, and I believe accurately, reads the films as an ode to the shifting fortunes of the United States under neoliberalism that this book takes as its ground. "Made in the 1960s and '70s," Dargis points out, the "Gran Torino was never a great symbol of American automotive might, which makes Walt's love for the car more poignant. It was made by an industry that now barely makes cars, in a city that hardly works, in a country that too often has felt recently as if it can't do anything right anymore except, every so often, make a movie like this one."[40] For Kenneth Turan of the *Los Angeles Times*, the film is "impossible to imagine without [Eastwood] in the title role.... Even at 78 Eastwood can make 'Get off my lawn' sound as menacing as 'Make my day,' and when he says 'I blow a hole in your face and sleep like a baby,' he sounds as if he means it."[41] Without what Smith calls Eastwood's "extrafilmic star image," these reviewers suggest, the film would be nothing.[42]

But Walt Kowalski does not "blow a hole" in anyone's face in *Gran Torino*; it is the white man who is sacrificed for the good of the community. That this difference was ignored by reviewers points to the enduring power of Eastwood as a mythic figure of hypermasculinity in American culture. That the script, by a first-time scriptwriter, Nick Schenk, purportedly was not written with Eastwood in mind merely confirms the point. As Smith, quoting Homi Bhabha, points out, "For many years in American culture, Eastwood's body has acted as the very type of the 'undifferentiated whole white body.' "[43] Comparing Eastwood's portrayal of Walt Kowalski to his earlier portrayals of such iconic characters as the Man with No Name and Dirty Harry Callahan, these critics are locating the film—and Eastwood's performance in it—as a career-defining piece of revisionism. When considering critical responses to Eastwood's recent work one cannot ignore that he is seventy-eight and must surely be approaching the end of his long and prolific career.[44] As Smith says, "Attendant upon this process of canonization, retrospection, and preservation is the possibility of Eastwood's death, the recognition that a career has in some sense passed, or passed on." That Smith's words were published over fifteen years ago, and in reference to an earlier cycle in Eastwood's career, suggests how powerfully Eastwood symbolizes hegemonic white masculinity in the United States—and for how long he has done so.[45] In *Gran Torino* the revisionist project of his late career is complete. Recalling the various models of masculinist identity he has previously portrayed, the film recasts those prior models by resolving not only the ideological but also the cultural work that they perform. Smith writes, "The elevation of Eastwood to auteur-father had been predicated upon his ability to sustain and regulate the traditions of Hollywood and upon his becoming their artisanal guardian."[46] Therefore Eastwood becomes both a repository for and a guardian of tradition while also embodying, in problematic ways, an outmoded mode of masculinist behavior. What seems clear is that the first of these roles helps to obfuscate the second. If this is indeed the case, if *Gran Torino* is, as Dargis suggests, elevated by the "spectral figures" of Dirty Harry et al., how is Dirty Harry elevated by Walt Kowalski? In other words, what cultural work does *Gran Torino* perform?

Comparisons to *Dirty Harry* such as those cited above are not hard to understand. Both films represent an authoritative white male, cast in a vigilante mold, in the midst of an American urban landscape in which the ties of community and a homogeneous white cultural identity have been eroded by the welfare state and multiculturalism. The advertising for *Gran Torino* also does much to encourage such comparisons between the two films. In posters, official production stills, and DVD packaging, images of Eastwood brandishing a rifle featured prominently. Utilizing a palette of dark grays, browns, and blacks the film's advertising suggested a serious and somber tone that is personified in the figure of Eastwood himself. Dressed in dark gray slacks and a dark gray T-shirt he is positioned prominently in the foreground of the posters, his face partially obscured by shadow. Rifle in hand, he scowls at the viewer from beneath a brush of steel-gray hair. He is, as Turan suggests, a seventy-eight-year old to be taken seriously. The film parlays the accretion of Eastwood's various male protagonists into an image of progressive white masculinity in contemporary America for which Walt then becomes exemplary. What viewers see when they look at Walt starring out at them from the promotional posters is a model of white masculinity that the film will work to redeem from the negative associations that most commonly accrue to it.

One obvious difference between *Dirty Harry* and *Gran Torino* is, of course, that Eastwood's character kills in the former and is killed in the latter. Unbeknown to the audience, or to the film's other characters, Walt arrives unarmed at his final showdown with the gang members who raped Sue. He tricks them into shooting him by reaching into his jacket pocket for what turns out to be a cigarette lighter. Thinking that he is reaching for a pistol (as he has at other moments in the film), the gang members shoot first. They have gunned down an unarmed, and therefore innocent white man, reproducing mainstream fears of minority violence while ensuring that the gang members will be punished for their rape of Sue (who, fearing further reprisals against her family, is unwilling to prosecute them herself). This resolution transforms the vigilante justice of Dirty Harry Callahan into a different form of self-sacrifice, in which the white man gives up his own life for the good of the community.[47] Walt begins the film bemoaning the disintegration of one community and ends it by sacrificing himself for the survival of another. That the community he helps to save is not properly his own (in the logic of the film) only goes to prove the extent to which white masculinity has been required to transform its ideological function in contemporary America.

Walt Kowalski (Clint Eastwood) as Christ. From *Gran Torino* (2008).

Because the community Walt saves is Hmong there is another level on which the film serves to recuperate American models of white masculinity. During an early conversation Sue tells Walt that the Hmong are not jungle people, as he believes, but mountain people, many of whom emigrated to the United States following the Vietnam War. This distinction locates Walt's struggles with masculinist relevance within a history of U.S. military engagement in Southeast Asia that does not end (as Walt seems to believe it does) with his generation's involvement in Korea during the 1950s. Instead the film situates Walt's inability to understand or accept the transformations in his community within a broader history of political isolationism or disinvestment. Symbols of Walt's service in Korea are prominent in the film. For example, during the wake for his dead wife he catches his grandchildren rummaging through a footlocker in his basement in which he keeps his service revolver, a rifle, and a medal of valor awarded him in Korea. Late in the film he pins the medal to Thao's chest in a pseudo-initiation into manhood. The cigarette lighter Walt holds in his hand as he is gunned down is another memento from his years in service and is embossed with a U.S. Cavalry crest. As he lies prostrate on the ground, his arms outstretched in a Christ-like pose, the perspective shifts from an overhead crane shot to a close-up in which his fingers unclench and the lighter can be seen, crest up, in his hand. If this is the final image of Eastwood on screen, the hypostasis Smith reads in his earlier performances here reaches its apotheosis.[48] In the next sequence, after Thao and

Sue arrive at the scene of the shooting, the camera focuses on the medal pinned to Thao's chest.

Marking the transition from one conflict in Southeast Asia to another, this editing seems to be an attempt to reconcile the nation's imperial past with what the film takes to be its multicultural present. The legacies of the Korean War transit through the legacies of the Vietnam War and come to rest on the body of a young Asian American. That Clint Eastwood serves as the proper embodiment of white masculinity through which such a transfer can take place confirms the powerful ways in which his body and his multiple personas, both on screen and off, signify manhood in American culture. If there is no longer a place for the Man with No Name, the outlaw Josey Wales, or Dirty Harry Callahan, perhaps there is for Frankie Dunn or Walt Kowalski, and that, it seems, is good enough. At the close of both *Million Dollar Baby* and *Gran Torino* the audience is left to bear witness to the sacrifices of white men on behalf of women and people of color, whose wounded, raped, and dismembered bodies testify to the benign authority of white masculinity.

6

Family Melodrama and the Sentimental Logics of Neoliberalism

Films aren't first responders: we're not like a news programme,
so if ten kids get killed by a car bomb in Iraq it's two and a half years
before the movie gets made.
GEORGE CLOONEY, *Sight and Sound*

WINNING FOUR Academy Awards and grossing over $207 million internationally, Stephen Soderbergh's *Traffic* (2000) was both a critical and a commercial success. With Altmanesque complexity *Traffic* weaves together three loosely interconnected narratives into a broadly conceived and carefully structured analysis of the war on drugs that preceded and was displaced by the post–September 11 War on Terror. Many of the reviews of the film in the mainstream press pointed (as did the director himself) to the film's stark realism and its stated refusal to offer easy solutions to the problems inherent in its subject matter—the U.S. war on drugs—as integral to its appeal. In his review of the film for the *New York Times*, for example, Stephen Holden called *Traffic* an "intricate thriller . . . [that] builds into a profound and gloomy meditation on greed, violence and contemporary ennui."[1] In an interview with Soderbergh for *Salon.com*, Stephen Lemons likened the film to the work of the famed Japanese director Akira Kurosawa by calling it "an epic, two-and-a-half-hour war on drugs 'Rashomon.'" In the same interview Soderbergh hinted at one reason why the film was deemed so important; he claimed that he was "trying to present as detailed and accurate a picture of the current drug war as possible," thereby citing the film's verisimilitude as central to its appeal.[2] A variety of reasons were given for the film's putative realism: it was primarily shot with hand-held cameras (by Soderbergh himself under the alias Peter Andrews), shooting took place in nine different cities and over one hundred locations, the film had a cast that numbered in the hundreds and that included cameo appearances from real politicians and DEA officials (who were also consulted about the script), and the dialogue for the scenes set in Mexico was filmed in Spanish using English subtitles.[3] Despite such claims, however, *Traffic* situates its political engagement within the discourse and politics of affect that have come to dominate late twentieth-century American culture by resolving the double disruptions of white patriarchy and the nation it imagines through a family melodrama motivated by the saving of an errant daughter.

The film deploys a patriarchal sentimentality that serves a recuperative function for bourgeois masculinity and as such is a powerful example of the pervasive paradigm of masculine sentimentality as a recuperative mode. Therefore, while *Traffic* mounts a coherent critique of U.S. policies toward the drug war, the conservative nature of its retreat into gendered sentimentality obscures the geopolitical relations it seeks to elucidate and belies any claims about the film's realism. The attempted critique of the drug war manifests itself as a family drama, the resolution of which rescues the nation by healing the prototypical American family through a recuperation of white patriarchy founded on a traditionally gendered model of domesticity. The film's reenfranchisement of a normative, heterosexual paternalism is concomitant with the preservation of the nation it narrates. By situating the resolution of the national crisis of the war on drugs within the domestic realm of the middle-class family home, *Traffic* produces a family melodrama that mirrors the national drama and provides that national drama with the fantasy of a proper resolution. The film achieves this fantasy resolution through the production of a narrative of male sentimentality that addresses the extent to which neoliberalism locates political action in personal deeds. The film resolves both the crisis of the bourgeois family and the war on drugs at the level of affective relations. As a means of reconciling the multicultural nation to the needs of white patriarchy, feeling becomes the ne plus ultra of masculine affectivity (and authority).

By citing the home as the proper ground for the resolution of the war on drugs, *Traffic* reworks contemporary disruptions of the logic of the separate spheres for the benefit of a beleaguered white patriarchy. The recent turn to masculine affect as a mode of patriarchal recuperation relies on a turn to sentiment that obfuscates the reenfranchisement of masculinity at its core. *Traffic* overcomes the tensions it imagines lie at the heart of the nation and the family through the production of a masculine affectivity that displaces the need for any real social or political change. As such, the film condones the core beliefs of a reactionary liberalism that takes the personal and the familial to be the proper sites of any political action and reinforces the conservative agenda of "family values" which it yokes to a Monroe Doctrine of hemispheric control. *Traffic* is a precursor to and an exemplar of a small cycle of films that, while they are understood to be explicitly political and left leaning, all find conservative resolutions to both geopolitical and domestic social problems. While the creators of such films imagine they are offering a critique of the neoconservative doctrine of the Bush administration and the conservative right, their capitulation to both neoliberal and traditional logics of nationalism finds them unable to escape the constraints of neoliberal structures of affect that are inherently conservative.

Heroine Addiction: Family Melodrama and the (Anti-)Politics of Affect

Traffic's national and domestic struggles are played out most clearly on the body of a woman, Caroline Wakefield (Erika Christensen), the teenage daughter of Ohio Supreme Court judge and newly appointed national "drug czar" Robert Hudson Wakefield (Michael Douglas). A high school honors student with a severe case of ennui, Caroline turns to hard drugs to alleviate her boredom. Her descent into drug use is cast as a family problem and a result of her parents' failing relationship and her father's inability to communicate with or show any interest in her. As her heroin addiction gets worse, she runs away from home and quickly turns to theft and prostitution to feed her habit. Alternating between Cincinnati and

Washington, D.C., this central plotline narrates Wakefield's attempts to find and rehabilitate his missing daughter and the concomitant attempt to reconcile his fractured home life with his new political appointment. The patriarchal nationalism *Traffic* evinces is predicated on the trope of woman as nation and Caroline as an avatar of the national body under threat. The continuing power of such narratives should come as no surprise. As the editors of the volume *Woman and Nation* have pointed out, while the breakdown of the separate spheres model of gender relations troubles gendered nationalisms, "the woman/feminine signifier continues to serve as an alibi or figure of resistance in the fraternal struggles for control of the nation-state and the national project."[4] The only hope for Caroline, the film suggests, is the renewed love and affection of her father. As important, however, is the fact that in the resolution of his quest to find and save his daughter Wakefield is also saved as he becomes a legitimate father and husband again.

Caroline also represents the work the white patriarch must do; what is most significant about this is that the white patriarch is turning to the domestic realm to reinaugurate his own authority. The putatively separate spheres of home and politics are broken down precisely in order to reconfirm white patriarchal power. Sentiment is working for rather than against patriarchy. In making this claim, I do not wish to uphold the longstanding division between the public and the private (to which the film adheres), but to suggest, as Cathy N. Davidson and Jessamyn Hatcher have, that these two realms are "intimately intertwined and mutually constitutive."[5] Situating Caroline at the center of Wakefield's struggle, the film yokes the traditional logic of gendered nationalism—typically predicated on just such a separate spheres logic—to what Lauren Berlant calls the "patriotically-permeated pseudopublic sphere of the present tense."[6] My argument is that the film both adheres to and disrupts a separate spheres discourse, thereby requiring its recontextualization. If, as Davidson and Hatcher claim, "power and subjectivity [are] mobile and uneven in their development and inconsistent in their deployment," it is necessary to understand how white masculinity gains a particular form of subject authority through its manipulation of the structures of affectivity that permeate contemporary politics and social life in the United States.

The domestic recuperation *Traffic* imagines rehearses a fantasy of national recuperation in which the feeling man inaugurates a "new" patriarchal authority predicated on a benign paternalism forged from neoliberal sentimentality. This recuperation relies on Wakefield's ability to recast his identity within the bounds of a masculine sentimentality in which the public and private spheres of national life connect at the site of the domestic. As such, *Traffic* betrays its commitment to a neoliberal ideology of personal responsibility. In order to save Caroline, Wakefield must allow his private life to affect his public life as a political man; he must become in public what he has not been in private: a caring, sentimental individual. This principal plotline constitutes a variation on the typical quest narrative recast in the terms of the late twentieth-century culture of intimacy. Not only does Wakefield literally leave the home and venture into the outside world, here cast as the inner city of Cincinnati, in order to find his errant daughter, but he also quests inward in order to find himself. These two journeys are interconnected and coterminous. Wakefield's quest for the reclamation of patriarchal authority is couched in a fantasy in which he learns how to feel. If traditionally, as Stanley Aronowitz suggests, "male power comes at the price of emotional isolation," in *Traffic* that power is recuperated through the reclamation of emotion.[7] As a dialectical journey in which the public and the private meet at the point of public intimacy, Wakefield's quest is typical of narratives that have always been enshrined in such an affective economy.[8]

For Wakefield the home has long ceased to function as what Christopher Lasch has called a "haven in a heartless world."[9] His marriage is on the brink of collapse; he and his wife, Barbara, argue constantly; his daughter finds him a bore; he has taken a job that requires him to be away from home much of the time. In the midst of an argument between Wakefield and his wife about his inability to reconcile his home and work responsibilities, the degree to which the home has ceased to function as a haven for Wakefield is made clear. Responding to Barbara's accusation that he "has to have three scotches just to walk in the house and say hello," Wakefield says that he drinks in order to prevent himself from "dying of boredom." "Why don't you go in and tell your daughter how bored you are?" Barbara responds. The home fails Wakefield because he has failed it. His family no longer functions as the personal face of his political identity because he cannot rely on it to function properly. Indeed Wakefield's primary concern about Caroline's drug use is initially a concern about its effect on his position as a public figure and the role he believes his family

Wakefield fights back tears during a White House press conference. From *Traffic* (2000).

should play as a symbol of his own integrity. "I'm not sending out the message that our family will accept this kind of behavior because we do not, correct?" he tells Barbara after Caroline spends a night in jail when one of her friends overdoses at a party. It is clear that Wakefield believes his family has failed him. He must learn that he has positioned his priorities incorrectly and that the family is the proper location of his emotional investment; he must reorient his affective engagement and bring together the public and the private spheres within a single sphere of affective politics. The drug war can be won, in other words, if he can learn how to feel. He achieves this goal by bursting into tears at the podium of the White House.

Wakefield's tears come toward the close of the film and follow his successful attempt to find Caroline and place her in a drug rehab program. On the day of his official inauguration as the administration's new drug czar he attends a press conference at the White House during which he is to give a speech outlining a "ten-point plan" for the successful pursuit of the war on drugs under his leadership. This scene not only shows Wakefield's transformation from career-minded pragmatist to caring family man as it takes place, but also functions as the affective center of the film for the audience, who are invited to share in his transformation. The scene is shot from an adjoining media control room through a large window with an open but clearly visible Venetian blind that partially obscures Wakefield from the viewer. As Wakefield begins to talk the scene cuts to a bank of video monitors in the control room from which his speech is being aired. These distancing effects place the viewer at a remove from Wakefield that structurally symbolizes his own isolation. It is only after he has begun to talk that the camera moves through the open door into the press room and the viewer is given an unobstructed and unmediated view of him at the podium. The shift from an obstructed to an unobstructed view reproduces and strengthens the affective logic of the scene in which Wakefield himself drops his guard and abandons his scripted speech. His new openness is portrayed for the audience in the transformation from a mediated to a face-to-face view.

In this scene Wakefield's inability to maintain the separation between his public and private lives is underscored and then thoroughly disrupted. He opens his speech with the hackneyed and politically vacuous statement, "We have to win this war [on drugs] to save our country's most precious resource—our children." Immediately, however, his resolve abandons him, and after a number of pauses and false starts he soon departs from his prepared script. "I can't do this," he says. "If there is a war on drugs then many of our family members are the enemy." Wiping away a tear he admits, "I don't know how you wage war on your own family." Wakefield's tears evidence the collapse of the distinction between his public and private selves, and for the remainder of the film that collapse is taken to be the signal event by which patriarchy reclaims its symbolic authority. In a discussion of George Bush Sr.'s predilection for weepiness that was the subject of a *Time* magazine article in 1994, Chapman and Hendler write, "Masculine affect, in contemporary American culture, can be deployed as a form of public display and political rhetoric." Such displays mark the contemporary American cultural moment, the authors suggest, because they mark a seeming departure from commonplace understandings of gender and sentiment: "Bush's tears are 'surprising' because sentimentality and the public display of emotion are conventionally seen as feminine characteristics." However, even though the "source of sentiment" is usually located in female bodies, such an understanding "occludes the meaning of such performances of masculine affect."[10] It is not that men do not cry, but that male sentimentality and affect are typically named as feminine, thereby maintaining the myth of masculine authority and isolation.

To rethink such an investment allows for a reconsideration of when, how, and why masculine affect works. What interests me here is not only how masculine affect produces "public displays," but also how such "public" displays always transit through and reinforce the private. As the case of Wakefield's tears clearly suggests, it is in the dialectical relationship between the public and the private that masculine authority is reclaimed. Able to publicly display the feelings he has previously hidden even privately, Wakefield manifests the empathy he must bring himself to feel in order to be able to stand by Caroline at the close of the film. Milette Shamir and Jennifer Travis suggest that sentimentality "is an affective economy where masculine emotion is 'scarce' and feminine emotion 'excessive,'" and as a result "the slightest expression of masculine feeling [is endowed] with inflated value."[11] Wakefield's tears mark the emotional center around which *Traffic*'s own logic of benign patriarchy turns. At this moment he transitions from a man who gets off on "face time with the president" and who can barely face the boredom of dinner with his family to a father who, as he tells the members of Caroline's rehab group in a later scene, "is just here to listen." As sentiment overrides political action Wakefield leaves the stage; he is shown walking alone through the streets of Washington, then taking a taxi to the airport to return home to his family.

The irony of Wakefield's admission that he does not "know how you wage war on your own family" (and indeed the source of the statement's affective power) is that that is precisely what he has spent much of the film doing. Only when the private pain of his daughter's drug addiction enters the public realm of his political office, however, does he realize that he cannot "do this." As the film shifts the attention of its affective resolution from the White House to the Wakefields' house, the public and the private are blurred through a discourse of tears as Wakefield's affective sentimentality is reencoded at a site in which the public/private dichotomy is partially broken down: the rehab center. As a private institution in which individuals are brought together to take responsibility for and overcome their addictions, the focus on the treatment center is indicative of the degree to which the film wishes to locate its political resolution at the level of the individual and the family. The treatment center is a place where Wakefield can make his tears matter, where he can transform sentimentality into a form of neoliberal self-regulation.

In the penultimate scene of the film Robert and Barbara Wakefield attend a group therapy session at the rehab center where Caroline has been admitted. After Caroline has spoken about her own experiences in front of the participants, the therapist asks Wakefield if he would like to share his thoughts. "My name is Robert," he says, "and my wife, Barbara, and I are here to support our daughter Caroline." After a pause in which the camera focuses in as he squeezes Barbara's hand, thereby including her in his statement, he concludes, "We're here to listen." The scene ends with Robert, hand in hand with Barbara, looking lovingly at Caroline, who has retaken her seat beside them. The family is once again complete. Wakefield's claim "We're here to listen" is doubly significant. On the one hand, it situates the film's notion of responsibility at the level of a civic-minded return to bourgeois family values routed through neoliberal policies of self-help and atomized social responsibility; on the other hand, it claims that "we," not "I," are here to listen. This shift signifies Wakefield's successful reenfranchisement of white patriarchy through his production of an affective sentimentality. At the end of the film (and in a way he has not been able to before) he can speak as the head of the family and for his wife as he reclaims ownership of his daughter. White patriarchal authority is hereby recuperated by being relinquished: Wakefield declines the opportunity to speak, listens instead, and reclaims the authority to speak for and to his family. As a father who is "here to listen," he has become a changed man. He has changed, however, not because of his frustrations with the political machine of Washington or the lack of funding for the war on drugs or the incommensurate focus on the drug problem by the Mexican authorities, but because he has personally experienced, through Caroline, the effects of drugs on families and individuals. By shifting the ground on which the war on drugs is to be fought from the traditional public, masculine sphere (the White House) to the private, domestic, feminized realm (the Wakefields' house) via the pseudo-public sphere (the treatment center), the film miniaturizes the geopolitical contest in a father's struggle to save his daughter. The film does not simply reestablish the public/private dichotomy of the separate spheres, however, but produces a dialectical relationship between them in which both are transformed.

These transformations of the public and the private ground *Traffic*'s primary axis of affectivity. Creating a homology between Wakefield's public and private lives, the film then offers the resolution of his private trials as a model for resolving the problems of the public sphere that he faces as the drug czar. The lessons the film believes Wakefield needs to learn in order to save his daughter are also the lessons it believes he (and the audience) must learn in order to save the nation and win the war on drugs. As Wakefield's public and private lives collide, an affective sentimentality trumps action through the production of a display of feeling which becomes, like the now reinvigorated figure of patriarchal authority, unimpeachable. Therefore, while Wakefield's public display does not necessarily work *within* the film (the status of his public life after this breakdown is never resolved), the correctness of his display functions as a central aspect of the film's affective logic. The audience, in short, is encouraged to understand that Wakefield has done the right thing.

Inner-City Blues, Tijuana Browns: *Traffic*'s Spatial Logics

Traffic establishes a series of spatial dichotomies—the inner city and the suburbs, Mexico and the United States, Tijuana and Washington, D.C.— that highlight its capitulation to hegemonic ideologies of domestic and foreign, inside and outside. The film uses a variety of filters and optical processes in order to produce visual markers that differentiate the three central plotlines and multiple locations. Mexico, for example, is represented in a rich sepia; Washington, D.C., and Cincinnati in a washed-out blue; and San Diego in vibrant color.[12] While the film uses these different colors as a sort of shorthand to ground the audience in its various plotlines and multiple locations, they also perform an ideological function. In these visual demarcations the film evidences a spatialized logic of national identity that parallels its definitions of public and private activity. As such, the spatialized logic of national space also operates on a hemispheric level, and Mexico and South America more generally are situated in relation to the United States in a subordinate relationship grounded in paternalism. Like Caroline, Mexico is a child in need of protection.

As Wakefield's personal quest produces a fantasy resolution to his crisis of domesticity, that affective fantasy serves as a rehearsal and a model for the film's concomitant resolution of the war on drugs, which is also understood by a familial logic in which the United States is a benign paternal figure to an infantilized Mexico (which seemingly stands in for all of South America). The sepia-tone footage (achieved with tobacco filters and complex processing of the film stock after filming) presents Mexico in relationship to the United States in a symbolic position of atavistic backwardness in which the role of benign paternalism that the film imagines for the United States appears both logical and natural. The problematic issue of Mexico's status as a major hub in the international drug trade, therefore, is similarly conceived of as an issue of parental neglect. Showing that the political, military, and financial resources of the United States are matched by the equal resources of the drug cartels, on the one hand, and negated by the corruption and incompetence of the Mexican authorities, on the other, the film offers a solution to the national problem that mirrors Wakefield's private turn to sentiment. The United States can significantly curb Mexico's participation in the drug trade if it helps save Mexican children from its temptations by allowing them the space to be children. Therefore, in the resolution to the narrative strand of the film that focuses on Mexico, the United States is positioned in a paternal role and Mexico's problems are seen to be solvable through a like turn to sentimental inaction. Like Wakefield, the United States becomes a good neighbor and a benign patriarch. The results are shown in the final scene: as a Mexican policeman looks on from the bleachers, Mexican children play baseball on newly groomed diamonds with new sporting equipment, provided by the United States in exchange for information about a major Tijuana drug cartel. This final scene's correlation to the prior (and penultimate) scene in the rehab center cannot be underestimated. Mexican and American children can both be saved by the paternal interventions of powerful American men. As the final credits roll, superimposed over the scene of Mexican children playing baseball, the viewer is encouraged to feel that the film's twin resolutions provide workable and coterminous solutions to the manifest problems of the U.S. war on drugs.

As the concatenation of Caroline's white body and the body of the nation reproduces a gendered logic of bourgeois nationalism, the bodies of those from whom she must be saved are also explicitly raced. The dichotomies of space and place the film goes to such trouble to produce also extend to the demarcation of raced and gendered bodies, and the naturalness of one disguises the essentialism inherent in the other. *Traffic*'s discourse on the drug trade positions Mexicans as producers, Mexican Americans as smugglers, African Americans as pushers, and upper-middle-class white teenagers as users. Therefore, while the film portrays the American inner city as an explicitly racialized location in which drugs are readily available, it is unable to imagine a drug addict who is not white. Drug abuse is understood to be a problem of the white middle classes and is related to the declining security of the bourgeois home. Middle-class white kids take drugs because they're bored and feel unloved. As Caroline tells her rehab group, drugs are easier for her to obtain than alcohol. Middle-class children can be saved from the plight of drug addiction by their parents. When Wakefield reclaims Caroline for the family, her redemption becomes the catalyst for his own. As in *Million Dollar Baby*, the white patriarch is redeemed through his redemption and reclamation of the white woman. By maintaining this racialized logic of the drug trade, the film can stand by its sentimentalized narrative of white patriarchal reenfranchisement, thereby eliding the structural realities of contemporary U.S. socioeconomic conditions and concomitant structures of race, class, and gender inequality as Caroline becomes the victim of a series of racial others who prey on susceptible middle-class white American teenagers.[13] The film further attenuates the complexities of America's racial and social problems through its capitulation to an explicitly racialized national imaginary that serves as the constitutive ground on which the struggle over Caroline's (national) body takes place.

Caroline's descent into drug abuse is symbolized most powerfully not when she robs her parents or prostitutes herself to a white businessman in order to feed her habit, but when she willingly engages in sexual intercourse with an African American drug dealer in exchange for heroin. In this pivotal scene the hypersexualized black male body becomes the abject site at which the national crisis Caroline signifies reaches its nadir. The scene begins with a striking shot/reverse shot that fully depicts the depths to which Caroline has sunk. The opening is shot from Caroline's perspective as she engages in intercourse with her drug dealer. The frame is two-thirds filled with the muscled and glistening shoulders, neck, and head of the dealer. The remaining third of the frame (and the focal point of the shot) consists of a bare light bulb, blinding white, hanging from the ceiling. The scene cuts to a reverse shot, filmed from behind the dealer. The frame is two-thirds filled with a close-up of the dealer's back and neck, the remaining third showing Caroline's face. Because of the framing of these shots Caroline is dwarfed by the dealer, pinned under his body, which is pure muscle and sinew. The dealer, naked throughout, is presented in this

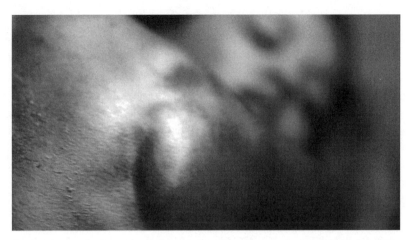

Caroline is overshadowed by the brute materiality of her dealer. From *Traffic* (2000).

scene as all body. Their intercourse is interrupted by a buyer who knocks on the door. The viewer sees the naked dealer, from Caroline's perspective, walking toward the door and then returning to pull the drugs from his stash. He returns to find Caroline taking a syringe filled with heroin from his bag. He injects her with the drug and the scene ends, as it began, with him on top of her. In both theme and composition this scene establishes an explicit connection between race, sex, and drug abuse. Caroline's encounter with her dealer is a moment of profound menace in which he has complete control over her. As a sexual predator the black drug dealer disrupts the white middle-class domestic realm, turning daughters into sexual objects. In this light it is significant that the dealer penetrates Caroline twice, once with his penis and once with his needle. Doubly monstrous, the dealer is all phallus, all embodiment, and his seduction of Caroline signals the depths to which she has sunk and the loss of innocence that her father will mourn. This reading of the scene is further suggested by the diegetic soundtrack. While the dealer is injecting Caroline with heroin, the sounds of children playing in the street outside are clearly heard, cementing just how far Caroline, still a child herself, is from home. It is at this moment that she truly loses her innocence and at which Wakefield has failed her most completely.

Wakefield's failure to protect Caroline is made concrete in a scene shortly after this, in which he confronts the dealer himself. The dealer pulls a gun on Wakefield, who interprets his encounter with the black man as an attempted mugging and offers him all the money in his wallet in exchange for information about his daughter. Seemingly more aware than Wakefield of the racial dynamics of the encounter, the dealer dismissively says that he would take his money if he wanted it and tells him to leave. "This is a business," he says. "Get the fuck out of here." Unable to counter the dealer's assertion, Wakefield can do nothing but leave. In this encounter Wakefield, like Caroline, becomes a victim of the racialized other of the American inner city. As Caroline's father he ceases to be the patriarchal figurehead of the state (the drug czar) and becomes a powerless victim of the drug trade. Divested of his judicial robes, the symbolic power he is used to wielding over black subjects disappears in the face of the raw physical power of a black man with a gun.

Wakefield is able to partially recuperate his masculine authority in the next scene, in which he finds Caroline in a hotel room she shares with her boyfriend, Seth (Topher Grace), and is given the first opportunity to reestablish his status as Caroline's father and protector. In a scene that completely reverses both Wakefield's and Caroline's earlier encounters with the drug dealer, he physically confronts a white businessman who has solicited Caroline for sex. Unlike the previous encounter, in which he was powerless, Wakefield is in control of this one. As he rushes to his daughter's side he tells the man, in an echo of his previous exchange with the dealer, "You get the fuck out of here." Taking Caroline's hand in his he bursts into tears and begs her to forgive him. Seth, who has been watching from the door, turns and walks away, thereby relinquishing his own authority over Caroline. Wakefield rescues Caroline by removing her from the inner city and its multiple depravations and placing her in the private rehab facility. The errant daughter is reclaimed by and for white patriarchy by being relocated to a privatized space of individual responsibility. At the close of the scene she is back in the arms of her father. The newfound ability to shed tears for his daughter and to ask for her forgiveness is what marks that father as a changed man and inaugurates his later public breakdown at the White House. Sentimentality recoups white masculine authority by citing the white patriarch as the exemplary affective figure. Able to cry for his daughter, Wakefield is allowed to cry for himself; redeeming her, he is able to redeem himself.

Hollywood's Third Way: Affect as Critique

Inasmuch as *Traffic* illustrates a pervasive turn to sentimentality in contemporary American political culture, it also suggests the ideologies inherent in that turn. Rather than signaling a reorientation of white masculinity as patriarchy that, having learned the lessons offered by the sociocultural transformations of American culture since the mid-1960s, is willing to relinquish its hegemonic authority, *Traffic* indicates how forcefully white masculinity attempts to recoup its losses. Given the stated progressivism of the film, the force of that recuperation further suggests a critical absence within contemporary American liberalism. This absence becomes clear when *Traffic* is considered in its cultural context; as I have already suggested, the film is exemplary but not alone in its turn to sentimentality and can be considered among the first in a cycle of films that mount explicitly liberal critiques yet turn on equally reactionary solutions. Having actors, directors, writers, and producers in common, *Good Night, and Good Luck* (2005), *Syriana* (2005), and *Crash* (2004) constitute part of a cycle of recent liberal interventions in the discourse of American cultural politics. Like *Traffic*, these films each betray a belief in patriarchal recuperation and find reactionary resolutions grounded in masculine sentimentality in the midst of their liberal critiques.

Syriana, directed and written by Stephen Gaghan (who wrote the screenplay for *Traffic*), relies, much like *Traffic*, on the complex interweaving of multiple plotlines for much of the force of its critique. Set in the present day, the film attempts to chart the interconnections between the oil industry, U.S. geopolitics, Islamic terrorism, and global migrant labor. The film anchors its multiple and often unresolved plotlines in the star performances of George Clooney, Matt Damon, and Jeffrey Wright, each of whom is the central focus of one of the film's central stories. Like *Traffic*, the film's narrative complexity serves as a critical device. The audience is intentionally bombarded with an excess of information in the form of characters, locations, jargon, and relationships. Speaking of the film's ambition and its intentional complexity, Gaghan points out that it was shot in over 220 locations, on four continents, and in five languages. This complexity at the level of form and production, he believes, prevents the film from slipping into the easy essentialism of black/white binaries.[14] Like others associated with the film, Gaghan believes that it asks thought-provoking questions while refraining from providing rote or simplistic answers. George Clooney, an actor in and an executive producer of the film, says, "It's worth bringing up issues that reflect the questions we're asking. And not answering them. We didn't answer anything in *Syriana*."[15] Clooney also said, "[*Syriana*] is going to get us in a lot of trouble."[16] Critics in the tributary media by and large agreed with these assessments of the film and took its putatively progressive agenda at face value. Writing for *Sight and Sound*, Graham Fuller refers to the film as "willfully complicated."[17] Peter Travers of *Rolling Stone* refers to the film as a "hot potato": "You see . . . with the exhilarating feeling that a movie can make a difference." Continuing the food metaphors, he writes, "*Syriana* is a tough nut that demands attention, refuses to ingratiate and keeps throwing curves. . . . It's the kind of give-'em-hell filmmaking that Hollywood left for dead, the kind that matters."[18] Kenneth Turan writes in the *Los Angeles Times*, "'Syriana' is a film of paradoxes, contradictions and complications. . . . The . . . reason 'Syriana' is structured the way it is is as an aid to verisimilitude. To be heedlessly thrown into things heightens the film's sense of reality, giving us the feeling that we are on the inside, deliciously eavesdropping on behind-closed-doors situations."[19] For both Travers and Turan, the film's realism produces an immediacy that heightens its import. As the kind of film "that matters," *Syriana* provides a platform for its makers to engage meaningfully with contemporary American geo- and cultural politics.

The ability to see complexity in the world or to represent it on screen through formal and plotting devices, however, in no way guarantees that the solutions one suggests will be equally complex. The film's multiple and interconnected plots, rapid-fire editing, and complex and jargon-laden dialogue often serve as merely the ground against which its more traditionally oriented individual narratives are resolved. Rather than refusing to provide answers, as Clooney suggests, the film simply provides the wrong ones. Despite Clooney's and Gaghan's claims and the opinions of the film's reviewers, the structures of feeling of bourgeois sentimentality and the reactionary therapeutics of family values evident in the film trump its more complex concerns with U.S. geopolitics. As Turan himself says, Gaghan uses melodrama to ground the film and to render its complexity understandable to the audience: "Gaghan [is] a natural storyteller, [who] build[s] in unashamedly emotional moments, often situations between fathers and sons, that provide dramatic handholds on an otherwise slick surface."[20] The formal and narrative complexities of the film's multiple plotlines are folded into a moral certitude at the level of the individual plot.[21]

Syriana creates its affective resonance through a focus on two stories of paternal failure and recuperation. In one of these stories, Robert Barnes (George Clooney) vainly attempts to reconcile his career as a CIA agent with the requirements of home and family. Barnes is a long-term CIA field operative with extensive experience in the Middle East. His wife (who is never shown on screen and from whom he seems to be estranged) is also a CIA field operative. Their son, Bobby (Max Mingella), is a high school senior who is about to leave for college. It is unclear where or with whom Bobby lives. Barnes has lost control of both his personal and his professional life. In one scene he argues with Bobby about where he will go to college. Bobby, who is on a campus tour of Princeton, seems to want to go somewhere away from his family, but Barnes wants him to attend the University of Maryland, close to home. Bobby complains to his father that he "just want[s] a normal senior year . . . a normal house, with Cinemax [and] a normal prom." When Barnes responds, "It's complicated, you know?" Bobby leaves in frustration. Barnes's response repeats one he made in the scene immediately prior to this one, in which he was called on to offer expert testimony to a Senate committee on the Middle East. Instructed by his boss to stick to the company line, he instead responds to the question "Are we going to have a nice secular, pro-business government [in Iran]?" with the opinion "It's possible, it's complicated." The conflation of geopolitics and family tension that the juxtaposition of these two scenes creates illustrates the degree to which the film wishes to yoke its political resolutions to the trials of domesticity. Nowhere is this more clear than in the plotline starring Matt Damon.

That plotline involves a young expatriate financial analyst, Bryan Woodman (Matt Damon), and subordinates its complex analysis of the relationship between the U.S. economy and the geopolitics of the Middle East to a family melodrama in which Woodman trades on the accidental death of his eldest son for financial gain. During a summer party hosted by an oil-rich emir, Hamed Al-Subaai (Nadim Sawalha), with whom he is trying to secure a business contract, Woodman's eldest son, Max (Steven

Hinkle), is electrocuted in a swimming pool with a faulty light. The emir has the Spanish estate on which the party took place razed to the ground, and Woodman takes the opportunity to turn his tragedy into a business opportunity when he meets the emir's son, Prince Nasir Al-Subaai (Alexander Siddig), and becomes his financial consultant. Woodman becomes increasingly estranged from his wife, Julie (Amanda Peet). At one point he ignores a call from her on his cell phone but takes a call from a business associate. During an argument that immediately precedes her return to the States with their younger son, Woodman tells Julie that the opportunity provided him by his relationship with the prince is "like someone put a giant ATM on [their] lawn." Disgusted, Julie replies, "Here's a question: How do you think it looks to profit off the death of a six-year-old?" Woodman chooses business over family and continues his relationship with the prince.

In these scenes the film explicitly locates the broader geopolitical issues with which it attempts to grapple in the confines of the bourgeois family home. Woodman gives up the security of home and family for the thrill of global finance; Barnes is incapable of maintaining a home because he has spent so long attending to the covert operations of geopolitics. At the film's end the problems of home and politics must be reconciled. Barnes sacrifices his life for the pursuit of democracy, dying in a CIA rocket attack carried out against the prince, who is attempting a coup against his younger brother, made emir by their ailing father. The United States sides with the younger brother because he is compliant with its business interests, whereas Prince Nasir has recast himself as a reformer who wishes to democratize his country. Woodman, on the other hand, survives the rocket attack and is given the opportunity to return home. Following the attack, he is seen walking across the desert toward the city, making his way to the airport and back to his family. In one of the closing scenes Woodman reunites with his wife and son. As he enters the house his return will make a home, the audio recording of the martyrdom video made by one of the young suicide bombers featured in another of the film's plotlines can be heard. As he walks in the door and his wife turns to face him, the posthumous voice of the dead bomber is heard saying, "From the dust a new person will be created." This new person is Bryan Woodman. Rather than produce an equivalency between the young suicide bomber who has sacrificed everything for a cause he seems to scarcely understand and the wealthy young American who realizes the sacrifice he is making before it is too late, the scene replaces one with the other. It is Bryan Woodman's plight that resonates with the viewer in these final moments. What is reconstituted at the end of the film is the American family. Like Robert Wakefield in *Traffic*, Woodman has learned the value of family, and the plot is resolved affectively by his return to the bourgeois nuclear family. Thus while these filmmakers are understood—and understand themselves—to be working at the limits of Hollywood, the (limited) critique their films produce has been fully incorporated into the new studio system. This is apparent in the high profile of these films at the major cinema awards.

In addition to the ideological formations that underpin their formal and narrative content, the production and distribution history of these films also suggest the degree to which the corporate structures of contemporary Hollywood have transformed the meaning of independent cinema. Exemplified by their technical innovations, complex and often multivalent plots, innovative camera work, distinctive directorial styles, and a stated commitment to a politically motivated social hyperrealism, such films have become the prestige products of contemporary Hollywood. What constitutes independent cinema in the United States has increasingly become the output of the independent wings of the major studios. Films such as *Traffic*, *Crash*, and *Good Night, and Good Luck* serve as the prestige offerings of the major studios. *Good Night, and Good Luck*, for example, is a production of Warner Independent Pictures, part of the Warner Bros. Entertainment group and therefore wholly owned by Time Warner, one of the world's largest multimedia conglomerates. USA Films, the company that distributed *Traffic*, is now owned by NBC Universal (of whom General Electric is the majority shareholder). While *Syriana* was a Warner Bros. production, and therefore not independent, Clooney claims that they were able to make the picture only because of his and Damon's star power and because the stars worked for a percentage.[22] Thus while these filmmakers consider themselves to be the heirs of the New Hollywood of the 1970s, they are actually evidence of the centralization the new studio system has produced and indicate the degree to which sociological critique has been tempered by the dictates of the corporate structures of the transnational media conglomerates. This phenomenon suggests not only the degree to which these films have met with mainstream critical and industry approval, but belies a number of the claims about their critical interventions made by filmmakers, actors, and critics alike.[23]

The success of these films during awards season—if not always at the box office—suggests that the types of intervention they are making have clearly met with approval from Hollywood and that their creators are understood, both within the industry and within the tributary media, to be operating at the forefront of their fields. For example, including *Traffic*, the films mentioned above garnered a total of seventeen Academy Award nominations and eight awards in a total of nine major categories. This tally becomes even more significant if we bear in mind the fact that *Good Night, and Good Luck*, *Syriana*, and *Crash* all exhibited in a single year, 2005, making them all eligible for that year's Academy Awards. As a result these ideologically similar films with cast members, screenwriters, and directors in common dominated a number of major categories at that year's Oscars. All three were nominated in the Original Screenplay category, for example. *Crash* won the award for Best Motion Picture, meaning that Paul Haggis became the first person to write the screenplays for two consecutive best picture winners (*Million Dollar Baby*, for which he wrote the screenplay, won the award in 2004). Haggis also won the award for Best Original Screenplay. George Clooney won the award for Best Supporting Actor for his role in *Syriana*. Other nominations include Best Motion Picture, *Good Night, and Good Luck*; Best Performance by an Actor in a Leading Role, *Good Night, and Good Luck*; Best Performance by an Actor in a Supporting Role, *Crash*; Best Director, *Crash* and *Good Night, and Good Luck*; and Best Cinematography, *Good Night, and Good Luck*.

That these nominations and awards were all presented to individuals is interesting because the films themselves were all advertised and reviewed as ensemble pieces with enormous casts. As has already been discussed, each relies not only on the complexity of their multiple plotlines, but also on the ensemble nature of their casts for their claimed political effects. Their success during the awards season, however, in which individuals and not ensembles are rewarded, belies any claims to democratic pluralism and progressivism made on their behalf. Not only, therefore, do the films offer plots that focus on the individual achievements of heroic individuals, but the filmmakers themselves are understood in a similar way. As directors, writers, producers, and actors, Soderbergh, Clooney, Haggis, and Gaghan are all understood to be auteurs who work within the Hollywood system in order to transcend it.[24] Indeed these films are typically understood to offer great entertainment precisely because the filmmakers are attempting to do something more. As A. O. Scott says of *Syriana* in his review of the film for the *New York Times*, "It aims to be a great deal more than a standard geopolitical thriller and thereby succeeds in being one of the best geopolitical thrillers in a very long time."[25] It is therefore not only because of the thematic materials of these films that they are understood to be progressive, but also because of the celebrated commitment of their lead actors, directors, and writers, all of whom are powerful and progressive men. Because the star power of Damon, Clooney, and Douglas accrues to the characters they play on screen, these characters tend to become larger than the ensemble and their fortunes more significant.

The casting of Michael Douglas as Robert Wakefield in *Traffic* is a case in point. From his performances in the romantic comedies *Romancing the Stone* (1984), *The Jewel of the Nile* (1985), and *War of the Roses* (1989), in each of which he costarred with Kathleen Turner, to *Basic Instinct* (1992), *Falling Down* (1993), *Disclosure* (1994), and *The Game* (1997), Douglas has come to exemplify the crisis of masculinity on the big screen.[26] The overwhelming amount of attention paid by the media to the fact that Douglas is married to his costar in *Traffic*, Catherine Zeta-Jones, and to the fact that Zeta-Jones was six months pregnant during filming illustrates the interconnections between celebrity and character. The arrest of his son for possession of cocaine was cited as a motivation for Douglas and a reason for the emotional intensity of his performance.[27] Thus while *Traffic* was widely discussed as an ensemble film and its multiple plotlines were a significant feature of discussions of the film in the media, the presence of Douglas often overshadowed these other aspects of the film. The recalibrated masculinity of his star persona fed into and amplified the transformation of the character he was called upon to play. Thus when Wakefield regains control of his family at the close of the film, this narrative closure is deemed proper as much because of Douglas's star persona as because of the requirements of the plot.

George Clooney's involvement in *Syriana* and *Good Night, and Good Luck* exemplifies the degree to which these films are the work of powerful men. Despite its ensemble cast and multiple plotlines, *Syriana* was often reviewed as a Clooney film. A. O. Scott's review for the *New York Times*, for example, is titled "Clooney and a Maze of Collusion" and begins with a description of the actor as "swaddled in 30 extra pounds and a thick gray beard."[28] Peter Travers writes, "The first surprise is Clooney himself. Bearded and bloated from the thirty-five pounds he packed on to play Barnes, he gives us a ground soldier who's been used and used up by the CIA's war on Middle East terrorism. . . . This is the best acting Clooney has ever done—he's hypnotic, haunting and quietly devastating."[29] Kenneth Turan points out that the film "hides glamorous George Clooney behind a rumpled exterior and a full beard."[30] What is perhaps most interesting here is the fixation on Clooney's body. As an actor who for the past fifteen years has been a perennial fixture on *People* magazine's "most beautiful people" list, Clooney is typically represented as an old school heartthrob and a man's man, who does not care about his looks and is all the more attractive for it. In the list in 2001 *People* quoted Wolfgang Petersen, who directed Clooney in *The Perfect Storm* (2000), saying of the actor, "When he is all the way through his 40s, I think he will be even more attractive." Citing Clooney's refusal to try to disguise his age, the magazine opined in closing that he "doesn't have to." Clooney's transformation for the role of Barnes in *Syriana* is seen as both a sign of his commitment to his craft and a sign of the film's commitment to accuracy. "Unrecognizable," Clooney does not offer a star turn in the film, but subordinates himself to the role. But, as the evidence of many of Clooney's earlier roles and the representation of him in the media as someone who does not care about his looks suggests, this is all part of Clooney's celebrity persona. He is beautiful because of, not in spite of, his ability to make himself so undistinguished.[31] In these roles Clooney as sex symbol is subordinated to Clooney as politically engaged filmmaker. As such, the relationship between his participation in *Syriana* and in *Good Night, and Good Luck* is significant here.

That *Syriana* and *Good Night, and Good Luck* were released so close together (in October and November 2005) meant that Clooney received a great deal of media attention, including numerous magazine covers. *Sight and Sound* referred to him on the cover of its March 2006 issue as "Hollywood's Mr. Politics" and included seven pages of discussion and interviews. In the magazine Clooney refers to himself as "an old leftie."[32] The subordination of discussions about his physical appearance to concerns with his political engagement provide evidence of the ways in which the investment with white patriarchy in the films is replicated in the tributary discussions of them. Like the other figures under discussion here, Clooney is represented as a politically motivated and powerful man, who by the force of his star power and his belief is able to get such projects made. This representation, as I have suggested throughout, relies on recidivistic models of gendered authority in which men are the proper conduits for political and social change.

If the Academy Awards are an indication of the esteem in which these films and their writers, directors, and stars are held, they highlight a troubling, albeit unsurprising, absence. Despite their impressive tally of nominations and awards, there are two major categories in which none of these films received a nomination: Best Performance by an Actress in a Leading Role and Best Performance by an Actress in a Supporting Role. Without a single female writer, director, or lead actor and with female supporting characters in clearly subordinate roles, it is small wonder that these films still take patriarchy to be the limit point of critical intervention.[33] The turn in these films to the healing confines of the bourgeois family home and their commitment to the reenfranchisement of patriarchal authority within that home are central to the solutions they offer and ground their critiques of American domestic and geopolitics. In their sentimentalized paternalistic logic of masculine action, these films return us to the scene with which this book began: Jack Bauer's problems of state and family. Like *24*, these films rely on reactionary modes of masculine action. Couched in the progressive transformations of paternal sentimentality, the new man looks very much like the old. There is of course no surprise in this. The reactionary nature of the resolutions offered by this putatively progressive liberal cinema suggests the profound degree to which the agendas of neoliberalism organize the contemporary political horizons of both the right and the left. As these films suggest, the forms of patriarchal intervention that motivate contemporary politics locate the resolution to political problems in the realm of domestic paternalism. Soderbergh, Clooney, Gaghan, and the others claim they inhabit the left of the contemporary political spectrum, yet the conservative resolutions their films offer are predicated on forms of masculinist empowerment and authority that belie any such claims.

If compassionate conservatism is a lure for the continued erosion of the welfare state and the paternalistic imperial project behind the Bush administration's invasions of Afghanistan and Iraq, the compassionate liberalism these films evidence offers few alternatives. As *Traffic*'s appraisal of the Clinton-era war on drugs morphs into *Syriana*'s negotiations with the Bush administration's War on Terror, these films' simpatico patriarchal assertions suggest the degree to which the neoliberal horizons of contemporary politics have long been in place. Hollywood liberalism has been transformed into a Clintonian Third Way undergirded by the tenets of neoliberalism. The critical profiles of *Traffic*, *Syriana*, and the other films under discussion indicate the degree to which the political has become the personal in the contemporary United States: affect is mistaken for action, technique is mistaken for critique, and melodrama is mistaken for sociopolitical insight.

If white masculinity has been able to find the validation for its own authority—which it believes it has lost—in the locations described in the earlier chapters of this book, its concurrent turn to the modes of authoritarianism described in these final pages offers both another example of the ways white masculinity reclaims power and another illustration of its reactionary tendencies. Working hard for a living, white masculinity has relocated its authority in the cultural representations of closeted homosexuals, of the socioeconomic travails of white trash, in the celebratory figure of the blue-collar laborer, in the platonic love of an Irish father, and in the sentimental purviews of the private sphere patriarch. The various popular cultural texts that I have examined suggest that white masculinity's appeals to injury, cries for recognition, and critiques of power have found a resonance in American culture that serves as a lure for its revanchism. I have pinpointed and analyzed some of the cultural locations in which white masculinity's reclamation of authority can be found in order to illustrate—and thus resist—the force of white masculinity's lability.

NOTES ⤡

Introduction

1 Palahniuk, afterword, 215. The novel was first published by Norton in 1996.

2 Throughout this book the term *white masculinity* refers to a process through which or a location in which heteronormative white masculinity attains or regains privilege. The term is not meant to describe actual individuals per se, although the authority that accrues to those individuals who do conform to the ideal of this process or location should not be underestimated.

3 Savran, *Taking It Like a Man*, 5.

4 For an interesting analysis of the specific relationship between the American novel and contemporary sociocultural transformations, see Fitzpatrick, *The Anxiety of Obsolescence*, particularly 137–41, 217–33.

5 Wellman, "Minstrel Shows," 321.

6 Lipsitz, "Listening to Learn," 630.

7 Hill, *After Whiteness*, 93.

8 Faludi, *Stiffed*, 53.

9 See, for example, ibid., 51–101.

10 Ibid., 86.

11 All statistics from the U.S. Department of Labor, Bureau of Labor Statistics, online.

12 See Hill, "Introduction," 9.

13 Wellman, "Minstrel Shows," 316.

14 Dyer, *White*, 9.

15 DiPiero, *White Men Aren't*, 2.

16 Savran, *Taking It Like a Man*, 4.

17 For more on this, particularly the literature on recognition and redistribution, see, Fraser, *Redistribution or Recognition?*

18 See Robinson, *Marked Men*, particularly 1–22.

19 Lipsitz, "Listening to Learn," 369.

20 Frankenberg, "Introduction," 6.

21 Wiegman, "Whiteness Studies," 117.

22 This is evident, for example, in the slippery nature of the term *whiteness* as it is used to describe majority privilege. Academic studies of whiteness are often concerned primarily with white *masculinity*; at the same time the popular discourse around the "crisis of masculinity" almost exclusively names *white* male dissatisfaction.

23 Frankenberg, "Introduction," 5.

24 Hill, "Introduction," 5.

25 Ibid., 2.

26 Cherniavsky, "Introduction," xxii.

27 Roger Ebert, "Brokeback Mountain," *Chicago Sun-Times*, online (accessed 29 July 2009).

28 *Brokeback Mountain* was nominated for eight Academy Awards, including Best Motion Picture and acting nominations for Heath Ledger and Jake Gyllenhaal, and won three, including for Best Director. The film's success at the Oscars was met or exceeded at numerous other award ceremonies, including the British Academy of Film and Television Arts and the Golden Globes. In all the film won eleven major domestic awards in the core categories of best film, direction, writing, and performance. With a production budget of only $14 million it was also a commercial success, grossing $83 million on domestic release and another $95 million from foreign markets. (These figures do not include DVD sales and rentals.) *Brokeback Mountain* was noticeably more profitable than any of the other major prestige films of 2005. For example, it exceeded the domestic gross of the Academy Award's Best Motion Picture rival and eventual winner, *Crash*, by just under $30 million. While it couldn't compare with the staggering domestic revenues of the year's major blockbusters—*Star Wars: Episode Three* ($380 million), *Harry Potter and the Goblet of Fire* ($290 million), and *King Kong* ($218 million)—the film's box office receipts were healthy for a prestige picture of its kind.

29 Stephen Holden, "Brokeback Mountain," *New York Times*, 9 December 2005; Owen Gleiberman, "Brokeback Mountain," *Entertainment Weekly*, online (accessed 29 July 2009).

30 McMurtry and Ossana, "*Brokeback Mountain*," 67. All other references are given parenthetically in the text.

31 Wiegman, "Whiteness Studies," 117.

32 Despite the length of their affair and the profound effect it has on their lives, neither of the film's protagonists considers himself to be anything but straight. The morning after their first sexual encounter Ennis warns Jack, "I'm no queer." "Me neither," Jack reassures him. This is a stance that, despite its emotional and psychological toll, both men attempt to maintain throughout the duration of their relationship. It is also a stance that the film does its best to uphold through both plot and staging. Despite winning an MTV Movie Award for Best Kiss, the film's portrayal of same-sex intercourse is one of violence. Not only are Jack's and Ennis's interactions often literally followed by fistfights, but the sexual act itself is brutal and violent. This is one of many indications that the film cannot condone its own logic of homosexual enfranchisement. By coding male-male sex as violent and irrational the film simultaneously locates it in commonly understood discourses about homosexuality and deviancy *and* recodes the homosexual as the homosocial.

33 This is not to say that the film does not, or cannot, function in different ways for different viewers. Any popular culture text is complex and open to various interpretations. As such, the film can offer solace to a young gay man who identifies with the plight of its protagonists while the film also uses that plight to tell a very different story.

34 Perhaps we might revisit Roger Ebert's claim for a moment and suggest of Jack and Ennis that it is not so much that their tragedy *is* universal, but that it is their tragedy *to be* universal.

35 I would like to thank Elizabeth Dillon for suggesting this subtitle—the pithy part, anyway.

36 Fusco, "Fantasies of Oppositionality," 8.

1   Jack Bauer's Extraordinary Rendition

1 After a brief postponement because of the events of September 11, 2001, *24* first aired in the United States on Fox TV on 6 November 2001.

2 Agamben, *State of Exception*, 18.

3 At the time of writing, *24* has been on the air for seven seasons. Aside from key moments from later seasons, in this discussion I limit myself to an analysis of the first two seasons.

4 While the shift from Balkan terrorists of the first season to the Muslim extremists of the second suggests the show's capitulation to the altered socio-political landscape after September 11, it is worth noting that *24* does not produce a fully demonized portrayal of Muslim extremism until the fourth season.

5 To reiterate, while the first season of *24* was written and produced prior to the events of September 11, the continuities from one season to the next, before and after September 11, are startling.

6 Ray argues, "American culture's traditional dichotomy of individual and community [has] generated the most significant pair of competing myths: the outlaw

and official hero. Embodied in the adventurer, explorer, gunfighter, wanderer, and loner, the outlaw hero stood for that part of the American imagination valuing self-determination and freedom from entanglements. By contrast, the official hero, normally portrayed as a teacher, lawyer, politician, farmer, or family man, represented the American belief in collective action, and the objective legal process that superseded private notions of right and wrong." Ray, *A Certain Tendency*, 58–59.

7   Pease, "The Global Homeland State," 12.

8   J. Butler, *Precarious Life*, 51.

9   Foucault, "Governmentality," 211 (my italics).

10   J. Butler, *Precarious Life*, 54, 55, 66.

11   The administration showed an ambivalent relation to the law from the start and, remarkably, was forthright about its instrumental uses of international law. In an interview with Tim Russert on *Meet the Press* on 16 September 2001, Vice President Richard Cheney said, "We also have to work, though, sort of the dark side, if you will. We've got to spend time in the shadows in the intelligence world. A lot of what needs to be done here will have to be done quietly, without any discussion, using sources and methods that are available to our intelligence agencies, if we're going to be successful. That's the world these folks operate in, and so it's going to be vital for us to use any means at our disposal, basically, to achieve our objective" (White House website, accessed 23 April 2009). In an interview for the PBS show *Frontline*, a former White House associate counsel to President Bush, Bradford Berenson, made the following statement regarding the Geneva Conventions: "But once you appreciate and understand that this is in fact an existential threat to our government and to our way of life, that it is a military conflict, even if of an unconventional character, the answers to a lot of these questions about how to deal with detainees become fairly clear-cut. Under the international laws of armed conflict, you are entitled to capture and hold *until the end of hostilities* individuals who are fighting against you. You are not required to charge them with a crime. You are not required to provide them with a lawyer or access to your courts. And you are not required to let them go return to the battlefield and fight against you and prolong the armed conflict and all of the suffering that that inevitably entails" (pbs.org, accessed 23 April 2009, my italics).

12   See "Gonzales Helped Set the Course for Detainees," *Washington Post*, online (accessed 23 April 2009).

13   Brennan and Ganguly, "Crude Wars," 25.

14   J. Butler, *Precarious Life*, 55.

15   Ibid., 62.

16   Dana D. Nelson reminds us that the president himself is, or at least should be, a *functionary*. "The president is not the leader of [a] democracy," Nelson points out, "he is the executive of the institutions that are designed to support represen-

tative democratic self-governance." Nelson, "The President and Presidentialism,"
11–12.

17 Pease, "The Global Homeland State," 16.

18 See ibid.; J. Butler, *Precarious Life*, 67.

19 Agamben, *Means without End*, ix–x.

20 Žižek, "The Depraved Heroes of *24*."

21 J. Butler, *Precarious Life*, 61.

22 W. Brown, *Regulating Aversion*, 82.

23 Bruzzi, *Bringing Up Daddy*, 156.

24 May, "Echoes of the Cold War," 50.

25 This moral clarity is also foregrounded in relation to Bauer's work life when the
audience discovers that he is distrusted by some of his coworkers because he had
recently turned in a number of corrupt agents.

26 Ray, *A Certain Tendency*, 63.

27 Scott McClellan, White House Press Briefing, White House website (accessed
23 April 2009).

28 Ray, *A Certain Tendency*, 63.

29 George W. Bush, "Guard and Reserves 'Define Spirit of America,'" Remarks
to Employees at the Pentagon, 17 September 2001, state.gov (accessed 23 April
2009).

30 I discuss these issues further in relation to the figure of the firefighter and the
"everyday hero" in the next chapter.

31 Bush, "Guard and Reserves 'Define Spirit of America.'"

32 Nelson, "The President and Presidentialism," 6.

33 Ibid.

34 Alan Dershowitz, "The Present International Rules of War Enable and Protect
Terror," *Baltimore Sun*, 28 May 2004.

35 CNN *Late Edition with Wolf Blitzer*, 8 September 2002, online (accessed 23 April
2009).

36 In the next chapter I discuss the issue of time and September 11 in further detail
with reference to the narratives of exceptionalism that locate responses to the
events of that day in a possible future in which the United States and its citizens
will not fail to act.

37 Susan Sontag, "Regarding the Torture of Others," *New York Times*, 23 May 2004,
section 6, p. 25.

38 George W. Bush, "Remarks by President Bush to the Troops in Iraq," 13 June
2006, state.gov (accessed 23 April 2009).

39 R. D. Kaplan, *Warrior Politics*, 130–31.

40 Taylor, "The Unthinkable Made Real."

41 The show's ability to present the actions of its protagonist through a lens of startling moral clarity in which the correct response is always clear belies the severe
tolls it exacts on its other characters. Thus while Bauer is occasionally troubled

by his actions—but never prevented from carrying them out in the name of a higher moral purpose—the central female characters in season 1 are repeatedly subjected to kidnapping, assault, rape, torture, and murder.

42 Žižek, "The Depraved Heroes of *24*."

43 In a bizarre twist—and proof, if it were needed, of the power of popular culture—the U.S. military was forced to ask the creators of *24* to tone down the torture scenes in the show. In February 2007 Brigadier General Patrick Finnegan, a lawyer and teacher at the U.S. Military Academy at West Point, visited the show's creators. "The disturbing thing," Finnegan said, "is that although torture may cause Jack Bauer some angst, it is always the patriotic thing to do." "U.S. Military Tells Jack Bauer: Cut Out the Torture Scenes . . . or Else!," *The Independent*, 13 February 2007, 3. Just six months previously, however, Michael Chertoff, secretary of the Department of Homeland Security, appeared on a panel with the cast and creators of *24* hosted by Rush Limbaugh (who opined that the creators of the show "got lucky with 9/11 happening shortly after the show started"). "Factual Terrorism Fight Collides with Fictional '24' on Panel," *Boston Globe*, 24 June 2006, C7.

44 Young, "Ground Zero," 18.

45 George W. Bush, "Iraq and the Global War on Terror," Address to the Nation, 28 June 2005, state.gov (accessed 23 April 2009).

2 Future Perfect

1 I am intentionally using the term *fireman* rather than the gender-neutral *firefighter* because the gendered construction of the term is integral to the heroic figure produced.

2 Rowe, "Culture, U.S. Imperialism, and Globalization," 575.

3 Žižek, *Welcome to the Desert of the Real*, 47.

4 Kammen, "The Problem of American Exceptionalism," 6.

5 Tocqueville, *Democracy in America*,

6 A. Kaplan, "Homeland Insecurities," 83.

7 Simpson, *9/11*, 13.

8 Earlier in their history comic book publishers were forced to deal with the relationship between the fantasies they sold and reality. During the Second World War, for example, the industry had to find ways to create patriotic stories without upstaging actual fighting men and women. Superman's alter ego, Clark Kent, for example, was declared 4-F after he failed a vision test because of his X-ray vision. Like many other superheroes Superman spent the war working on the home front, breaking up espionage rings and thwarting plots against the domestic United States. See Wright, *Comic Book Nation*, 43–55.

9 The speed with which these commemorative volumes appeared is remarkable, for, as Joseph Witek has noted, given the logistics of publishing lead times and the "political reticence of comics publishers and syndicates," it is rare for comics

to "respond so immediately to particular real-life events." Witek, "Long Form/ Short Form," 281.

10 Amy Kiste Nyberg, "Of Heroes and Superheroes," *Media Representations of September 11* (Westport, Conn.: Praeger, 2003), 176–77.

11 The most famous response to September 11 in sequential art must be Art Spiegelman's *In the Shadow of No Towers*. In that volume, a collection of ten comics originally published in the German newspaper *Die Ziet* and a supplement of newspaper comic strips from the early twentieth century, Spiegelman addresses questions of trauma and representation alongside a broad-scale condemnation of the Bush administration's responses to the terrorist attacks. Spiegelman, however, is doing something very different from the writers I examine here.

12 See Daniels, *Superman*.

13 However, as one would expect of any cultural form with such a long and rich history, the comic book superhero was not a static construction. From the origins of the form to the present, writers and artists have explored the ideological beliefs that stand behind the heroic figures they create. That the recent turn to the superhero after September 11 elides so much of this history illustrates the degree to which American culture has turned to a series of specific and unproblematic constructions of heroism and masculinity. For an alternative vision of the figure of the superhero in recent American culture, see, for example, Loeb and Sale, *Superman for All Seasons;* Seagle and Kristiansen, *It's a Bird*. For recent novelistic treatments that reimagine the superhero figure and its historical origins, see Lethem, *The Fortress of Solitude*; Cantor, *Great Neck*; DeHaven, *It's Superman*; Chabon, *The Amazing Adventures of Kavalier and Clay*.

14 Ray, *A Certain Tendency*, 58–59.

15 For more on this subject, see chapter 1.

16 Martin and Shohat, "Introduction," 2.

17 The superhero as vigilante reached its apotheosis in the Reagan era, the 1980s, in Frank Miller's seminal *Batman: The Dark Knight Returns*. Series such as Miller's *Dark Knight* and Alan Moore's *Watchmen* and *Batman: The Killing Joke* deconstructed the ideological beliefs that stood behind the traditional superhero figure and created superheroes of startling psychological depth whom they used to examine American society. Grounded in the individualism of Reagan-era America, these figures found darkness at the core of American heroic ideals.

18 Seagle, Rouleau, and Sowd, "Unreal," 15–17. It is worth pointing out that "Unreal" is the opening story in the collection and appears in a section called "Nightmares."

19 Kleid et al., "Letters from a Broken Apple," 127.

20 Unlike the other major publishers of superhero comics, such as DC Comics and Image, which situate their superheroes in fictional locales such as Gotham City or Metropolis, Marvel's principal superhero series are all set in New York City, suggesting one reason why Marvel felt the need to address the events of September 11 in a more sustained fashion than most of the other comic publishers.

21 See marvel.com (accessed 23 April 2009).

22 Volpp, "The Citizen and the Terrorist," 159.

23 For more on baseball after September 11, see Kraus, "A Shelter in the Storm."

24 See Ignatiev, *How the Irish Became White*, particularly 92–123.

25 See the National Conference of Law Enforcement Emerald Society website for more information (accessed 23 April 2009).

26 Gerstle, "Pluralism and the War on Terror."

27 It is perhaps worth noting that the writers and artists of early superhero comics in the late 1930s and 1940s were predominantly second-generation Jewish immigrants. Moreover the majority of them lived and worked in New York. Therefore, as the generation of immigrants who made good on the promise of America in the decade after the Great Depression, the histories of these men resonate through the everyday hero and, much like the superheroes they created, further serve to incorporate New York into the "homeland" by harking back to the city's halcyon days. See Jones, *Men of Tomorrow*.

28 Stein, "Days of Awe," 194.

29 A. Kaplan, "Homeland Insecurities," 88.

30 Halberstam, *Firehouse*, 5.

31 Ibid., 8.

32 Floren, "Too Far Back for Comfort." Floren goes on to argue that, while all 343 firefighters who lost their lives on September 11 were male, this fact reflects FDNY hiring practices more than it does the merits or abilities of female firefighters. Floren also claims that, of the 11,500 firefighters in New York City, currently only 25 are women.

33 May, "Echoes of the Cold War," 50.

34 As the shock of September 11 has receded, fractures have begun to appear in this fantasy construction and—as evidenced, for example, in recent court cases involving the widows of deceased firemen and a related episode of the television series *Law and Order*—the widow has become a more problematic figure than this construction allows.

35 Franklin's photograph first appeared in the Bergen County, New Jersey newspaper, *The Record*, on 12 September 2001. Within days his photograph (or ones similar to it) had been reproduced in countless other publications.

36 Sturken, "Memorializing Absence." It is also important to note how quickly the Pentagon dropped away as a target, arguably because, as the center of U.S. military authority, it signifies literally what the representation of the Twin Towers seeks to hide symbolically: the hegemony of U.S. military and economic imperialism.

37 *People Weekly*, 24 September 2001, 1.

38 This proposed memorial itself exposed the ethnic work performed by the figure of the New York City fireman after September 11. An early model for the proposed memorial (which was never actually constructed) attempted to paint a more racially inclusive picture by changing the ethnicities of the firemen it portrayed.

The memorial's designers were criticized for this attempt at racial inclusivity by citizens who, under the guise of respecting the memories of those who died and risked their lives on September 11, insisted that the faces of the actual firemen in the original picture (all of whom were white) should be used for the statue.

39 *People Weekly*, 24 September 2001, 136.

40 See Sontag, *On Photography*, 27–50.

41 This de-historicization also produces an epiphenomenal *re*-historicization because, in the words of Amy Kaplan, it "locates [the United States] in world history rather than as an exception to it" ("Homeland Insecurities," 57). While Kaplan is specifically discussing the use of the term *Ground Zero* to describe both the site on which the World Trade Center once stood and the events of September 11 in time, the evocation of America's involvement in World War Two similarly situates the events of September 11 in a historical narrative as the symbolic and the actual collide.

42 Kennedy, "Framing September 11," 276.

43 This moral absolutism replicates the spurious patriotic logic in which any criticism of the War on Terror is considered an attack on U.S. troops.

44 For more on this term, see Pease, "National Narratives."

45 Caruth, "Recapturing the Past," 153.

46 J. Butler, *Precarious Life*, 181.

47 Jameson, "The Dialectics of Disaster," 58–89.

48 Caruth, *Unclaimed Experience*, 7.

49 It is worth noting that *The Call of Duty* couldn't sustain the logic of emergency service worker as everyday hero. As *The Call* (a short-lived monthly title bringing together the main characters from the three *The Call of Duty* series) makes clear, to sustain the series the everyday heroes had to become traditional superheroes. "They saved Manhattan from certain doom," stated one ad for the new series, "but will they be able to save themselves? The saga of Marvel's everyday heroes continues in *The Call*. As they become something more than human, the fight begins to retain their humanity." "Something more than human" is hardly "everyday," and the real-life heroes have become actual superheroes, replete with costumes, masks, superpowers, and alter egos. There is, unfortunately, nothing surprising about the fact that the everyday hero became a bona fide superhero at exactly the moment when the United States began a preemptive war against Iraq.

50 Pease, "The Global Homeland State," 18.

51 J. Butler, *Precarious Life*, 180.

52 Silverman, *Male Subjectivity at the Margins*, 55.

3   Men's Soaps

1 For salary details, see the *USA Today* website (accessed 23 April 2009).

2 Lowe, *The Body in Late-Capitalist USA*, 34.

3 *American Chopper* aired on the Discovery Channel for its first four seasons and

has since moved to a sister network, the Learning Channel (TLC), where, at the time of writing, the sixth season has just begun.

4 See Stilson, "It's All about the Family Thing," for a brief analysis of *American Chopper* viewing data.

5 I am intentionally using the term *fireman* rather than a gender-neutral term such as *firefighter* to highlight the fact that it is undoubtedly men who are being valorized in this commemorative affectivity. For an interesting discussion of this investment in gender specificity after September 11, see Floren's insightful comments in "Too Far Back for Comfort."

6 Although *American Chopper*'s status as a reality-based TV show is significant, genre is not the central focus of this analysis. Therefore, while I attend to the formal aspects of the show and do not wish to separate it from the broader cycle of reality television in which it is situated, I am more interested in questions of cultural politics that are not predicated solely on the genre conventions of reality TV. For a discussion of the reality TV cycle, see Murray and Ouellette, *Reality TV.*

7 Hill, *After Whiteness*, 93.

8 DiPiero, *White Men Aren't*, 3.

9 Nowhere is this more apparent than in the motorcycle industry itself. Harley-Davidson is currently the only American motorcycle manufacturer that has continually built motorcycles in the United States (in their factory in Milwaukee). Indian Motorcycles, the marquee American brand, has recently been revived and is building motorcycles in North Carolina; the first production model is expected in mid-2009. See, for example, Yates, *Outlaw Machine*, especially 116–44.

10 For more on the cultural history of the motorcycle in the United States, see Krens, introduction to *The Art of the Motorcycle.*

11 Flaherty, *American Chopper*, 15.

12 Lowe, *The Body in Late-Capitalist USA*, 18.

13 See the Harley-Davidson website (accessed 23 April 2009); Orange County Choppers website (accessed 23 April 2009).

14 Flaherty, *American Chopper*, 14.

15 The dynamic at work in this phenomenon closely replicates nineteenth-century discourses about the "vanishing Indian." As the blue-collar worker has all but disappeared, he or she is reconstituted as a nostalgic figure of mythic American purity. See, for example, Dippie, *The Vanishing American.*

16 Hartigan, *Odd Tribes*, 119.

17 Appadurai, *Modernity at Large*, 81.

18 Aronowitz, *How Class Works*, 27.

19 Interestingly, after the two pilot episodes Paulie is never shown at church again, and the show's attention to his leisure-time activities revolves around his love life.

20 Berlant, *The Queen of America*, 11.

21　Ibid., 3.

22　Denning, *Culture in the Age of Three Worlds*, 91.

23　Willis, *Learning to Labour*, 131. In his discussion of the relationship between time, money, and labor, Willis writes, "In middle class professions it is clear that the yearly salary is paid in exchange for the use of continuous and flexible services. Remuneration here is not based on the particular amount of time spent on the job and of course those 'on the staff' are expected to work overtime and at home for no extra cash. Such workers, their wage form makes clear, are being paid for what they *are*: for the use of their capacities, for their general potential as managers, accountants, etc. The social implications of the weekly wage packet are very different. The *general* capacity of labour power which is recognized by the salary form is here broken up into weekly lumps and riveted to a direct and regular reward. Weekly wages, not yearly salaries, mark the giving of labour. The quantity of the wage packet is the quantitative passing of time. Its diminution is loss of measured time, its increase 'overtime'" (131).

24　Ibid., 135.

25　Teresa Howard, "'American Chopper' Stars Climb aboard AOL," *USA Today*, 19 January 2004, B2.

26　The authenticity of Senior's old school roots is confirmed when he and Mikey restore one of Senior's first choppers, originally built in 1974. The bike was later featured in the Harley-Davidson enthusiast magazine *V-Twin Motorcycles*. See Garson, "Paul Sr.'s Pride and Joy."

27　Needless to say, this hasn't prevented him from turning it into a commodity identity. OCC now features a signature line of bikes, the Old School Paul Sr. Series, with an asking price of $55,000. See the Orange County Choppers website (accessed 23 April 2009).

28　Willis, *Learning to Labour*, 148, 147.

29　Appadurai, *Modernity at Large*, 82.

30　Mikey Teutul used the witty phrase "like Martha Stewart on a motorcycle" during a "best of" episode to describe his father's desire for cleanliness. While I do not discuss them here, a number of major arguments between Senior and Paulie center on issues of neatness and Paulie's inability to keep his work space tidy.

31　Quoted in Seate, *Outlaw Choppers*, 93, 12. There is of course a certain irony in the fact that Long makes this statement in a book that would not exist without the popularity of shows like *American Chopper*.

32　Ibid., 59 (my italics).

33　Ann Oldenburg, "Leaders of the Pack," *USA Today*, 25 March 2004.

34　See the Discovery Channel website (accessed 23 April 2009).

35　OCC-related products include T-shirts and baseball caps bearing the OCC logo, coffee-table books, Teutul bobble-head dolls, *American Chopper* DVDs, Full Throttle cologne, miniature models of the theme motorcycles built on the show, children's coloring books, and a video game in which the player gets to ride the bikes built on the show.

36 Denning, *Culture in the Age of Three Worlds*, 103.

37 Halliday, "Tuners Fit In with Customizing Fare," 8.

38 Perhaps because the Teutuls do not possess the same skills as James and because their design ethos is so different from his, they are not positioned in exactly this way. Paulie refers to the companies that supply parts to OCC as "vendors," and the company relies more on the just-in-time methods of late capitalism than the nostalgic individualism of James's solo productions. Parts are brought in from various locations and only final assembly takes place on site.

39 In this light it is interesting to note that one of the few work-related injuries seen on *American Chopper* involves an OCC employee, Rick Petko, getting his hand caught in a drill. Despite his young age, Senior believes that Rick is "old school" like him, a belief that is confirmed for both Senior and the viewer by the fact that Rick returns to work immediately after visiting the emergency room for stitches. For a discussion of hands and the laboring body, see Zandy, *Hands*.

40 For more on this topic, see chapter 2.

41 See ouboces.org for more information about the program (accessed 23 April 2009).

42 Three hundred forty-three is the number of firefighters who lost their lives on September 11, 2001.

43 Wiegman, "Whiteness Studies," 116.

44 Flaherty, *American Chopper*, 60.

4 Eminem's White Trash Aesthetic

1 Eminem is a stage name. The rapper's real name is Marshall Mathers; he also uses the pseudonym Slim Shady. Throughout this chapter I use Eminem as the default and Marshall Mathers, Slim Shady, or "Eminem" (in quotation marks) to discuss specific uses of these names.

2 At the time of writing, the much anticipated new album, *Relapse*, was about to be released.

3 In "Shady Agonistes," James Keller notes that the "rags to riches paradigm is ubiquitous within hip hop." This is not surprising, given that hip-hop, while understood to be a part of black American culture, is still a part of an American culture construed more broadly, in which such narratives have always held a prominent place. As Tricia Rose points out, "Rappers who criticize America for its perpetuation of racial and economic discrimination also share conservative ideas about personal responsibility." Rose, *Black Noise*, 2.

4 I do not wish to rehash the history of hip-hop, which has been well documented elsewhere. Instead I draw on that history as and where appropriate. For the reader interested in that general history, see Chang, *Can't Stop Won't Stop*; George, *Hip Hop America*; and Rose, *Black Noise*. Interestingly, Chang's book, though published in 2005, contains no mention of Eminem. *Total Chaos*, his subsequent edited collection on the "art and aesthetics of hip-hop," contains just a single

mention of Eminem, and that in an essay about theater and only in relation to Anthony Mackie, the actor who plays Papa Doc in *8 Mile*. See Davis, "Found in Translation," 74. See also the films *Wild Style* (dir. Charlie Ahearn 1982) and *Scratch* (dir. Doug Pray, 2001).

5 Over the course of his career Eminem's mainstream appeal has grown tremendously. A search for "Eminem" on the website of the celebrity news magazine *Entertainment Weekly* turns up almost a thousand unique hits.

6 The history of hip-hop is as deep and complex as that of any other significant cultural form. That hip-hop is in many ways a black cultural form cannot and should not be denied. However, from the very beginning of the hip-hop phenomenon in the mid-1970s white audiences, performers, producers, and patrons have contributed to the formation and development of the culture. Figures such as Rick Rubin, the cofounder with Russell Simmons of Def Jam Records and the producer of many seminal hop-hop albums and singles, were important to the culture. The explosion of hip-hop as a global phenomenon can also be attributed in part to the ways that African American culture has been internationalized by cultural and economic globalization. On race and hip-hop, particularly in the early years of the culture, see George, *Hip Hop America*, especially 56–75. On the global spread of black American culture and hip-hop, see Basu and Lemelle, *The Vinyl Ain't Final*.

7 Katja Lee writes that Eminem's "rap suggests an awareness of authenticity as an inhabited rather than inherent position and of identity as a posturing of self." Lee, "Reconsidering Rap's 'I,' " 352.

8 Walsh, "An Interview with Saul Williams," 732.

9 Hartigan, *Odd Tribes*, 159.

10 Wray, *Not Quite White*, 1. For a history of the origins of the term *white trash*, see 41–46.

11 Hartigan, *Odd Tribes*, 160.

12 Negra, "The Irish in Us," 1.

13 Rose, *Black Noise*, 11.

14 Lynette Holloway, "The Angry Appeal of Eminem Is Cutting across Racial Lines," *New York Times*, 28 October 2002, C1.

15 Gleiberman, "Is Eminem the Elvis Presley of Today?" Chris Ayres also likened Eminem to Elvis. See Ayres, "All Change as Eminem Hailed as New Elvis," *The Times (London)*, 9 November 2002.

16 See Wray, *Not Quite White*, 47–95.

17 See Gilman, "Nietzsche, Bizet, and Wagner."

18 Wray, *Not Quite White*, 16.

19 Quinn, *Nuthin' but a "G" Thang*, 14, 143.

20 Hartigan, *Odd Tribes*, 24.

21 The CD was released with two alternate covers; the other contains a photograph of Eminem sitting on the front porch of a wood-sided house.

22 In this light it is interesting that one of Eminem's full-length CD releases is called

Encore (2004, Interscope Records) and his first "greatest hits" album is called *Curtain Call* (2005, Interscope Records), continuing the link between performance and celebrity. Derived from the alliterative qualities of his given name (Marshall Mathers) and the popular candy M&Ms, the stage name Eminem already contains connotations of consumption and product branding.

23 See Browne, "'Stan' by Your Man."

24 The relationship between rapper and fan that is mediated through the poster is similarly evoked in the song "Sing for the Moment" when Eminem raps, "It's why we sing for these kids that don't have a thing / Except for a dream and a fucking rap magazine / Who post pinup pictures on their walls all day long / Idolize their favorite rappers and know all their songs" (*The Eminem Show*, Aftermath Records, 2002).

25 See chapter 3. See also Berlant, *The Queen of America*; Oullette, "'Take Responsibility for Yourself."

26 "Dream On" appeared on Aerosmith's eponymous first album (*Aerosmith*, 1973, Sony), was a top ten Billboard Chart single in 1975, was named one of the "500 Songs That Shaped Rock and Roll" by the Rock and Roll Hall of Fame (see the Hall of Fame website, accessed 29 April 2009), and was included in *Rolling Stone* magazine's "500 Greatest Songs of All Time" (see the magazine's website, accessed 29 April 2009). Aerosmith also holds a significant place in the early history of commercial rap after hip-hop group Run-D.M.C. remade their early single "Walk This Way" (1975) in 1986. The release was the first rock/hip-hop hybrid and helped propel hip-hop into the mainstream. See Rose, *Black Noise*, 51; George, *Hip Hop America*, 61. Aerosmith's own lucrative co-optation of the blues hardly needs mentioning.

27 See Aaron, "Don't Fight the Power."

28 Eminem's predilection for confessional modes has also produced an autobiography, *The Way I Am*. In it he describes the security his success has provided: "[This] was the first time in my life I'd had a real home that I could call my own and nobody was going to be able to throw me out." Excerpted before publication on the *Entertainment Weekly* website (accessed 29 July 2009).

29 See J. M. Butler, "'Luther King Was a Good Ole Boy.'"

30 Because of this, I believe Hartigan is incorrect when he suggests that Eminem's chief threat is that he "ominously invokes a 'fuckin' army marching' of similarly debased whites rising up against the conventions and decorums of the white mainstream." Hartigan, *Odd Tribes*, 162. It is not the threat of class revolt that the white mainstream is concerned with, but the revolt of their own children; it is, as Eminem points out, that he "speaks to *suburban* kids" (my italics).

31 Lynne Cheney became a target for Eminem after she repeatedly mentioned the rapper in her testimony in front of the Senate Committee on Violence in the Media in 2000. Tipper Gore was a founding member of the organization Parents Music Resource Center, which advocated for the inclusion of parental advisory labels on CD covers to warn against violent and sexual content matter.

See "Lynne Cheney Addresses Senate Commerce Committee on Violence in the Media," CNN website.

32 See the Billboard website (accessed 29 April 2009); allmusic.com (accessed 29 April 2009).

33 See boxofficemojo.com (accessed 29 April 2009). Throughout the remainder of this book, all box office totals are from this source. As Charles R. Acland points out in *Screen Traffic*, U.S. "domestic" distribution figures always include Canada, and this fact should be borne in mind throughout. Acland, *Screen Traffic*, 7.

34 Shickel, "Eminem's Eight Mile High."

35 Hoberman, "Signs of the Times," *The Village Voice*, 5 November 2002.

36 Elvis Mitchell, "A Youth's Rise from Rap to Riches," *New York Times*, 8 November 2002.

37 See Clemens, *Made in Detroit*, 12; Hartigan, *Racial Situations*, 24–26. See also city-data.com (accessed 23 April 2009).

38 Clemens, *Made in Detroit*, 8, 34, 40, 42. See also Faludi, *Stiffed*, 51–101. One could argue that being white entitled Clemens to write and find a publisher for his book. His is just one of a recent spate of memoirs documenting what it was like growing up white in a black city or neighborhood. See also Conley, *Honky*.

39 Some in the academy share this understanding. Houston A. Baker Jr. has said of rap, "Unlike rock and roll, rap can not be hastily and prolifically appropriated or 'covered' by white artists. For the black urbanity of the form seems to demand not only a style more readily accessible to black urban youngsters, but also a representational black urban *authenticity* of performance." Baker, *Black Studies*, 62, italics in the original. Baker's italicizing of the word *authenticity* suggests, to this reader anyway, a mixture of certainty and uncertainty that might undermine such a claim.

40 Perhaps in keeping with this ethos, at one point in the film Douglas Sirk's *Imitation of Life* (1959) is shown playing on the television in Rabbit's mother's trailer.

41 Forman, " 'Represent,' " 203.

42 See the Cranbrook website (accessed 29 April 2009).

43 See Denning, *The Cultural Front;* Lott, *Love and Theft;* Roediger, *Towards the Abolition of Whiteness*.

5   The Fighting Irish

1 The film was a critical and commercial success. Produced and distributed in the United States by Warner Bros., the film first opened in limited release on 15 December 2004 (allowing it to be entered in that year's Academy Awards) and then nationwide on 28 January 2005. *Million Dollar Baby* earned a final domestic gross of $100,492,203 (slightly exceeded by a foreign gross of $116,271,443). It was nominated for seven Academy Awards and won four (Best Motion Picture, Best Director [Eastwood], Best Actress in a Lead Roll [Swank], and Best Actor

in a Supporting Roll [Freeman]). The film also received almost universal critical claim from film critics working in the mainstream press.

2 Negra, "The Irish in Us," 1.

3 In part as a strategy for keeping secret the abrupt plot twist that occurs two-thirds of the way through the film, *Million Dollar Baby* was explicitly marketed as the story of Maggie Fitzgerald. The film's posters present Maggie as the central protagonist and reviewers generally described the plot in ways that foregrounded her rise and eventual fall.

4 Hartigan, *Odd Tribes*, 24.

5 Because lemon meringue pie—and its provenance—is central to the concluding scene of the film, the relevance of this early exchange between Maggie and Frankie is more significant than its function as an indicator of Maggie's tutoring might suggest. Lemon meringue pie becomes a symbol of Frankie's desire for an authentically individualistic life, outside the bounds of common society.

6 Aronowitz, *How Class Works*, 22.

7 Carter, *The Heart of Whiteness*, 35.

8 It is remarkable just how little we learn about Maggie's opinions, feelings, and desires from Maggie herself. Almost everything we know about her comes from Scrap directly or his retellings of Frankie's opinions.

9 Carter, *The Heart of Whiteness*, 38.

10 It is worth noting, however, that Maggie is not overtly sexualized in the film. Her platonic love affair with Frankie, in which she is both lover and daughter, precludes such an investment. The audience is not supposed to desire Maggie so much as it is encouraged to understand her newly athletic body to be a sign of her successful control and regulation of that body. While *Million Dollar Baby* is, in many ways, a love story, it is not erotic in any way. What is most significant here, then, is not the transformation of Maggie into a sexual object, but her transformation into a citizen.

11 Interestingly the conclusion of the film and its portrayal of an assisted suicide caused a great deal of consternation for the religious right, who took the film as an endorsement of euthanasia. As Frank Rich reports in a piece he wrote for the *New York Times*, right-wing talk radio turned on Eastwood and attempted to cut into the film's profits by "giving away" the ending on air. Rich opines, "There hasn't been a Hollywood subversive this preposterous since the then 10-year-old Shirley Temple's name surfaced at a House Un-American Activities Committee hearing in 1938." Frank Rich, "How Dirty Harry Turned Commie," *New York Times*, 13 February 2005, section 2, p. 1.

12 Wiegman, "Intimate Publics," 860.

13 The observant viewer will have noticed that Frankie first utters this term under his breath during Maggie's first professional fight.

14 Cannon, "The Heavyweight Champion of Irishness," 90.

15 Negra, "Irishness, Innocence," 361.

16 Carby, "What Is This 'Black,'" 329.

17 Gibbons, "Race against Time," 96.

18 Ignatiev, *How the Irish Became White*, 3.

19 Presumably lacking Frankie's ability to navigate the treacherous terrain of high culture, Scrap is only ever seen reading superhero comic books.

20 On this movement (and Yeats's place in it), see Fallis, *The Irish Renaissance*; Marcus, *Yeats and the Beginning of the Irish Renaissance*.

21 Hunter, "Return to 'La bonne vaux,'" 80.

22 Yeats, *Autobiographies*, 153, quoted ibid., 71.

23 Hunter, "Return to 'La bonne vaux,'" 73.

24 McAllister, "Clint Eastwood's Boxing Movie."

25 Sklar and Modleski, "*Million Dollar Baby*: A Split Decision," 7.

26 The role Freeman plays in *Million Dollar Baby* can also be seen as a reprise of the role he played alongside Eastwood in the director's revisionist western, *Unforgiven* (1992).

27 I will leave it to the reader to assess the significance of the fact that Mackie is the actor who plays Papa Doc in *8 Mile*.

28 That these reviewers are all men, and almost all middle-aged, is perhaps no surprise.

29 Kenneth Turan, "In 'Million Dollar Baby,' Clint Eastwood Delivers a Lean, Emotionally Daring Tale Set in the Unforgiving World of Boxing," *Los Angeles Times*, 15 December 2004.

30 A. O. Scott, "3 People Seduced by the Bloody Allure of the Ring," *New York Times*, 15 December 2004.

31 Ty Burr, "A Sublime Meeting of Director, Star, and Script Makes 'Baby' a Masterwork," *Boston Globe*, 7 January 2005.

32 Denby, "High Rollers."

33 Frayling, *Clint Eastwood*, 100.

34 Dyer, *Heavenly Bodies*, 8.

35 Smith, *Clint Eastwood*, 207, 209. Smith devotes some time to a discussion of an early Eastwood film, *The Beguiled* (1971), in which Eastwood's character, McBurney, has a leg amputated after being pushed down a flight of stairs. Smith, rightly, discusses this amputation as a symbolic castration (78–79). It is hard to view the loss of Maggie's leg separately from this earlier moment.

36 Asian men are often feminized in American culture, and the film's desire to transform Thao from an effeminate Asian boy into a self-assured American man should be considered in this light. See, for example, Eng, *Racial Castration*.

37 Recent revisits to hoary old franchises such as *Die Hard*, *Rambo*, and *Indiana Jones* suggest that, while ultimately untrue, this was as good a possibility as any.

38 By comparison *Changeling*, released in October 2008, starring Angelina Jolie and directed by Eastwood with a budget of $55 million, realized just under $36 million in gross domestic box office receipts (but achieved gross foreign sales of $77 million).

39 Travers, "Gran Torino."

40 Manohla Dargis, "Hope for a Racist, and Maybe a Country," *New York Times*, 12 December 2008.

41 Kenneth Turan, "Clint Eastwood, at 78, Shows He's Still a Formidable Action Figure," *Los Angeles Times*, 12 December 2008.

42 Smith, *Clint Eastwood*, 210.

43 Ibid., 241.

44 Perhaps an indication of the late stage of Eastwood's career, a number of recent or forthcoming volumes attempt career retrospectives. These include Drucilla Cornell's scholarly monograph, *Clint Eastwood and Issues of American Masculinity*. Popular books include Marc Eliot's *American Rebel: The Life of Clint Eastwood* and Howard Hughes's *Aim for the Heart: The Films of Clint Eastwood*. The difference between these last two titles perhaps suggests the complex ways in which Eastwood registers in American cultural life.

45 Smith, *Clint Eastwood*, 248. Interestingly, as Smith points out, Eastwood's films during the mid-1980s (in which his status as an auteur and a leading figure in American cinema was established) were neither commercially nor critically successful (245). The same cannot be said of his films since *Unforgiven*. A brief list of total domestic and foreign box office receipts for some of those films should suffice to establish Eastwood's refound commercial success: *Unforgiven* (1992), $159 million; *In the Line of Fire* (1993), $177 million; *The Bridges of Madison County* (1995), $182 million; *Space Cowboys* (2000), $129 million; *Mystic River* (2003), $157 million; *Million Dollar Baby* (2004), $217 million; *The Changeling* (2008), $113 million; *Gran Torino* (2008), $263 million. This list is only partial and does not tell the whole story. Films such as *Flags of Our Fathers* (2006), with a production budget of $90 million, and the companion film, *Letters from Iwo Jima* (2006), were less commercially successful but did much to cement Eastwood's critical stature and to keep him in the public eye during the prolific period from 2004 to 2008. On the other hand, many of his more successful pictures during this period were made with very low production budgets ($33 million for *Gran Torino*, $30 million for *Million Dollar Baby*, for example). Suffice it so say that, as both actor and director, Eastwood has experienced something of a career resurgence since the early 1990s.

46 Smith, *Clint Eastwood*, 264.

47 Edward Gallafent points out that in each of the *Dirty Harry* films violence perpetrated against women is an important motivating factor in the hero's actions. To the degree that Walt's actions are motivated by a desire to see Sue's rapists brought to justice, *Gran Torino* could be understood to update and revise the models of heroic action available in the earlier films. See Gallafent, *Clint Eastwood*, 38.

48 That the final *image* of Eastwood in the film is of the actor spread-eagled on the ground in a Christ-like pose would seem to be enough to confirm this point. It is not, however, the final time he is heard. The film closes with an overhead shot of Thao, driving along beside Lake Michigan in the Gran Torino, which Walt has

left him in his will. As the car disappears down the road the film's theme song begins to play before the credits start to roll. The first verse of the song is sung not by the song's co-writer, Jamie Callum (who sings the remainder of the song), but by its other co-writer, Eastwood himself. Literally disembodied, the voice of Eastwood outlasts his bodily onscreen presence like a haunting remainder. (While he does not develop the point very far in relation to Eastwood specifically, Smith also devotes some attention to the question of the voice in cinema. See Smith, *Clint Eastwood*, 219–22.)

6 Romancing the Nation

1 Stephen Holden, "Traffic," *New York Times*, 27 December 2000.

2 Lemons, "Stephen Soderbergh."

3 The list of politicians and DEA agents who play themselves in the film includes Governor Bill Weld; Senators Don Nickles, Harry Reid, Barbara Boxer, and Orrin Hatch; and ex-DEA official Craig N. Chretein.

4 Alarcón, Kaplan, and Moallem, introduction, 6.

5 Davidson and Hatcher, introduction, 8.

6 Berlant, *The Queen of America*, 4.

7 Aronowitz, "My Masculinity," 320.

8 One has only to watch John Ford's *The Searchers* for proof of the point.

9 Chapman and Hendler, introduction, 3.

10 Ibid., 1, 2. See also Shamir and Travis, introduction; Nelson, "Representative/ Democracy." For a succinct overview of the history and criticism of male affect in American culture, see Chapman and Hendler, introduction, 2–8.

11 Shamir and Travis, introduction, 2.

12 These effects are considered to be such an important and distinct part of the film that the Criterion Collection edition of the DVD contains, as part of its extensive supplementary features, a film-processing demonstration that shows how the look of the Mexican scenes was achieved.

13 In this regard the film compares poorly to the more sophisticated portrayals of the drug trade found in HBO's acclaimed series *The Wire* or its predecessor, *The Corner*.

14 Jaafar, "Ali Jaafar Talks to Stephen Gaghan," 20.

15 Jaafar, "Ali Jaafar Talks to George Clooney," 17.

16 See Travers, "Syriana."

17 Fuller, "Confessions of a Dangerous Mind," 16.

18 Travers, "Syriana."

19 Kenneth Turan, "Syriana," *Los Angeles Times*, 23 November 2005. This feeling of "being on the inside" also extends to the audience's knowledge of film history. At one point a group of young Pakistani immigrant workers are seen watching the film *The Outsiders* (1983; dir. Francis Ford Coppola). In the following scene one of the young men quotes from the film when asked his name by a security guard

following an altercation. As such, the film also produces a cinephilic insider's perspective that adds to the illusion of complexity by offering knowledgeable viewers a gratifying sense of their own expertise.

20 Turan, "Syriana."

21 While I do not discuss the film in detail here, *Crash* likewise bases its entire sociological critique on the concept of complexity: a racist cop can love his father, a socially progressive cop can harbor deep-rooted racist feelings, a working-class Hispanic man can look like a gang member yet love his daughter, and so on. *In the Valley of Elah* (2007), Paul Haggis's next directorial effort after *Crash*, could also be considered in this group.

22 Jaafar, "Ali Jaafar Talks to George Clooney," 17.

23 By and large the films all did fair business at the box office (in relation to their production budgets). *Crash* achieved domestic box office receipts of $54.5 million from a budget of $6.5 million; *Good Night, and Good Luck* realized domestic receipts of $31.5 million from a budget of $7 million. *Syriana*, with a budget of $50 million, only just broke even with domestic receipts of $50.8 million (and foreign sales of $43 million).

24 See, for example, the interviews with Clooney and Gaghan cited above.

25 A. O. Scott, "Clooney and a Maze of Collusion," *New York Times*, 23 November 2005.

26 This is particularly the case with *Falling Down*, which has received a great deal of critical attention. See, for example, Clover, " 'Falling Down' and the Rise of the Average White Male"; Davies, "Gender, Ethnicity and Cultural Crisis"; Gabriel, "What Do You Do When Minority Means You." See also Kennedy, *Race and Urban Space*, 33–42.

27 Bowes, "Traffic Speeding Ahead."

28 Scott, "Clooney and a Maze of Collusion."

29 Travers, "Syriana."

30 Turan, "Syriana."

31 Clooney's performances in the Coen brothers films *O Brother, Where Art Thou?* (2000), *Intolerable Cruelty* (2003), and others can be read as an interesting commentary on the actor's celebrity persona. In many of them he is intentionally made physically or characteristically grotesque and his status as a sex symbol is undercut or otherwise played with.

32 Jaafar, "Ali Jaafar Talks to George Clooney," 18.

33 I am talking solely about the three films eligible for the Academy Awards in 2005. Because Zeta-Jones's character is central to the third plotline in *Traffic*, that film's inclusion in this discussion could potentially yield a slightly different story. The media's focus on her marriage to Douglas and on her pregnancy, however, perhaps says all that needs be said on this point.

BIBLIOGRAPHY ❧

Aaron, Charles. "Don't Fight the Power." *Da Capo Best Music Writing of 2002: The Year's Best Writing on Rock, Pop, Country, Jazz, and More*, edited by Jonathan Lethem and Paul Bresnick. New York: Da Capo Press, 2002.

Acland, Charles R. *Screen Traffic: Movies, Multiplexes, and Global Culture*. Durham: Duke University Press, 2003.

Agamben, Georgio. *Homo Sacer: Sovereign Power and Bare Life*. Translated by Daniel Heller-Roazen. Stanford: Stanford University Press, 1998.

———. *Means without End: Notes on Politics*. Translated by Vincenzo Binetti and Cesare Casarino. Minneapolis: University of Minnesota Press, 2000.

———. *State of Exception*. Translated by Kevin Attell. Chicago: University of Chicago Press, 2005.

Alarcón, Norma, Caren Kaplan, and Minoo Moallem. Introduction to *Between Woman and Nation: Nationalisms, Transnational Feminisms, and the State*. Durham: Duke University Press, 1999.

Appadurai, Arjun. *Fear of Small Numbers: An Essay on the Geography of Terror*. Durham: Duke University Press, 2006.

———. *Modernity at Large: Cultural Dimensions of Globalization*. Minneapolis: University of Minnesota Press, 1996.

Aronowitz, Stanley. *How Class Works: Power and Social Movement.* New Haven: Yale University Press, 2003.

———. "My Masculinity." *Constructing Masculinity*, edited by Maurice Berger, Brian Wallis, and Simon Watson. New York: Routledge, 1995.

Austen, Chuck, et al. *The Call of Duty.* Volume 1: *The Brotherhood and the Wagon.* New York: Marvel Comics, 2002.

———. *The Call of Duty.* Volume 2: *The Precinct.* New York: Marvel Comics, 2002.

Baker, Houston A., Jr. *Black Studies, Rap, and the Academy.* Chicago: University of Chicago Press, 1993.

Baldwin, Davarian L. "Black Empires, White Desires: The Spatial Politics of Identity in the Age of Hip-Hop." *That's the Joint! The Hip-Hop Studies Reader*, edited by Mark Anthony Neal and Murray Forman. New York: Routledge, 2004.

Balibar, Etienne, and Immanuel Wallerstein. *Race, Nation, and Class: Ambiguous Identities.* New York: Verso, 1991.

Basu, Dipannita, and Sidney J. Lemelle, eds. *The Vinyl Ain't Final: Hip Hop and the Globalization of Black Popular Culture.* London: Pluto Press, 2006.

Berger, Maurice, Brian Wallis, and Simon Watson, eds. *Constructing Masculinity.* New York: Routledge, 1995.

Berlant, Lauren. *The Female Complaint: The Unfinished Business of Sentimentality in American Culture.* Durham: Duke University Press, 2008.

———. "Poor Eliza." *American Literature* 70.3 (1998), 635–68.

———. *The Queen of America Goes to Washington City: Essays on Sex and Citizenship.* Durham: Duke University Press, 1997.

Bowes, Peter. "Traffic Speeding Ahead." BBC website (accessed 29 July 2009).

Brennan, Timothy, and Keya Ganguly. "Crude Wars." *South Atlantic Quarterly* 105.1 (2006), 19–35.

Brown, Jeffrey A. *Black Superheroes, Milestone Comics, and Their Fans.* Jackson: University Press of Mississippi, 2001.

Brown, Wendy. *Regulating Aversion: Tolerance in the Age of Identity and Empire.* Princeton: Princeton University Press, 2006.

Browne, David. "'Stan' by Your Man." *Entertainment Weekly Online*, 16 March 2001. (accessed 23 April 2009).

Bruzzi, Stella. *Bringing Up Daddy: Fatherhood and Masculinity in Post-war Hollywood.* London: BFI, 2005.

Buck-Morss, Susan. *Thinking Past Terror: Islamism and Critical Theory on the Left.* New York: Verso, 2003.

Busiek, Kurt, and Stuart Immonen. *Superman: Secret Identity.* New York: DC Comics, 2004.

Butler, J. Michael. "'Luther King Was a Good Ole Boy': The Southern Rock Movement and White Male Identity in the Post–Civil Rights South." *Popular Music and Society* 23.2 (1999), 41–62.

Butler, Judith. *Bodies That Matter: On the Discursive Limits of "Sex."* New York: Routledge, 1993.

————. *Precarious Life: The Powers of Mourning and Violence.* New York: Verso, 2004.

Cannon, Eoin. "The Heavyweight Champion of Irishness: Ethnic Fighting Identities Today." *New Hibernia Review* 10.3 (2006), 87–107.

Cantor, Jay. *Great Neck.* New York: Knopf, 2003.

Carby, Hazel. "What Is This 'Black' in Irish Popular Culture?" *European Journal of Cultural Studies* 4.3 (2001), 325–49.

Carson, David A. *Grit, Noise, and Revolution: The Birth of Detroit Rock 'n' Roll.* Ann Arbor: University of Michigan Press, 2006.

Carter, Julian B. *The Heart of Whiteness: Normal Sexuality and Race in America, 1880–1940.* Durham: Duke University Press, 2007.

Caruth, Cathy. "Recapturing the Past: Introduction." *Trauma: Explorations in Memory.* Baltimore: Johns Hopkins University Press, 1995.

————. *Unclaimed Experience: Trauma, Narrative, and History.* Baltimore: Johns Hopkins University Press, 1996.

Chabon, Michael. *The Amazing Adventures of Kavalier and Clay.* New York: Random House, 2000.

Chang, Jeff. *Can't Stop Won't Stop: A History of the Hip-Hop Generation.* New York: St. Martin's Press, 2005.

————. *Total Chaos: The Art and Aesthetics of Hip-Hop.* New York: Basic Civitas Books, 2007.

Chapman, Mary, and Glenn Hendler. Introduction to *Sentimental Men: Masculinity and the Politics of Affect in American Culture.* Berkeley: University of California Press, 1999.

Cherniavsky, Eva. "Introduction: The Body Politics of Capital." *Incorporations: Race, Nation, and the Body Politics of Capital.* Minneapolis: University of Minnesota Press, 2006.

Chomsky, Noam. *9/11.* New York: Seven Stories Press, 2002.

Clemens, Paul. *Made in Detroit: A South of 8-Mile Memoir.* New York: Doubleday, 2005.

Clinton, Bill. *My Life.* New York: Knopf, 2004.

Clover, Carol J. "'Falling Down' and the Rise of the Average White Male." *Women and Film: A Sight and Sound Reader,* edited by Pam Cook and Phillip Dodd. London: Scarlett Press, 1993.

Conley, Dalton. *Honky.* Berkeley: University of California Press, 2000.

Cooke, Darwyn. "Human Values." *9–11: September 11th, 2001: The World's Finest Comic Book Writers and Artists Tell Stories to Remember.* New York: DC Comics, 2002.

Cornell, Drucilla. *Clint Eastwood and Issues of American Masculinity.* New York: Fordham University Press, 2009.

Daniels, Les. *Superman: The Complete History. The Life and Times of the Man of Steel.* San Francisco: Chronicle Books, 1998.

Davidson, Cathy N., and Jessamyn Hatcher. Introduction to *No More Separate*

Spheres! A Next Wave American Studies Reader, edited by Cathy N. Davidson and Jessamyn Hatcher. Durham: Duke University Press, 2002.

Davies, Jude. "Gender, Ethnicity and Cultural Crisis in *Falling Down* and *Groundhog Day*." *Screen* 36.3 (1995), 214–32.

Davis, Eisa. "Found in Translation: The Emergence of Hip-Hop Theatre." *Total Chaos: The Art and Aesthetics of Hip-Hop*, edited by Jeff Chang. New York: Basic Civitas Books, 2006.

Dawson, Ashley, and Malini Johar Schueller, eds. *Exceptional State: Contemporary U.S. Culture and the New Imperialism*. Durham: Duke University Press, 2007.

DeHaven, Tom. *It's Superman*. San Francisco: Chronicle Books, 2005.

Denby, David. "High Rollers." *The New Yorker*, 20–27 December, 2004.

Denning, Michael. *The Cultural Front: The Laboring of American Culture in the Twentieth Century*. New York: Verso, 1998.

———. *Culture in the Age of Three Worlds*. New York: Verso, 2004.

Diner, Robyn. " 'The Other White Meat': Princess Superstar, Irony, Sexuality, Whiteness in Hip Hop." *Canadian Review of American Studies* 36.2 (2006), 195–209.

DiPiero, Thomas. *White Men Aren't*. Durham: Duke University Press, 2002.

Dippie, Brian T. *The Vanishing American: White Attitudes and U.S. Indian Policy*. Lawrence: University Press of Kansas, 1991.

Dudziak, Mary L., ed. *September 11 in History: A Watershed Moment?* Durham: Duke University Press, 2003.

Dyer, Richard. *Heavenly Bodies: Film Stars and Society*. London: Routledge, 1986.

Dyer, *White: Essays on Race and Culture*. London: Routledge, 1997.

Eight Mile. Directed by Curtis Hanson. 2003.

Eliot, Marc. *American Rebel: The Life of Clint Eastwood*. New York: Harmony, 2009.

Eminem. *Angry Blonde*. New York: Harper Entertainment, 2000.

———. *The Eminem Show*. Aftermath Records, 2002.

———. *The Marshall Mathers LP*. Interscope Records, 2000.

———. *The Slim Shady LP*. Aftermath Entertainment/Interscope Records, 1999.

———. *The Way I Am*. New York: Dutton, 2008.

Eng, David. *Racial Castration: Managing Masculinity in Asian America*. Durham: Duke University Press, 2001.

Fallis, Richard. *The Irish Renaissance*. Syracuse: Syracuse University Press, 1977.

Faludi, Susan. *Stiffed: The Betrayal of the American Man*. New York: Perennial, 1999.

———. *The Terror Dream: What 9/11 Revealed about America*. New York: Metropolitan Books, 2007.

Fishman, Robert. "Half the Story: Paul Clemens, *Made in Detroit: A South of 8 Mile Memoir*." *Technology and Culture* 48.2 (2007), 404–6.

Fitzpatrick, Kathleen. *The Anxiety of Obsolescence: The American Novel in the Age of Television*. Nashville: Vanderbilt University Press, 2006.

Flaherty, Mike. *American Chopper: At Full Throttle*. Des Moines: Meredith Books, 2004.

Floren, Terese M. "Too Far Back for Comfort." *Firework: The Newsletter of Women in the Fire Service* 19.10 (2001), 1–2.

Forman, Murray. "'Represent': Race, Space and Place in Rap Music." *That's the Joint! The Hip-Hop Studies Reader*, edited by Mark Anthony Neal and Murray Forman. New York: Routledge, 2004.

Foucault, Michel. "Governmentality." *Power: Essential Works of Foucault, 1954–1984*. Edited by James D. Faubion. London: Penguin Books, 2001.

Frankenberg, Ruth, ed. *Displacing Whiteness: Essays in Social and Cultural Criticism*. Durham: Duke University Press, 1997.

———. "Introduction: Local Whitenesses, Localizing Whiteness." *Displacing Whiteness: Essays in Social and Cultural Criticism*, edited by Ruth Frankenberg. Durham: Duke University Press, 1997.

Fraser, Nancy. *Redistribution or Recognition? A Political-Philosophical Exchange*. London: Verso, 2003.

Frayling, Christopher. *Clint Eastwood*. London: Virgin Publishing, 1992.

Fuller, Graham. "Confessions of a Dangerous Mind." *Sight and Sound*, March 2006, 14–16.

Fusco, Coco. "Fantasies of Oppositionality." *Afterimage* 16.9 (1988), 6–9.

Gabriel, John. "What Do You Do When Minority Means You? *Falling Down* and the Construction of 'Whiteness.'" *Screen* 37.2 (1996), 129–51.

Gallafent, Edward. *Clint Eastwood: Actor and Director*. London: Studio Vista, 1994.

Garson, Paul. "Paul Sr.'s Pride and Joy." *V-Twin Motorcycles*, June 2005.

George, Nelson. *Hip Hop America*. New York: Penguin Books. 1998.

Gerstle, Gary. "Pluralism and the War on Terror," *Dissent*, spring 2003.

Gibbons, Luke. "Race against Time: Racial Discourse and Irish History." *Oxford Literary Review* 13 (1991), 95–117.

Gilman, Sander L. "Nietzsche, Bizet, and Wagner: Illness, Health, and Race in the Nineteenth Century." *Opera Quarterly* 23.2–3 (2007), 247–64.

Gilmore, Paul. *The Genuine Article: Race, Mass Culture, and American Literary Manhood*. Durham: Duke University Press, 2001.

Gleiberman, Owen. "Is Eminem the Elvis Presley of Today?" *Entertainment Weekly*, 22 December 2000.

Gordon, Avery F., and Christopher Newfield, eds. *Mapping Multiculturalism*. Minneapolis: University of Minnesota Press, 1996.

Guralnick, Peter. *Sweet Soul Music: Rhythm and Blues and the Southern Dream of Freedom*. Boston: Back Bay Books, 1999.

Halberstam, David. *Firehouse*. New York: Hyperion, 2002.

Halliday, Jean. "Tuners Fit In with Customizing Fare." *Advertising Age*, 31 May 2004.

Hartigan, John, Jr. *Odd Tribes: Toward a Cultural Analysis of White People*. Durham: Duke University Press, 2005.

———. *Racial Situations: Class Predicaments of Whiteness in Detroit*. Princeton: Princeton University Press, 1999.

Hauerwas, Stanley, and Frank Lentricchia, eds. *Dissent from the Homeland: Essays after September 11*. Durham: Duke University Press, 2003.

Hendler, Glenn. *Public Sentiments: Structures of Feeling in Nineteenth-Century American Literature*. Chapel Hill: University of North Carolina Press, 2001.

Hill, Mike. *After Whiteness: Unmaking an American Majority*. New York: New York University Press, 2004.

———. "Introduction. Vipers in Shangri-la: Whiteness, Writing, and Other Ordinary Terrors." *Whiteness: A Critical Reader*, edited by Mike Hill. New York: New York University Press, 1997.

Hughes, Howard. *Aim for the Heart: The Films of Clint Eastwood*. New York: I. B. Tauris, 2009.

Hunter, C. Stuart. "Return to 'La bonne vaux': The Symbolic Significance of Innisfree." *Modern Language Studies* 14.3 (1984), 70–81.

Ignatiev, Noel. *How the Irish Became White*. New York: Routledge, 1995.

In the Line of Duty: A Tribute to New York's Finest and Bravest. New York: Regan Books, 2001.

Jaafar, Ali. "Interview: Ali Jaafar Talks to George Clooney." *Sight and Sound*, March 2006, 16–18.

———. "Interview: Ali Jaafar Talks to Stephen Gaghan," *Sight and Sound*, March 2006, 19–20.

Jackson, John L., ed. *Racial Americana*. Special issue of *South Atlantic Quarterly* 104.3 (2005).

Jameson, Fredric. "The Dialectics of Disaster." *Dissent from the Homeland: Essays after September 11*, edited by Stanley Hauerwas and Frank Lentricchia. Durham: Duke University Press, 2003.

Jones, Gerard. *Men of Tomorrow: Geeks, Gangsters, and the Birth of the Comic Book*. New York: Basic Books, 2004.

Kammen, Michael. "The Problem of American Exceptionalism: A Reconsideration." *American Quarterly* 45.1 (1993), 1–43.

Kaplan, Amy. "Homeland Insecurities: Reflections on Language and Space." *Radical History Review* 85 (winter 2003), 82–93.

Kaplan, Amy, and Donald E. Pease, eds. *Cultures of United States Imperialism*. Durham: Duke University Press, 1993.

Kaplan, Robert D. *Warrior Politics: Why Leadership Demands a Pagan Ethos*. New York: Random House, 2002.

Kaysen, Susan. *Girl, Interrupted*. New York: Vintage Books, 1994.

Keller, James. "Shady Agonistes: Eminem, Abjection, and Masculine Protest." *Studies in Popular Culture* 25.3 (2003), online (accessed 23 April 2009).

Kennedy, Liam. "Framing September 11: Photography after the Fall." *History of Photography* 27.3 (2003), 272–83.

———. *Race and Urban Space in Cotemporary American Culture*. Edinburgh: Edinburgh University Press, 2000.

Kleid, Neil, et al. "Letters from a Broken Apple." *9–11: Emergency Relief*. Gaineseville: Alternative Comics, 2002.

Kraus, Rebecca S. "A Shelter in the Storm: Baseball Responds to September 11." *Nine: A Journal of Baseball History and Culture* 12.1 (2003), 88–101.

Krens, Thomas. Introduction to *The Art of the Motorcycle*. New York: Solomon R. Guggenheim Foundation, 1998.

Lee, Katja. "Reconsidering Rap's 'I': Eminem's Autobiographical Postures and the Construction of Identity Authenticity." *Canadian Review of American Studies* 38 (2008), 351–73.

Lemons, Stephen. "Steven Soderbergh." *Salon.com*, 20 December 2000 (accessed 23 April 2009).

Lethem, Jonathan. *The Fortress of Solitude*. New York: Doubleday, 2003.

Lhamon, W. T., Jr. *Raising Cain: Blackface Performance from Jim Crow to Hip Hop*. Cambridge: Harvard University Press, 1998.

Lipsitz, George. *Footsteps in the Dark: The Hidden Histories of Popular Music*. Minneapolis: University of Minneapolis Press, 2007.

———. "Listening to Learn and Learning to Listen: Popular Culture, Cultural Theory, and American Studies." *American Quarterly* 42.4 (1990), 615–36.

———. *The Possessive Investment in Whiteness: How White People Profit from Identity Politics*. Philadelphia: Temple University Press, 1998.

Loeb, Jeph, and Tim Sale. *Superman for All Seasons*. New York: DC Comics, 1999.

López, Ian Haney. *White by Law: The Legal Construction of Race*. Revised edition. New York: New York University Press, 2006.

Lott, Eric. "All the King's Men: Elvis Impersonators and White Working-Class Masculinity." *Race and the Subject of Masculinities*, edited by Harry Stecopoulos and Michael Uebel. Durham: Duke University Press, 1997.

———. *Love and Theft: Blackface Minstrelsy and the American Working Class*. New York: Oxford University Press, 1993.

———. "White Like Me: Racial Cross-dressing and the Construction of American Whiteness." *Cultures of United States Imperialism*, edited by Amy Kaplan and Donald E. Pease. Durham: Duke University Press, 1993.

Lowe, Donald M. *The Body in Late-Capitalist USA*. Durham: Duke University Press, 1995.

Marcus, Phillip L. *Yeats and the Beginning of the Irish Renaissance*. Ithaca: Cornell University Press, 1970.

Martin, Randy, and Ella Shohat. "Introduction: 911—A Public Emergency." *Social Text 72* 20.3 (2002), 1–8.

May, Elaine Tyler. "Echoes of the Cold War: The Aftermath of September 11 at Home." *September 11 in History: A Watershed Moment?*, edited by Mary L. Dudziak. Durham: Duke University Press, 2003.

McAllister, Mike. "Clint Eastwood's Boxing Movie Takes Its Time . . . and Is Worth it." *Sports Illustrated Online* (accessed 23 April 2009).

McClintock, Anne. *Imperial Leather: Race, Gender, and Sexuality in the Colonial Contest.* New York: Routledge, 1992.

McMurtry, Larry, and Diana Ossana. "*Brokeback Mountain*, the Screenplay." *Brokeback Mountain: Story to Screenplay.* London: Harper Perennial, 2006.

Michaels, Walter Benn. *The Shape of the Signifier: 1967 to the End of History.* Princeton: Princeton University Press, 2004.

———. *The Trouble with Diversity: How We Learned to Love Identity and Ignore Inequality.* New York: Metropolitan Books, 2006.

Miller, Frank. *Batman: The Dark Knight Returns.* New York: DC Comics, 1997.

Million Dollar Baby. Directed by Clint Eastwood, 2004.

Murray, Susan, and Laurie Ouellette, eds. *Reality TV: Remaking Television Culture.* New York: New York University Press, 2004.

Nadel, Alan. *Containment Culture: American Narratives, Postmodernism, and the Atomic Age.* Durham: Duke University Press, 1995.

Neal, Mark Anthony, and Murray Forman, eds. *That's the Joint! The Hip-Hop Studies Reader.* New York: Routledge, 2004.

Negra, Diane. "The Irish in Us: Irishness, Performativity, and Popular Culture." *The Irish in Us: Irishness, Performativity, and Popular Culture*, edited by Diane Negra. Durham: Duke University Press, 2006.

———. "Irishness, Innocence, and American Identity Politics before and after September 11." *The Irish in Us: Irishness, Performativity, and Popular Culture.* Durham: Duke University Press, 2006.

———. *Off-White Hollywood: American Culture and Ethnic Female Stardom.* New York: Routledge, 2001.

Negra, Diane, ed. *The Irish in Us: Irishness, Performativity, and Popular Culture.* Durham: Duke University Press, 2006.

Nelson, Dana D. *National Manhood: Capitalist Citizenship and the Imagined Fraternity of White Men.* Durham: Duke University Press, 1998.

———. "The President and Presidentialism." *South Atlantic Quarterly* 105.1 (2006), 1–17.

———. "Representative/Democracy: Presidents, Democratic Management, and the Unfinished Business of Male Sentimentalism." *No More Separate Spheres! A Next Wave American Studies Reader*, edited by Cathy N. Davidson and Jessamyn Hatcher. Durham: Duke University Press, 2002.

9–11: Emergency Relief. Gainesville: Alternative Comics, 2002.

9–11: September 11th, 2001: The World's Finest Comic Book Writers and Artists Tell Stories to Remember. New York: DC Comics, 2002.

Nyberg, Amy Kiste. "Of Heroes and Superheroes." *Media Representations of September 11*, edited by Steven Chermak, Frankey Y. Bailey, and Michelle Brown. Westport, Conn.: Praeger, 2003.

Ong, Aihwa. *Neoliberalism as Exception: Mutations in Citizenship and Sovereignty.* Durham: Duke University Press, 2006.

Ouellette, Laurie. "'Take Responsibility for Yourself': *Judge Judy* and the Neoliberal Citizen." *Reality TV: Remaking Television Culture,* edited by Susan Murray and Laurie Ouellette. New York: New York University Press, 2004.

Paglen, Trevor, and A. C. Thompson. *Torture Taxi: On the Trail of the CIA's Rendition Flights.* Hoboken: Melville House, 2006.

Palahniuk, Chuck. Afterword to *Fight Club.* New York: Vintage Books, 2006.

Pease, Donald E. "The Global Homeland State: Bush's Biopolitical Settlement." *boundary 2* 30.3 (2003), 1–18.

———. "National Narratives, Postnational Narration." *Modern Fiction Studies* 43.1 (1997), 1–23.

Perry, Imani. *Prophets of the Hood: Politics and Poetics in Hip Hop.* Durham: Duke University Press, 2004.

Poniewozik, James. "My Wheels, My Self." *Time,* 5 March 2004.

Quinn, Eithne. *Nuthin' but a "G" Thang: The Culture and Commerce of Gangsta Rap.* New York: Columbia University Press, 2005.

Rasmussen, Birgit Brander, Eric Klinenberg, Irene J. Nexica, and Matt Wray, eds. *The Making and Unmaking of Whiteness.* Durham: Duke University Press, 2001.

Ray, Robert B. *A Certain Tendency of the Hollywood Cinema, 1930–1980.* Oxford: Oxford University Press, 1985.

Robinson, Sally. *Marked Men: Masculinity in Crisis.* New York: Columbia University Press, 2000.

Roediger, David R. *Towards the Abolition of Whiteness: Essays on Race, Politics, and Working Class History.* New York: Verso, 1994.

———. *The Wages of Whiteness: Race and the Making of the American Working Class.* Revised edition. London: Verso, 1999.

———. *Working towards Whiteness: How America's Immigrants Became White: The Strange Journey from Ellis Island to the Suburbs.* New York: Basic Books, 2006.

Rose, Tricia. *Black Noise: Rap Music and Black Culture in Contemporary America.* Middletown, Conn.: Wesleyan University Press, 1995.

Rowe, John Carlos. "Culture, U.S. Imperialism, and Globalization." *American Literary History* 16.4 (2004), 575–95.

Russo, John, and Sherry Lee Linkon, eds. *New Working-Class Studies.* Ithaca: Cornell University Press, 2005.

Samuels, Shirley. *The Culture of Sentiment.* New York: Oxford University Press, 1992.

Savran, David. *Taking It Like a Man: White Masculinity, Masochism, and Contemporary American Culture.* Princeton: Princeton University Press, 1998.

Seagle, Steven T., and Teddy Kristiansen. *It's a Bird.* New York: DC Comics, 2004.

Seagle, Steven T., Duncan Rouleau, and Aaron Sowd. "Unreal." *9–11: Emergency Relief.* Gainesville: Alternative Comics, 2002.

Seate, Mike. *Outlaw Choppers.* St. Paul, Minn.: Motorbooks International, 2004.

Shamir, Milette, and Jennifer Travis, eds. *Boys Don't Cry: Rethinking Narratives of Masculinity and Emotion in the U.S.* New York: Columbia University Press, 2002.

Shamir, Milette, and Jennifer Travis. Introduction to *Boys Don't Cry: Rethinking Narratives of Masculinity and Emotion in the U.S.*, edited by Milette Shamir and Jennifer Travis. New York: Columbia University Press, 2002.

Shickel, Richard. "Eminem's Eight Mile High." *Time*, 7 November 2002.

Silverman, Kaja. *Male Subjectivity at the Margins.* London: Routledge, 1992.

Simpson, David. *9/11: The Culture of Commemoration.* Chicago: Chicago University Press, 2006.

Sklar, Robert, and Tania Modleski. "*Million Dollar Baby*: A Split Decision." *Cineaste,* summer 2005.

Slotkin, Richard. *Regeneration through Violence: The Mythology of the American Frontier, 1600–1860.* Eugene: University of Oklahoma Press, 2000.

Smith, Paul. *Clint Eastwood: A Cultural Production.* Minneapolis: University of Minnesota Press, 1993.

Sontag, Susan. *On Photography.* London: Penguin Books, 1979.

Spiegelman, Art. *In the Shadow of No Towers.* New York: Pantheon, 2004.

Spigel, Lynn. *Welcome to the Dreamhouse: Popular Media and Postwar Suburbs.* Durham: Duke University Press, 2001.

Stam, Robert, and Ella Shohat. *Flagging Patriotism: Crises of Narcissism and Anti-Americanism.* New York: Routledge, 2007.

Stecopoulos, Harry, and Michael Uebel, eds. *Race and the Subject of Masculinities.* Durham: Duke University Press, 1997.

Stein, Howard F. "Days of Awe: September 11, 2001 and Its Cultural Psychodynamics." *Journal for the Psychoanalysis of Culture and Society* 8.2 (2003), 187–99.

Stilson, Janet. "It's All about the Family Thing." *Television Week*, 27 October 2003.

Sturken, Marita. "Memorializing Absence." Social Science Research Council, online (accessed 23 April 2009).

———. *Tourists of History: Memory, Kitsch, and Consumerism from Oklahoma City to Ground Zero.* Durham: Duke University Press, 2007.

Taylor, Charles. "The Unthinkable Made Real." *Salon.com* (accessed 23 April 2009).

Thompson, Hunter S. *Hell's Angels: A Strange and Terrible Saga.* New York: Modern Library, 1999.

Tocqueville, Alexis de. *Democracy in America and Two Essays on America.* Translated by Gerald E. Bevan. London: Penguin Books, 2003.

Toole, F. X. *Million Dollar Baby: Stories from the Corner.* New York: Ecco Press, 2005.

Travers, Peter. "Gran Torino." *Rolling Stone*, online (accessed 20 July 2009).

———. "Syriana." *Rolling Stone*, online (accessed 3 August 2009).

Various artists. *Music from and Inspired by the Motion Picture 8 Mile.* Shady/Interscope Records, 2002.

Virilio, Paul. *Ground Zero*. New York: Verso, 2002.

Volpp, Leti. "The Citizen and the Terrorist." *September 11 in History: A Watershed Moment?*, edited by Mary L. Dudziak. Durham: Duke University Press, 2003.

Walsh, Robert. "An Interview with Saul Williams." *Callaloo* 29.3 (2006), 728–36.

Weheliye, Alexander G. *Phonographies: Grooves in Sonic Afro-Modernity*. Durham: Duke University Press, 2005.

Wellman, David. "Minstrel Shows, Affirmative Action Talk, and Angry White Men: Marking Racial Otherness in the 1990s." *Displacing Whiteness: Essays in Social and Cultural Criticism*, edited by Ruth Frankenberg. Durham: Duke University Press, 1997.

Wiegman, Robyn. *American Anatomies: Theorizing Race and Gender*. Durham: Duke University Press, 1995.

———. "Intimate Publics: Race, Property, and Personhood." *American Literature* 74.4 (2002), 859–85.

———. "Whiteness Studies and the Paradox of Particularity." *Boundary 2* 26.3 (1999), 115–50.

Williams, Christopher G. "Losing Himself in the Music: Will the Real Marshall Mathers Please Stand Up?" *Popular Culture Review* 15.1 (2004), 79–89.

Willis, Paul. *Learning to Labour: How Working Class Kids Get Working Class Jobs*. London: Gower, 1977.

Witek, Joseph. "Long Form/Short Form: Narratives Strategies of Some 9/11 Comics." *International Journal of Comic Art* 5.2 (2003), 281–95.

Wood, Ellen Meiksins. *Empire of Capital*. New York: Verso, 2003.

Wray, Matt. *Not Quite White: White Trash and the Boundaries of Whiteness*. Durham: Duke University Press, 2006.

Wright, Bradford W. *Comic Book Nation: The Transformation of Youth Culture in America*. Baltimore: Johns Hopkins University Press, 2001.

Wurtzel, Elizabeth. *Prozac Nation*. New York: Houghton Mifflin, 1994.

Yates, Brock. *Outlaw Machine: Harley-Davidson and the Search for the American Soul*. New York: Broadway Books, 1999.

Yeats, W. B. *Autobiographies*. London: Macmillan, 1961.

———. "The Lake Isle of Innisfree." *The Poems*. Ed. Richard J. Finneran. London: Macmillan, 1989.

Young, Marilyn B. "Ground Zero: Enduring War." *September 11 in History: A Watershed Moment?*, edited by Mary L. Dudziak. Durham: Duke University Press, 2003.

Zandy, Janet. *Hands: Physical Labor, Class, and Cultural Work*. New Brunswick, N.J.: Rutgers University Press, 2004.

Žižek, Slavoj. "The Depraved Heroes of *24* Are the Himmlers of Hollywood." *The Guardian*, online (accessed 23 April 2009).

———. *Welcome to the Desert of the Real*. London: Verso, 2002.

INDEX

McVeigh, Timothy, 104

melodrama: *American Chopper* and, 79–93; *Brokeback Mountain* as, 11–17; domesticity and, 21; *Gran Torino* and, 150–56; *Million Dollar Baby* as, 131–49; *Syriana* and, 172–73, 180; *Traffic* as, 157–71; *24* as, 27–48. See also domesticity

Miller, Frank, 187n17

Miller Electric, 82–85, 96, 99

Million Dollar Baby, 22, 131–56, 168, 176; Academy Award nominations for, 195n1; affect in, 145–46; assisted suicide in, 196n11; Catholicism in, 144; consumption in, 137–38; genre components of, 135–36; Irishness in, 131–32, 138–48; melodrama in, 141–48; possessive individualism in, 135, 137; U. S. race relations in, 146–48; white trash and, 131–36; Yeats in, 142–44

"Million Dollar Baby," 132

Mitchell, Elvis, 120

Moment of Silence, A, 52

Monroe Doctrine, 159

Monster Garage, 78, 93

Moore, Alan, 187n17

Motorcycle Mania, 78, 94

MTV, 78

multiculturalism, 3, 19, 59–62, 132, 154

Mummy Returns, The, 120

"My Name Is" (Eminem), 107

Mystic River, 149

N.W.A. (Niggaz with Attitude), 107

NAPA Autoparts, 78, 82

Naudet, Gideon, 59

Naudet, Jules, 59

NBA (National Basketball Association), 77

Negra, Diane, 103, 132

Nelson, Dana D., 40–41, 138–39, 184n16

neoliberalism, 13, 18–19, 22–23, 27–31, 86, 93, 100, 122, 152, 157–58, 179–80

New England Patriots, 77–78

Newsweek, 50

New York City, 19–20, 49–50, 53, 57–67

New Yorker, 53, 148

New York Times, 11, 148, 152, 157, 177–78

New York Yankees, 77

NFL (National Football League), 77

Nicholson, Jack, 147

Nike, 78, 133

9/11. See September 11, 2001

9/11 (film), 59

9–11: Artists Respond, 52

9–11: Emergency Relief, 52–53, 57

9–11: September 11th, 52, 55–56

"'97 Bonnie and Clyde" (Eminem), 106–9, 112–14

Nyberg, Amy Kiste, 53

OCC (Orange County Choppers), 78, 81–84, 87–88, 90–100

O'Neal, Shaquille, 94

On Walden Pond, 143

Opera Quarterly, 105

Orange County Choppers (OCC), 78, 81–84, 87–88, 90–100

Orange County Ironworks, 84, 87–88

Outlaw Choppers, 91

Overhauling, 78

Oxford English Dictionary, 10

Palahniuk, Chuck, 1–3, 6, 101

Parker, Alan, 140

particularity, 6–8, 17, 132

patriarchy, 19, 22–23, 61–62, 131, 144–46, 150, 158–65, 170–71, 179

patriotism: blue-collar workers and, 10, 82–83; comic books and, 52; as spectacle, 31; in *24*, 28

Paulie. See Teutul, Paul, Jr.

Pearl Harbor, 67

Pease, Donald E., 30, 33, 72

Pentagon, 38, 64, 67, 72

People Weekly, 66, 178

United Nations, 32
universalism, 6, 8, 10, 67, 78–79; *Brokeback Mountain* and, 10–11, 17
USA Patriot Act, 46
U.S. citizenship. *See* citizenship
U.S. Department of Labor, 4–5
U.S. exceptionalism. *See* exceptionalism
U.S. News and World Report, 50
USS *Abraham Lincoln*, 40

Vanilla Ice, 104
Vietnam War, 155–56
Vietnam War veterans, 79
Village Voice, The, 120
Volpp, Leti, 58

"Wagon, The." *See Call of Duty, The*
Wallace, George, 118
Warner Bros., 152
War of the Roses, 177
War on Drugs, 157
War on Terror, 18–19, 27–47, 65–67, 157, 180
Watergate scandal, 118
Wellman, David, 3, 5
West Coast Choppers (WCC), 90, 94
"White America" (Eminem), 118–19
whiteness, 5; academia and, 182n22; Eastwood and, 131–56; *8 Mile* and, 119–27; Eminem and, 101–27; Irishness and, 59–60, 131–41; masculinity and, 1–23, 59–60; *Million Dollar Baby*

and, 131–50; as minority identity, 21–23, 59–60, 103–4, 119–27; September 11 and, 18–19, 49–73; as universal, 7–9. *See also* Irishness; masculinity; white trash
white trash, 7, 20–23, 82, 180; Eminem as, 21, 101–27; Irishness and, 131–45; *Million Dollar Baby* and, 151. *See also* masculinity; whiteness
Wiegman, Robyn, 8, 14, 99, 137
Wild One, The, 80
Williams, Saul, 103
Willis, Paul, 88–90, 191n23
Witek, Joseph, 186n9
Woman and Nation, 160
work. *See* labor
Working Fire, 50
World Series, 77
World Trade Center, 60–61, 64–67; Statue of Liberty and, 65–69; steel reclaimed from, 99; as Twin Towers, 65, 67
Wray, Matt, 103
Wright, Jeffrey, 171

Yeats, John Butler, 131
Yeats, W. B., 131, 141–44
Young, Coleman, 101
Young, Marilyn B., 46

Zeta-Jones, Catherine, 177
Žižek, Slavoj, 33, 46, 50, 73

HAMILTON CARROLL is a lecturer in American
literature and culture at the University of Leeds.

Library of Congress Cataloging-in-Publication Data

Carroll, Hamilton
Affirmative reaction : new formations of white masculinity
/ Hamilton Carroll.
p. cm. — (New Americanists)
Includes bibliographical references and index.
ISBN 978-0-8223-4929-7 (cloth : alk. paper)
ISBN 978-0-8223-4948-8 (pbk. : alk. paper)
1. Men, White—United States—Attitudes.
2. Whites—Race identity—United States.
3. Masculinity—Social aspects—United States.
4. Masculinity in popular culture—United States.
I. Title. II. Series: New Americanists.
E184.A1C377 2011
305.800973—dc22   2010031778